T0313930

Contents

WARFARE
WELFARE

Also by Marcus G. Raskin

The Limits of Defense, with Arthur Waskow (Doubleday, 1962)

Vietnam Reader, with Bernard Fall (Random House, 1965)

A Citizen's White Paper on American Policy in Vietnam (Vintage Books, 1965)

After 20 Years: Alternatives to the Cold War in Europe, with Richard J. Barnet (Random House, 1965)

An American Manifesto, with Richard J. Barnet (New American Library, 1971)

Being and Doing: An Inquiry Into the Colonization, Decolonization, and Reconstruction of American Society and Its State (Random House, 1971)

Washington Plans an Aggressive War, with Ralph L. Stavins and Richard J. Barnet (Vintage Books, 1971)

Notes on the Old System: To Transform American Politics (David McKay Co., 1974)

The American Political Deadlock: Colloquium on Latin America and the United States: Present and Future of Their Economic and Political Relations (Institute for Policy Studies, 1975)

Next Steps for a New Administration (Transaction Publishers, 1976)

The Federal Budget and Social Reconstruction: The People and the State (Transaction Books, 1978)

The Politics of National Security (Transaction Publishers, 1979)

The Common Good: Its Politics, Policies, and Philosophy (Routledge & Kegan Paul, 1986)

New Ways of Knowing, with Herbert J. Bernstein (Rowman & Littlefield, 1987)

Winning America: Ideas and Leadership for the 1990s, with Chester Hartman (South End Press, 1988)

Essays of a Citizen: From National Security State to Democracy (M. E. Sharpe, 1991)

Abolishing the War System: The Disarmament and International Law Project of the Institute for Policy Studies and the Lawyers Committee on Nuclear Policy (Aletheia Press, 1992)

Presidential Disrespect: From Thomas Paine to Rush Limbaugh—How and Why We Insult, Scorn, and Ridicule Our Chief Executives, with Sushila Nayak (Carol Publishing Group, 1997, 2008)

Visions and Revisions: Reflections on Culture and Democracy at the End of the Century (Interlink Publishing Group, 1998)

Liberalism: The Genius of American Ideals (Rowman & Littlefield, 2003)

In Democracy's Shadow: The Secret World of National Security, with Carl LeVan (Nation Books, 2005)

The Four Freedoms Under Siege: The Clear and Present Danger from Our National Security State, with Robert Spero (Praeger, 2006, and Potomac Books, 2008)

Also by Gregory D. Squires

Chicago: Race, Class and the Response to Urban Decline, with Larry Bennett, Kathleen McCourt, and Philip Nyden (Temple University Press, 1987)

Capital and Communities in Black and White: The Intersections of Race, Class, and Uneven Development (SUNY Press, 1994)

Insurance Redlining: Disinvestment, Reinvestment, and the Evolving Role of Financial Institutions (Urban Institute Press, 1997)

Color and Money: Politics and Prospects for the Community Reinvestment Movement in Urban America, with Sally O'Connor (SUNY Press, 2001)

Urban Sprawl: Causes, Consequences, and Policy Responses (Urban Institute Press, 2002)

Organizing Access to Capital: Advocacy and the Democratization of Financial Institutions (Temple University Press, 2003)

Why the Poor Pay More: How to Stop Predatory Lending (Praeger, 2004)

Privileged Places: Race, Residence and the Structure of Opportunity, with Charis E. Kubrin (Lynne Rienner, 2006)

There Is No Such Thing as a Natural Disaster: Race, Class, and Hurricane Katrina, with Chester Hartman (Routledge, 2006)

The Integration Debate: Competing Futures for American Cities, with Chester Hartman (Routledge, 2010)

Introduction

The Ground on Which We Stand:
States of Warfare and Welfare

Marcus G. Raskin

The United States has been at war for more years than it has been at peace. War is not a "last resort." War is not something we fall back on when diplomacy, economic sanctions, and other tools fail. War is the normal state of affairs. We have our justifications. We are defending essential interests. We are spreading freedom abroad. We are making the world safe for democracy, and from the aggressive instincts of imperialistic and totalitarian regimes. If our record of accomplishments in these areas is mixed, the costs are clear. Particularly in recent years, the United States has seen its standing in the global community fall precipitously, even if it is the strongest military and economic force. And the arsenal for democracy is hurting at home, with the economic fallout from our efforts to conduct war on at least two fronts, and the collapse of financial service industries being just the latest indicators.

The Middle East and Asian military quagmires, along with the steepest economic decline since the Great Depression, have been joined by a newfound hope for the future in the historic presidential election of 2008. Such contradictory sentiments are nothing new. In fact, tensions between war and peace, civility and civil unrest, prosperity for some and poverty for many, and many other local and global tensions have been the norm throughout U.S. history.

As President Barack Obama sought to turn the page of history, his opponent Senator John McCain also claimed that change was coming. What does it mean when we hear the phrase "turn the page" or "change"? To what purpose and why? After all, during the election of 1944, Franklin Delano Roosevelt's Republican opponent— the youthful governor Thomas Dewey—announced that it was "time for a change." Change was an important word used by most candidates. But in *Warfare Welfare*, we have gone one step further. By the readings we have chosen, we have sought to ask whether there is anything we can know and use from recent history that would be of

1

help in attempts made by poets, scholars, students, and politicians alike to speculate or shape the future. Or is it that we know so many different things that it is hard to discern underlying truths among all of them and therefore what should be discarded as trivial or worse?

The first thing to note is that the modern political awakening sought not only to see government as something other than a band of thieves holding power for themselves and their friends, but also a measure of justice, emerged from modern revolutions that promised much and delivered more than was intended. Of course, those aware of the faint voice of Saint Augustine heard his echo—he was the one who said that without justice government is but a band of thieves. In modern revolutions, the shadow of tragedy and cruelty was present, but the length of that shadow depended on each revolution and the cultural forces that built up to that revolution. The question invariably came down to the relationship between justice, war, human affections, equality, and economic distribution (either through the state and governmental apparatus, or outside of it in the so-called private sector or the vague conglomerate now known as " civil society"). Whether it is our own situation pierced by a moment's thought, twenty-four-hour news cycles, or newspapers, we know that these are the underlying problems that cannot be magically wished away. And since that is so, it is of value to set the frame for these readings in the struggles of the past and their prior, but similar relationships that we can now discern in the present.

The United States has long prided itself as a beacon of freedom and democracy in a dangerous and undemocratic world. Yet its long history of imperialistic ventures has compromised its standing in the world, and undercut visions of freedom and democracy at home. Drawing from classical readings in political theory, primary documents including key court decisions, and social science research, the introductory chapter and the balance of the book demonstrate how a permanent war economy has denied the United States the ability to in fact spread democracy abroad and has exacerbated a host of social problems at home. Only by ending war as an acceptable form of conduct can any meaningful progress be made on the foreign or domestic challenges facing the United States The concluding chapter offers steps to replace the warfare system.

AMERICAN EXCEPTIONALISM, AND THE EXCEPTIONS

If there has been a strong democratic impulse throughout U.S. history, many undemocratic, if not savage and violent actions, have frequently dotted the American landscape. Reformist sentiments have long been part of the history and culture of the United States. However, reactionary, violent, and imperialist threads have also been part of the American tapestry.

The American Revolution erupted as a diverse nation steeped in ideas of liberty, slavery, faith, productive work, and linkage between the personal and the collective good. Some of these progressive impulses were found in early attempts at political transformation, none more important than attempts of the underclasses of the "mother country" England between 1640 and 1660. These underclasses organized a major assault on the deity of the King and the riches of the few. It was not only the staid Puritans who escaped England and shaped the United States in covenants with God and each other. The Massachusetts Puritans knew and used violence not only against Native Americans, but their dissenters as well. They could not countenance Anne Hutchinson, the mother of fifteen children, as a citizen of the Massachusetts Bay colony. She was expelled as a devil and user of witchcraft who supported Roger Williams in the establishment of a place in the wilderness known as Rhode Island. Her beliefs were those of a free thinker who refused to accept the integration of church and state. She identified with the poor, the wretched, and the women she counseled as a midwife. It was during that extraordinary period (1640–1660), which was described as the world turned upside down, that many of the ideas we honor in the welfare state developed, namely that the individual good cumulatively must be reflected in the collective decency of how a people organizes its social relationships and obligations.

We must not forget the tragedy that often befalls authentic heroes. Hutchinson, after disagreement with colleagues in Rhode Island, took her children to New York. She was caught in a land-grab battle between Dutch settlers and Indians. The Dutch carried out several murderous raids against the Indians. And soon, the Indians retaliated against the Dutch settlers and their ways of commerce. Hutchinson, along with six of her children, was killed in the geographic area of what would in our time be recognized as part of New York City. (Indeed, there is now the Anne Hutchinson highway named after her, which for travelers may be thought of as an escape route to and from New York.) Such brutal political events are part of the collective history of American struggle around religion and class.

After the American revolution, Rhode Island came to be known as " rogue island" because its penurious inhabitants were unable to pay their debts to wealthy landowners and lenders from other colonies.

Indebtedness is more than a series of dots through American history and development. Wartime debt precipitated the Shays's Rebellion, which necessitated the use of armed force to disperse revolutionary war veterans. The capital of the United States changed from Philadelphia to Washington, D.C., and the city was laid out along wide boulevards by the French architect L'Enfant to ensure that the armies could control and shoot at the mobs if they got out of hand. In the early 1930s, thousands of bonus marchers who sought payment for fighting in the American expeditionary force of World War I had their encampment destroyed during the Hoover administration by General Douglas MacArthur and Major Dwight Eisenhower, his aide. (MacArthur would later become the boss of the emperor of Japan after World War II, and Eisenhower would be given command of all allied armed forces in Europe.)

By the twentieth century, it was clear that Americans were part of a polyglot nation comprised of Poles, Hungarians, Germans, Jews, Russians, Slovaks, French, and Italians all tied to different parts of the United States and undertaking a wide variety of activities from mining and steel to rail construction and farming. Some came to the United States under false pretenses. Their way was paid by large corporations, which preferred Eastern European workers dependent on the corporations over Blacks from the South. Despite the fact that many Chinese worked and died building the railroads for such corporations as Union Pacific, Chinese immigrants were also excluded after the Chinese Exclusion Act. Immigrants from different nations who stayed in America were held together by the "New Patriotism," which meant finding a means for their children to be physically safe and materially better off than parents. Their ambition was wrapped in the goals of a better and more secure life for their children and the boundaries of individualism as defined by the expanse of the United States.

Beneath this story was another one. It had to do with the costs of patriotism and the actualities of the American state, its function as an expansionary nation that prided itself on its exceptionalism, and the various elements of its military, economic, social and cultural power. The common thrust of these elements was both feared and envied at different times among other nations. It had not escaped their attention that the United States, through cunning, mass murder, and Indian removal, destroyed the millions of Indians who founded their cultures there. As the United States matured domestically, there was tension between the various groups that exhibited themselves on the school playground, in alleys, at the workplace, in churches, and implicit agreements of live and let live. These "treaties" were enforced through political parties that reflected and protected different ethnic groups, sometimes through ticket balancing and municipal jobs granted by political bosses. As in all political systems, bribes, extortion, threat, and other forms of corruption were present in greater or lesser degree depending on historical time and cultural fashion. The United States was no exception.

There were many who disagreed with the formulation and practice of the American purpose as it had developed among the ambitious and the powerful. Often dissenting voices were drowned out. At other times, their concerns for the common good were co-opted by established institutions that had no trouble tailoring ideals for their purposes, so long as such ideals did not upset the pyramid of power. On the other hand, dissenters saw themselves as catalytic organizers seeking immediate reforms or comprehensive change. Although these dissenters too strummed the national guitar of patriotic consciousness, there were nuances and differences that individuals and groups believed informed their personal conscience and actions. Patriotic consciousness and conscience had distinctive meanings to several figures who arguably influenced a more humane direction in warfare and welfare. This may be said of Jane Addams and Emily Balch, hardly household names even during their respective creative lives.

Balch won the 1946 Nobel Peace prize for her work against war and her allied work on the development of settlement houses in Boston. She took an uncompromising stand against World War I, which she saw as an intolerable interruption in the possibility of progress of Americans—especially for Irish and Portuguese immigrants, who were part of the new subjugated immigrant class. She lost her professorship at Bryn Mawr for her antiwar stance.

In Chicago, Jane Addams had a remarkably similar career. In 1931, she received the first Nobel Peace prize awarded to an American woman for her antiwar activism and exemplary work in binding public welfare to the building of community. Addams was the cofounder of Hull House in Chicago with Ellen Gates Starr. Besides the usual amount of begging and fundraising, Addams and Starr lived in Hull House and opened it to thousands of needy people each week who required counseling, food, and social services. Addams sought the development of strong local communities protected by a welfare state. There was no task that she found demeaning or degrading. She used her class position and the appearance of wealth as protection in a city that sought class stratification accompanied by the demands of a measure of civic democratic pride. Addams took a paying job from the Chicago city government as garbage inspector in order to improve the sanitation conditions of Chicago's neighborhoods. Her friend in the establishment of Hull House was John Dewey, the premier philosopher of modern America, as it moved from the small town to the city. Both Dewey and Addams saw linkages between education and the development of a multicultural American nation, which had to be built on economic and social welfare offered by the state, and the collective actions of community. Addams's cofounder, Ellen Starr, was a strong trade unionist working for better conditions in factories. However, in 1930 she left this struggle to join a nunnery. (Women of strong religious faith continued to play a powerful role in relation to the working class. They sought to change the Catholic church, as was the case with Dorothy Day, now beatified and soon to be made a saint.)

The work of these remarkable women was the organic outgrowth of the Seneca Falls convention of 1848, which brought a few hundred women and some men together near Albany New York to announce the Declaration of Sentiments. This notable document written by feminists Elizabeth Cady Stanton and Lucretia Mott, was patterned after the Declaration of Independence. It championed equality between women and men and detailed wrongs such as women's lack of property rights, their inability to vote without voting recognition, and direct legal power to protect their person. White males in the United States never exceeded in numbers the combined population of Blacks, Native American Indians, Asians, Hispanics, and women, once they were finally counted. This stubborn fact no longer seems to go unnoticed.

WARFARE AND WELFARE AT HOME AND ABROAD

The contradictory tendencies between freedom and democracy on one hand, and imperialism and violence on the other, are not distinctively American traits. In many ways, Americans learned and adopted these tendencies from friends and foes alike.

In 1848, the year of the Declaration of Sentiments, revolutionary turmoil was prevalent in Europe. In Austria restrictions on student life created revolutionary turbulence championed students. These ideological signposts were defined in terms of personal dignity, civil rights, and personal well-being. It was in this context that people turned to the purposes of the French revolution of 1789—a revolution that had different, sometimes contradictory, features.

In an early stage, the French revolution sought to bring about a redistribution of power, privilege, and virtue in the form of equality among property owners. There was another view, that an organized representative body could be replaced by the people themselves who submit their own complaints rather than through representatives with their own interests. The Sans Culottes, as they were called, brought forward a reservoir of citizens who in fact were the largest number of people in France. Historians have thought that this changed the nature of the French revolution from a bourgeois to a people's revolution.

Prior to Napoleon's commitment to traditional ideas of military power and imperialism, the stage of the French revolution sought to define itself in terms of the "will of the people." Yet in that framework, who would best know and capture the meaning of "will of the people"? Was it going to be through rhetoric and redefinition of legitimacy which, while—shunting aside the landed noble pensioners dependent on the corruptions of the ancien régime—ended in Napoleon's reign of terror, and continuous wars? Or was it better expressed through the Jacobin attempt to control the Assembly and make clear that it could be replaced by radical democracy?

In the early twentieth century, the old Bolsheviks captured an already existing revolution with the slogan "Bread, Land, and Peace." They called for land reform, pulled the tsarist armies out of World War I, and guaranteed food for work. At the time, Russia was a cauldron of dissenting socialist, anarchist, communist, and democratic points of view. When the smoke cleared, there was no interest in continuing the war with Germany, or German workers who were thought to be internationalist—as many communists saw themselves. But, to pull out of the war, the slogan "Bread, Land, and Peace" required that the Bolsheviks deliver. This was no easy task, for it meant that part of the Russian empire would have to be surrendered to Germany. This dismemberment through the Treaty of Brest-Litovsk caused Russian concern as it meant the strengthening of the heavily industrialized state that Germany would become. History's competing creative fugal forces gave rise to a civil war among various factions in Russia, including the social democrats and constitutionalists who objected to giving away so much to the Germans in the peace of Brest-Litovsk. The British eagerly supported the tsarist forces that wanted to continue the war with Germany, for the British feared a strong Germany in the future. Attempts were made by thirteen nations, including the United States, to keep the Russians in the war. These interventionist nations had multiple goals. For example, Japan and Poland sought to carve up pieces of the Russian empire. The United States had a less voracious role. Its forces were involved in specific tasks, namely keeping open the Trans-Siberian Railway. For a time, the United States joined the British, Czechs, and Japanese against the Bolsheviks. The leader of the American expeditionary force, Maj. Gen. William Graves, received a special order from President Wilson not to interfere in the internal political matters of the fledging revolutionary state. Graves ended up praising the Bolsheviks for their "honor" compared to the other interventionist forces and the Russian armies under the control of General Kolchak and Admiral Denikin. And so, the United States pulled out of the alliance.

Certain facts should be kept in mind. Cholera and influenza were rampant in the first years after World War I. An estimated 45 million people died worldwide. From Europe to the United States and the Soviet Union, the pandemic had political implications but no successful medical cure. Thus, a cordon sanitaire against the Russian people and the Soviet Union (RFSR as it was first known) was instituted as the answer to both influenza and communism.

Rhetorically, the Soviets in power sought mightily to overcome economic inequality. But it was not long before the obvious became clear. There were distinct differences in pay scales, as well as differences in privileges, accorded to particular groups. As a rule, women were at the bottom rung of economic well-being, having to do multiple jobs at home and outside of the overcrowded and poorly constructed apartments in which they lived. Wages for technicians were on a scale of one to fifteen times greater than that of the average worker in the first twenty years of the Soviet regime. This condition did not change, even during the relatively economically prosperous Khrushchev era. Nor did the problem of drunkenness improve.

From its first days, the Bolsheviks could not escape massive violence, starvation, and internecine struggle which led to the destruction of the "old Bolsheviks" who made the revolution a fight to the death between Stalin and his brilliant military commander Leon Trotsky. Stalin hounded Trotsky and caused him to be murdered in Mexico on the eve of World War II. Stalin's thermidor and Hitler's attack against the Soviet Union through Operation Barbarossa caught the Soviet army off guard after its decimation through internal Stalin purges. This appeared to suggest that the Soviets would be ground up quickly by the German pincer attack. But such was not to be the case. The Soviets stopped the German army a few miles from Moscow and therein began a whole new story in the history of politics, national patriotism, and warfare. The cost was astonishing in terms of sheer suffering.

Russia and its Soviet sphere lost 25 million dead in World War II and suffered the destruction of its entire infrastructure. It would not be overstated that Russia had become a nation of widows and orphans. Russia had already lost 10 million people in World War I, plus the destruction of millions of poor and middle-class farmers caught in the industrializing process. What remained in Russia throughout the Stalinist Cold War, and post—Cold War period was a commitment to the welfare state, which it increasingly was unable to afford because of the costs of preparing for war and fears of nuclear encirclement and war from the West.

Nineteenth-century revolutionaries doubted that Russia could ever be fertile ground for revolution because there was no strong working class. So where would revolutionaries turn for their practical utopia? In the nineteenth century, a European journalist named Karl Marx, who wrote for the *New York Herald Tribune*, talked about the dead hand of the past and how it laid itself on the future. Marx, the revolutionary, saw the United States as the hope of the future and a nation open to revolution. He certainly did not see Russia, which he saw as a primitive state, as this hope. He believed that a government never had to be larger than the one the United States had before the Civil War. An early twentieth century doctor from Vienna, Sigmund Freud reminded us that we had an unconscious that directed our conscious lives. This was not an argument that set well with Americans convinced of their own capacity to build and secure a new nation. Theirs was a world that had no time for demons: always there, perhaps, but manageable, especially by those who looked forward rather than inward or backward.

AMERICAN EXCEPTIONALISM IN MODERN TIMES
When the outcome of World War II was no longer in doubt, the important political scientist, economist, and activist for Indian independence the indefatigable Harold Laski—the Fabian upper-middle-class British Jewish intellectual who led the British

Labour Party—studied the United States. What he saw was a nation that had been critical in saving Great Britain from Nazism and fascism by joining with it against Germany and acting as a go between in relations with the Soviet Union. But Laski also saw something else. He was amazed at the grandeur of the American nation, its size, riches, the independence of its people, the progressive character of part of its business class, and the strength of the labor movement. The head of the Communist Party in the United States, Earl Browder, called for and succeeded in disbanding the Communist Party by stating that American progressive capitalists were dissimilar from capitalists in Europe. Browder was heavily criticized by the leaders of the French Communist Party at Moscow's orders and soon lost his position in the American Communist Party for his views of American exceptionalism.

Laski saw with clarity that the United States was an unfinished society scarred by class and race divisions, but held together by Franklin Roosevelt's pragmatist public philosophy and program of the welfare state. Yet Laski was aware that there was not smooth sailing for the crippled Roosevelt who won forty-six of the forty-eight states in his reelection of 1936. Roosevelt took this victory as a signal to challenge the Supreme Court, which had declared as unconstitutional his far-reaching economic programs in the first term. He called for increasing the number of Supreme Court judges, causing a furor in the Senate. Though he lost this battle, in the next few years the Supreme Court reversed its positions on various issues important to FDR's economic program, although he feared breaking the coalition inside the party when liberals unsuccessfully called for an anti lynching law. By 1941, Doctor New Deal gave way to Dr. "Win the War according to FDR." The dire sense of the time was spelled out in *Behemoth*, a book by Franz Neumann—a legal theoretician at the radical intellectual Frankfurt Institute who later taught at Columbia University. Neumann dissected the emergence of Nazis and then the way Hitler and his group organized power with the intention of violently stamping out whole classes and groups of people by war and race purification, eugenics, and the encouragement of burning troublesome books and businesses owned by Jews. This later came to be known as genocide, a condition that infected the German people with passive avoidance of reality and Nazi induced hatred of the "other." Neumann, a labor lawyer, believed that the fundamental struggles with Hitler's group centered on the conflict over labor unions and their independence. When Hitler came to power, he revealed much of his purpose, his intention to destroy an independent labor movement, and his attempt to destroy labor laws and labor lawyers who might have continued to carry ideas of independence and struggle against the Fuhrer. Neumann left Germany for England and there studied with the ubiquitous Harold Laski—who had also taught Kennedy at the London School of Economics.

Laski had an enormous effect on the independence movement of the Indians against Great Britain. It was said that Nehru left an empty chair at Congress party and ministerial meetings for "Laski's spirit." Spirits of Indian struggle for independence and revolutions aside, Franz Neumann left Laski to work in the United States for the Office of Strategic Services (OSS), a spy and research network where he did basic research on alleged Nazi war criminals for Justice Robert Jackson—the American prosecutor at Nuremberg. The Nazis defended themselves by pointing out that the United States had destroyed the Indian nation and they claimed that they had gotten the idea of ethnic cleansing (a later term) from the United States and concentration camps from the Soviets. Neumann had been assigned by James Donovan, the head of the OSS, to show Hitler's persecution of the Catholic Church—although the evidence on this question was mixed. Neumann also researched material about Hermann Goering who was the leading Nazi at Nuremberg. Neumann had hoped the Germans would bring the cases against the former Nazis in German courts, but the cold war intervened to abort this aspiration and former Nazis on both sides of the Iron Curtain were often given a pass in international and German tribunals if they were found "useful" to one side or the other. It is of more than historical importance to understand the sharp discussions in the United States about the Nazis.

By the late nineteen thirties, a fierce argument broke out inside and outside the American government and society on whether the United States would have to stop Hitler. In 1940, FDR had promised that American boys would be kept out of war in Europe. But, as Hitler advanced on other nations, FDR concluded that the United States was in danger. His own ambassador to Chile and the Spanish Republic, a professor and Jefferson scholar from the University of Chicago, Claude Bowers, warned FDR that there was no likelihood that a peaceful settlement could be worked out with Hitler and that war was inevitable. FDR was also told that the isolationist and seemingly Nazi sympathies of Ambassador Joseph Kennedy followed the line of a pro fascist segment of the British upper class. Kennedy was recalled so that mixed messages would no longer be given to the British. Such questions affected the biographies of intellectuals such as Neumann and Herbert Marcuse—a colleague in the preparation of materials about Nazism.

After government service, Neumann returned to Columbia where he partnered with C. Wright Mills and the political philosopher Herbert Marcuse—a colleague from the Frankfurt Institute who believed in many of the tenets of Marx and Freud. Mills's roots were distinctly different. He was a Waco, Texas American who had earned his PhD at the University of Wisconsin. There, he wrote on the philosophy of pragmatism as a profoundly radical conception. The University of Wisconsin social sciences lived under the spell of John R. Commons and Selig Perlman. Both in their own way believed that the question of control over property and means to accommodate differing interests of social classes was necessary for American stability.

But there were other aspects of American life which fed into the question of people's future: what a person could own, and where or what school or job a person might get. It was race and it could not be denied. Race as a concept has toxic meanings. For Blacks, it is the story of slavery, of forced rape by white slave owners, of stealing land, and—as W. E. B. Du Bois pointed out—lying about the history of Reconstruction after the Civil War, demeaning the decade of freedom (during which time Blacks held public office). White authors presented Reconstruction as a period of mismanagement and destruction of all that was decent in the antebellum South to generations of high school and college students. The emergence of Black Codes to control Blacks, of an early guerrilla force of white Southern confederate soldiers to harass and burn Black homesteads, of chain gangs and corvée labor of Blacks who were rented out to build steel mills in Birmingham, became a piece of the continuing American struggle that included lynchings, assassinations, and white expropriation of land.

Aggrieved Black farmers found a certain amount of justice in both the Carter and Clinton administrations after Agriculture Secretary Gilman arranged for reparations through federal funds. But in the aftermath of Hurricane Katrina, the same white land grab appeared. Chester Hartman and Gregory Squires are activist sociologist planners whose ideas fit with Mills rejection of a sociology that reinforces a status quo for the powerful, and who do so either out of parochial personal interest or inattention to the needs of the people who have been continuously disenfranchised and shortchanged in terms of benefits. The poorest section of New Orleans, the Ninth Ward, suffered the most damage because of faulty levees, federal mismanagement, and the vision of speculators to make New Orleans the fun city for tourists, white people, and the upper classes. This was to be accomplished by dispersion and removal of Black residents arranged in ways to ensure that their homes would never be rebuilt and trailer camps, which were provided, would in fact be centerpieces for disease and crime.

President George Bush's declaration that FEMA Director Brown was doing a fine job stands as a dreary statement of uncaring, a misunderstanding of the role the Corps of Engineers plays in the decaying American infrastructure, and the failure of sociologists and most social scientists to organize around the Katrina disaster. A question may be asked why sociologists, more than other committed scholars, should have been involved. The answer may be found in the wide scope of concern among sociologists, such as Squires, who see themselves as looking and participating in situations with a moral but not moralistic purpose. The Comtean sociologists who poached on philosophy and the sciences, or the participant pragmatist sociologists that were reflected in the Chicago school of sociology crossed boundaries of thought and practice, whether in the study and participation of family, therapy, music, or finding ways for the marginal worker and neighbor to organize their social life. If the sociologist conceived of humanity collectively or concentrated on the individual human as the center of thought and study, it meant that the sociological subject matter was boundless. For Mills, it was as boundless as one's "sociological imagination," and it even extended to questions of war. That sociology had a singular method applicable in all cases and all subject matter was not likely. What was true for Mills was that questions of war and peace could not be left to nuclear war strategists or warriors. Their lives, ideologies, and the consequences of their work cried out for analysis. There were early-twentieth-century questions of structure, such as the nexus between power, money, and status. But, there were also thermonuclear weapons that if used could destroy hundreds of millions of people within a few hours. It was this newly understood sense of pragmatic consequences which cried out for action without losing one's way because of blind scientism. These issues played heavily in the United States, where nuclear weapons had been used in Hiroshima and Nagasaki for a number of reasons.

Gar Alperovitz, in his groundbreaking work *Atomic Diplomacy* and other important writings, detailed the way the United States intended to use nuclear weapons as a tool of diplomatic and military threat. Such weapons constituted a warning to the Soviets that the United States had the will to use nuclear weapons in any future conflict with the Soviet Union, and that if it wanted to keep the Japanese emperor as a figurehead responsible to the American general Douglas MacArthur it would do so even though agreements had been reached to stick to unconditional surrender as the price for ending the war. It is important to note that the Hiroshima and Nagasaki bombs were constructed differently—one in Tennessee and the other in Washington state. The bomb used on Hiroshima was a uranium bomb whereas the Nagasaki bomb was configured with plutonium. Each represented different scientific and political interests. But the primary military concern was that the war in Japan was dragging and Members of Congress heard criticism from mothers, soldiers, and newspaper writers that there was no reason American soldiers who had fought valiantly in Europe should be shipped to Japan. After the bloody fight in Okinawa, there was fear that the United States might suffer thousands of casualties, and nuclear weapons were thought to be an American lifesaver along with massive nonnuclear fire bombing of Tokyo.

Lawyers attempted to understand this brutal reality by distinguishing *jus ad bellum* (law concerning acceptable justifications to use armed force) from *jus in bello* (law concerning acceptable conduct in war). In the first case, the Nuremberg trials were based on treaties broken which Germany as a sovereign nation had ratified and signed before the war. The Kellogg Briand Pact, sometimes called the Pact of Paris, committed signatories to forswear aggressive war. *Jus in bello* related to the rules of warfare intended to protect the lives of innocent civilians. Although "legitimate targets" were recognized, the Nazis did not follow those rules in the way they fought World War II. Nor did the allies. The difference was that the Nazis lost the war and for a short period the West thought of themselves as absolved until it was clear that United States government officials feared the symmetrical arguments of Justice Jackson and the decision of the Nuremberg tribunal. Their words would come to haunt many Americans during the Iraq and Vietnam wars. Military officials had no interest in, nor did American presidents want, American soldiers tried in foreign or international courts for war crimes. And so, the United States torpedoed the idea of international criminal courts if it could reach to American armed forces.

Today we increasingly see the domestic costs of the warfare state. During his long and productive life at Columbia University, engineer Seymour Melman was appalled at the effects of the arms race on American life. He coined the term "overkill," which described in a pithy slogan that the United States and humanity were being eaten away by a bacterial virus of nuclear weapons. Like C. Wright Mills, Melman saw nuclear strategy as crackpot realism, having nothing to do with the palpable need to convert the United States and the world into what he called a "peace race." With others, he predicted the collapse of the Soviet Union because of the arms race and warned that the United States was in mortal danger of making the same mistakes the Soviets did. The problem for the United States was that its leaders could eschew what was happening domestically, trumpeting invincibility over the failed Soviet system— a point made by Melman in his book *Profits without Production*. He was not a fan of the financial service "industry" because it created mountains of debt personally and nationally without any concern for what this would do to the everyday lives of working people and their families. The connections between warfare (e.g. Iraq) and the workings of our financial system (e.g. bailouts for Bear Stearns, Fannie Mae, Freddie Mac, AIG, and ultimately the financial system generally) have become all too evident in recent times.

Democracy, freedom, and progress are traditional American values that have long been compromised by imperialism, exploitation (often associated with race, gender, and class), and violence. War continues to be a routine mechanism by which the United States attempts to resolve conflict and preserve its position in the world. Yet war is a tool that in fact undermines both objectives. Perhaps the deepening economic crisis and the groundbreaking election of 2008 will provide a much-needed wake-up call. We choose to envision a more optimistic future.

It should not come as a surprise to the reader that Melman, Noam Chomsky, and this writer were close friends—seeing many public problems in similar ways, but from different experiences. With other writers in this book, as for example, Gar Alperovitz, John Dewey, and W. E. B. Du Bois and Institute for Policy Studies colleagues, John Cavanagh, Robin Broad, Barbara Ehrenreich, and many others, the dialogue continues. And with children, grandchildren, students, and friends perhaps we will learn how to keep riding the bicycle so we don't fall off and build institutions, projects, and social inventions worthy of a humanity in desperate need of a break.

PART I
THE WARS ABROAD

1

The Traditions of America

Harold J. Laski

Most of the heritage of past civilizations has gone into the making of American democracy. Europe and the Far East have alike nourished its rise and development; it has strains from the African continent which lie deep in its foundations. In the four and a half centuries since it emerged into the historic consciousness, it has passed from the epoch in which it was an object of colonial ambition to the epoch where it stands, independent, at the summit of political power. And in that momentous period there can be no sort of doubt but that its impact has changed the outlook of mankind wherever there has been the power to reflect on the meaning of human affairs. No state, until our own day, has done so much to make the idea of progress a part of the mental make-up of man. No state, either, has done more to make freedom a dream which overcame the claims both of birth and of wealth. It has been, in an impressive way, a refuge for the oppressed, alike in the political and in the religious field, for at least the period since the Pilgrim Fathers landed on the rocky shores of New England. It has offered to the common man an opportunity of self-advancement such as he has never known elsewhere until the Russian Revolution of 1917. Few countries have ever developed material resources on so vast a scale. Few countries have ever been able to move so swiftly from the circumference to the centre in their impact upon civilization. If it has often been hated and even more often envied, there has always been a perception, even in the hatred and the envy, that it occupied a unique position among the nations of the world. Now it stands close to the zenith of its fortunes. For something like the next generation it is difficult to doubt that world politics will be set in the context of American purposes. Upon the use it decides to make of its overwhelming productive power, no small part of the fate of Europe and Asia, perhaps of Africa as well, is bound overwhelmingly to depend.

There is hardly a type of European humanity which has not contributed its quota to the shaping of American tradition. The Spaniard made his mark on California; the Dutchman on New York; the Englishman on the Atlantic coast; the German in Pennsylvania; the Swedes in the Northwest; the Irish in New York and Chicago; the French in Louisiana and, for a period, in the Mississippi Valley. And as America developed economically, the call of the West and the endless spaces which craved for settlement brought Poles and Ruthenians, Serbs and Croats, Italians and Greeks. Already, by the time that independence had been won in 1783, the United States was a microcosm to which almost every European adventurer contributed his quota; after independence it was like a vast pit into which was poured whatever there was in Europe of the spirit of enterprise and adventure. Possibly it is true that until some such time as the Civil War the predominant mould into which this immense variety was poured in endless succession was shaped by the English tradition. The way of thought, in institutions, in religion, in science, and in literature, was perhaps more fully English than any other outlook. The language made for that primacy; so, also, did the pattern of the political framework.

But it was always English with a difference. Even the first generation of emigrants from the British Isles wore their Englishry with a difference. That is obvious in the case of men like Tom Paine, and it is still more obvious when the American is native-born. If it be true that it is not very difficult to think of George Washington as in temperament and habit a wealthy English squire, no one can doubt that Samuel Adams and Jefferson, Franklin and John Jay, are Americans in a sense which makes their English inheritance an element only in the final character they displayed. No one can read the literature of America, even up to the outbreak of the War of Independence, without seeing that a new national type has emerged upon the historic stage. He has an experimentalism in temper, a passion for making his own way in life, a zeal for self-assertion which were all of a world removed from the England he had defeated. The environment in which he functions breaks the cake of custom, which, had the English connection remained, he would doubtless have been eager to preserve. The conservatism of Alexander Hamilton was probably as profound as that of Lord Eldon in England; but it is very obviously an American conservatism. The radicalism of Thomas Jefferson goes back to foundations which Charles James Fox would have been proud to accept; but it is already a radicalism which has grown in a very different direction from any which Fox would have found it easy to follow. Chief Justice Marshall defended the claims of property with a zeal that must have made the members of the English bench feel that here was a spiritual partner in their legal effort; but there are elements in the method by which he defends his approach which would have been hardly intelligible to an English judge of his time. John Adams may analyse the weaknesses of democracy with a zeal that William Windham would have applauded had he been aware of it; but it is difficult to think that he would have grasped the basis upon which Adams approached his problems.

And if, by 1783, the peaks of the mountain ranges have already become so different, it is natural that the valleys are even more different. What is outstanding in the ordinary American, by the time the Peace of Versailles was signed in that year, is that he does not assume the duty to remain in the position in which he was born. Most English radicals of the time look backwards for their inspiration; as late even as Dickens it is goodwill and generosity that will solve the social problem. The English thinker who desires to reorganize the foundations of his community upon a new basis, like Robert Owen, or his disciple William Thompson, is not only rare; it is even suspected that he is a little mad. The average radical, O'Connor, Hunt, or Cobbett, is not only a man whose ideals are of the pre-Industrial Revolution; he is tempted to think that the ideal England means a recovery of the past rather than a search for the future.

That is in no sense true of the analogous American type. He is confident that he is in himself a person of social significance. He is rarely interested in his past because he is so certain that his future will bear no relation to it. The tradition that he has inherited is that of a dynamic civilization in which he is assured that whatever was yesterday, it will be different again tomorrow. He assumes as a part of his inheritance that he will have the right continually to go forward. He does not accept the postulates of a society where, as in the Europe from which he largely came, birth or inherited wealth may make all the difference to the hopes he may venture to form. No doubt it is true that there has been in American history that craving for the recognition of a special status, the desire to possess the inherent right to command, of which the remains lingered on in the South until they were broken to pieces in the Civil War. No doubt, also, the formulation of hope has been different in the level towards which it might reach in special groups like the Negroes and the American citizens of Oriental origin, in the Jews, and, to some degree and in some places, the Roman Catholics. But even when these exceptions have been made the dynamic quality of the American tradition is as notable as it is unmistakable. From the very outset the psychological roots of the American idea have been built upon the foundation of expansionism. There was expansion territorially; there was expansion in the power to utilize the vast resources which, until 1929, seemed to have no limit. There was, too, a cultural expansion symbolized, perhaps, above all, in the faith in education and the intensity with which applied science has been accepted as a normal part of living.

The very bigness of America has an importance in the formation of its tradition which it is not easy to overestimate. It creates the belief that America is different, is somehow exceptional, that there is reserved for its citizens another destiny from that which is to befall the Old World. The spaciousness of the United States as a physical entity makes the idea of unlimited horizons, of constant discovery, of novelty that is always imminent, part of the background against which each American is set. However much the colonial period may be dependent upon European ways of thought, their adaptation to American use always involves some change of greater or lesser profundity. This is, I think, because at the base of the tradition is, even when unconsciously, the thought in every man that he is somehow a pioneer, and, therefore, the growth of a conviction that there is no problem he cannot tackle. If he is an immigrant he is a pioneer because he has made the break with the Old World; if he is the child of an immigrant he is a pioneer because he is affirming in his own person the finality of the break; and if he is an American, like the remarkable Adams family, of long standing, he is a pioneer because he belongs to the small group of men who have shaped the contours of the New World.

This concept of the pioneer penetrates every nook and cranny of the American tradition. It explains why the ordinary American rarely assumes that any career upon which he embarks is, outside such special professions as medicine and the churches, the final career in which he will end. Thomas Jefferson is a polymath who attains distinction in every subject he touches; Benjamin Franklin is only less eminent as a diplomat and statesman than as a scientist; when Charles Carroll wishes to build himself a house in Baltimore, he does not send for an architect but for books on architecture, out of which he composes one of the loveliest houses in the New World. Almost as a boy, Alexander Hamilton is a distinguished officer on Washington's staff; he is then, within four years, as brilliant a political philosopher as the party of property has produced in the United States; he is as brilliant an administrator as the Treasury Department has known; and few advocates have won for themselves a higher position at the American Bar. Or there is Andrew Jackson, farmer, merchant, lawyer, soldier, congressman, and, finally, president of the United States. Towering above all is the majestic figure of Abraham Lincoln, lonely, aloof, tragic, who grows from the illiteracy of a home where there is little but failure and poverty to impose himself not merely on the mind of America, but on the mind of all civilization, as the supreme figure in the democratic tradition of the nineteenth century. As one examines the significance of these men, it is impossible not to conclude that they represent a new category in the conventional distribution of the human beings who search for the means to rule their fellow-citizens.

For, if we compare them with their European analogues, the characteristics they display are utterly different. Washington, perhaps, and the Adams dynasty are of the type that in the England or France of the early nineteenth century might have attained political distinction. Of all the others, I think it is true to say that either they would not have dreamed of a political career, or, had they dreamed of it, there is little likelihood that there would have been any avenue through which they could have passed to positions of authority. Here again, there is inherent in the American tradition the spaciousness of hope and the exhilaration that hope conveys; and it is the greatness of this quality that it brings out in so many the zest for adventure, the sense of ambition, the willingness to break the routines in which they have been enclosed. Indeed, it is notable that where the routine is over-valued it tends to become an object of satire or of indignation; one has the conviction of this in the interrelations between what is old-established convention in Boston or Philadelphia or Charleston, and the challenge which seeks to adapt it to new claims.

The American tradition is, in essence, an individualistic tradition which has tended to look upon the State with doubt or suspicion. In part, of course, this attitude stems from the religious background of the seventeenth century; the pioneers were men and women seeking to escape from a persecuting government to which their truths were unacceptable. That does not mean for a moment that the pioneers were generally in favor of toleration; the attitude of Massachusetts to Anne Hutchinson and Roger Williams and the first group of Quaker missionaries is sufficient evidence that the growth of toleration was alike slow and painful. But its growth was called for by the conditions which Americans confronted. There was a common danger from the Indian tribes; there was the variety of national origin of the settlers themselves, and the impossibility, in its light, of maintaining for long any rigid form of orthodoxy. No doubt the general basis of the American tradition was the Christian heritage from Europe; and no doubt, also, the clergy occupied a specially important place in its making. But it was rarely possible for any of the thirteen colonies to maintain for very long the union of some given Church with the State. And the outcome of this tendency to separation was to emphasize the idea that the individual should find his own pathway to salvation. The release this effected in the sphere of belief had inevitable repercussions far beyond its boundaries.

The first object of the settler on American soil was to be the master of his environment. He had to build his house, to sow his crops; and his wife had to provide the largest part of those needs which could only slowly come to count upon the results of the division of labor. The consequence of this was that few Americans, comparatively, lived by owning merely; and this fact conferred upon the idea of toil a claim to dignity, a sense of self-reliance, which gave the idea of individualism a special sanctity. By the War of Independence about one American in ten lived in a town. This meant that most of them assumed that they must depend upon themselves for the provision of services we now regard as a normal function of the government. And from this it followed that the individual citizen became what he could make himself, so that he tended to think of any restraint placed by authority upon his power to develop his fortunes as in itself a harmful thing. The tradition, therefore, looked upon the government as, above all, an organ of defence and order. And this attitude was even intensified by the colonial experience of restraints imposed upon the economic prospects of American citizens by the restrictive legislation of the mother-country. No doubt Great Britain was a safeguard as long as the government of France left it uncertain whether the civilization of the New World was to owe allegiance to London or to Versailles. But once the Seven Years' War had drawn to its victorious close, the sovereignty of Parliament became a clear restraint of opportunity, the more deeply resented the more vigorously it was applied. It is not fanciful to argue that no small part of the ease with which the doctrine of natural rights obtained acceptance in the eighteenth century arose from the fact that it seemed to restrain the exercise of an authority which was obviously a factor limiting the fulfillment of opportunities men like the merchants and farmers saw in front of them. To urge, therefore, that the government was best which governed least was to open gates which seemed to colonial America closed for no other reason than the protection of vested interests, and to limit the field of government action became almost a religious act when it was attained by victory in a revolutionary war.

This individualistic tradition is reinforced in a number of ways. It is democratic in the sense that, despite all pride of ancestry and wealth, the sheer abundance of land made it impossible to keep the planter aristocracy a closed caste. And, in any case, it was rare even for the wealthy planter to succeed unless he himself had a pretty shrewd judgment of men and the capacity to handle the details of his commerce. The outcome of this was to give trade a status which it never achieved in a society in which, as in France or England, the ruling class was composed of gentlemen of leisure, soldiers and sailors, eminent churchmen, and an occasional lawyer of the type of Lord Mansfield, a great advocate and greater judge. It was democratic, too, in that the rise of the educational system was not accompanied by that suspicion that learning might "make servants insubordinate to their masters" which, even now, is not wholly extinct in Britain. The eighteenth century gave a general and intense impetus to the idea of self-help; and the fame of men like Nathaniel Ames and Benjamin Franklin proved the practical value of this virtue.

Self-help, moreover, in a frontier civilization necessarily meant versatility. The farmer was coping, as he settled down to life, with new land, new plants and animals, and a climate which required inventiveness as almost its first demand. If, in general, the intellectual life out of which the American tradition was founded was more narrow than most of its historians are ready to admit, it was still a life in which the spread of new ideas was extraordinarily rapid and the growth of a sense that the future was bright remarkably widespread. The belief in progress was practically universal; even sour John Adams did not doubt that America was destined "for the illumination and the emancipation of the slavish part of mankind all over the earth." That is the theme, also, of Joel Barlow's epic, *The Vision of Columbus*, written in 1787. Countless ballads tell the same story. In America man and woman reach a stature that comports with the dignity inherent in human nature. There is a sense of self-confidence, a conviction that the world is theirs for the taking, which are both unmistakable.

The American War of Independence coincided with, is, indeed, a part of, the Age of Enlightenment. It therefore is natural to find that there is a new faith in reason, a growth in the humanitarian temper, a sense of initiative and exertion, all of which have had an important role to play in the shaping of the tradition. If the war dealt a heavy blow to the cultural life of America, it also evoked an energy and effort among humble men which was of the first importance for the future. The very fact that men like Thomas Paine could exercise so profound an influence both on the character and the purpose of the struggle meant that natural rights, hostility to monarchy, and faith in the validity of freedom became a part of the mental constitution of Americans. The influence of the greatest of the figures in the Virginian dynasty, Thomas Jefferson, was directed to the formal separation of Church and State; and this, in its turn, not only made for religious toleration, but also laid the basis for that faith in education for the common people which Americans have never lost. No doubt it is true that conservatives like John Adams and Fisher Ames had no thought of an America in which the common man would play a vital part; they desired the rule of "gentlemen" on the ground, as Adams said, that "the people of all nations are naturally divided into two sorts, the gentlemen and the simple men." Fisher Ames wrote bitterly of the pretensions of the poor to positions for which the well-born and the rich were the proper candidates; and the *Diary of Governor Morris* is full of contempt for the ordinary folk who, without careful discipline, would drift into insubordination and shiftlessness. It was notable that he was even prepared to leave Paine to perish in a French prison when he was ambassador of the new republic to Paris.

But neither the well-born nor the rich defined the ideology of the American tradition. By 1800, it is beyond all doubt that it was to be shaped by ordinary men. The lawyers, the clergy, the rich merchants, and the great landowners might feel, like Hamilton, that the people was "a great beast"; but the victory of Jefferson in the great election of 1800 meant that the idea of an America would triumph in which the notion of an *élite* to whom government was confided would have no place. And with the victory of Jeffersonian democracy there begins to mature a cultural democracy that is indigenous and not foreign in its origin. The sense that this would be the case is already present in books like those of Crèvecoeur and Chastellux. It is announced with passion by poets like Philip Freneau, and by the eminent lexicographer Noah Webster. They think of America as young and Europe as old, of America as a country with a mighty future, and Europe as a decrepit continent which is bound to decline. Even though there is a recognition that it will be far from easy to build an independent American culture, they have the conviction that it must and can be done. Books like Jefferson's *Notes on Virginia*, indeed, are nothing so much as a stone deliberately laid in the edifice he sought to build; and it is significant that, as the nineteenth century began, Americans were already insisting that its history and geography should be the basis upon which its educational system should be built. Joel Barlow may have exaggerated the level of American achievement in his poems, but it is important that, as early as the year in which the Federal Convention met, he was claiming the cultural, as well as the political, independence of the United States.

What is important in these years of the Enlightenment is the conviction that Americans will first free themselves and then set an example to the rest of the world. The power of the moneyed class was very great; and pamphlets like those of Timothy Dwight of Yale University show that events like Shays' Rebellion and the French Revolution struck terror into the minds of the men of property. But the Federalists were beaten on the political field and Paine's *Age of Reason* swept through every element in the population from students in the colleges to the small farmers in Massachusetts and Georgia. Men like Paine and Volney prepared the ground which, on the one hand, made possible the remarkable influence of the British reformers Robert Owen and Frances Wright, and, on the other, made theological principles like those of Universalism and Unitarianism replace the rigid Presbyterian orthodoxy of Jonathan Edwards. There is a passionate advocacy of new ideas, feminism, humanitarianism, and scientific analysis. The American tradition rarely goes beyond the limits of the Deist principle; but it is natural, as the nineteenth century dawns, to see any novelty in ideas receive a welcome far more profound than any it was likely to secure in Europe.

Not, indeed, that the tradition is wholly democratic or radical. There are elements in it of a deep conservative strain. In one sense, it is difficult to deny that the French Revolution threw the men of solid property into a panic as great as any upon the European continent, and the deposit of its influences is traceable right down to our own day. The men who had not hesitated to throw off their British chains by war explain with passion the evil of violence and the nobility of order and property. There emerges the hostility between the little men, the debtors who lined up behind the appeal of Shays' Rebellion, and the creditor class whom Hamilton defended as the true source of civilized life. He, and the great Chief Justice, John Marshall, are the authors of an American tradition which venerates the men of property and birth as eagerly as do Burke and Joseph de Maistre. William Ellery Channing was in a profound sense a liberal, with a keen sense of the rights of labour, but even he insists that the "French Revolution had diseased the imagination and unsettled the understanding of man everywhere." If there is a revolutionary principle in the American tradition, based upon the rights of man, there is also a counter-revolutionary principle based upon the rights of property; and it is difficult not to feel that the shield which safeguards the counter-revolutionary principle was, in Jefferson's time, as it is a century and a half later, the revival of religious orthodoxy. It is interesting and significant that James Fenimore Cooper should urge the possession of piety as the quality most valuable in a husband. It is equally significant that President Dwight of Yale University appointed Benjamin Silliman to his chair in that university in order that the students might see that science and Christianity are the twin sides of a single outlook.

There is, indeed, a middle way within this bifurcated tradition. Until, at least, the Civil War, the main outlines of American civilization are set in terms of an aristocratic leadership. But these terms do not exclude a popularization of culture, whether in education, in science, in literature, or in religion. If the intellectual leaders of America tended to look to Europe for their inspiration, the masses, on the other hand, sought to build an America free from the trammels of the Old World. And this antithesis is, after all, natural enough. The Brahmins of Boston, for example, had leisure and security; their cosmopolitan outlook was the expression of the self-confidence these implied. But the masses of America, whether the native-born workers or the immigrants from Europe, were naturally eager to prove their Americanism by drawing their inspiration, whether in thought or act, from the soil they were turning from a wilderness into a settlement. One finds, accordingly, within the American tradition a dependence upon the European heritage at the apex of the social pyramid, and, at its base, a proud insistence upon the American right to see things with their own eyes and in their own way. The rich American must obtain his letters of credit in Paris or in Rome, in Naples or Madrid; the poor American emphasizes above all his freedom from the rigidity of the European scheme. So long as the resources of America seem infinite, there is little difficulty in arriving at a compromise between the two ways of looking at life. There is room alike for a patrician cosmopolitanism and a plebeian nationalism; and both of these outlooks reveal, on examination, a deep conviction that the American idea has somehow come to include all the discoveries of civilized living. It is because all types of American, both rich and poor, native and foreign-born, knew in their inner being that the promise of American life was certain of fulfillment that they had the faith which is vital to building a nation.

America inherited most of what the Old World had to offer; but it has been central to the American tradition that it has been unfettered by old methods. In part, that was because it confronted problems that were either in their essence new or that called for techniques with which the Old World was unacquainted. Adaptability is inherent in the personality of the American, and, with it, there has gone a zeal for what is new merely because it is new. From the outset of its history, the American people has had the sense that it was conquering a wilderness that it was, as it were, wresting from Nature an unlimited area of virgin soil. This meant that, in general, the human qualities most valued were those of the practical man rather than of the theorist. What was required was the man or woman who could meet an immediate situation with a solution that fitted the problem. Abstraction, philosophizing, these tended to delay the mastery of Nature, and this is why, I think, that theory developed comparatively late in the evolution of the American mind, and when it did develop assumed very characteristically that form of empiricism which rejected absolutes in favor of concrete solutions that worked in the particular instance. Wherever an American philosophy has been non-empiric in character, it has always, also, like Hegelian idealism, been non-American in origin.

It is this pragmatism in the tradition which explains why the American mind tends to give so emphatic a priority to the man of action over the man of theory. Throughout American history there has been a zest, an admiration, for the concrete and the particular. Abstraction, the faculty of large-scale generalization, tends, on the whole, to be regarded as sterile. For the environment has called for men who can do things, whether it is to clear a forest, or build a house, or construct a railroad. The contemplative mind is, in the tradition, associated very largely with the idea of a leisured class; and that idea, in its turn, has always had about it a suspicion of the aristocratic idea of which American civilization, above all after 1776, has been a living denial. And this priority of the practical has meant the supremacy, in American life, of the executive type, of the man who can organize, of the person who sees his way through an immediate problem. Even outstanding "intellectuals" in American history are notable, like Franklin and Thomas Jefferson, for their power to get things done. Not only does the "gentleman," in the English sense of that complex term, arrive relatively late in American history; it is hardly until Eli Whitney had made the ownership of slaves a profitable enterprise that the planters of the South accepted the notion that leisure was itself a career.

Even in our own day the tradition tends to look askance at the man whose business is ideas. Woodrow Wilson is held, partially at least, to have failed because he was a college professor; and it is the assumption of his critics that he therefore laced the practical common sense that is expected from a lawyer or a business man. It is natural enough to an American that a successful general should, like Jackson or Taylor, Harrison or Grant, go to the White House; and it is equally natural that a melancholy scholar like Henry Adams, who aims, above all, at the achievement of a philosophy of history, should be regarded as a decorative ornament for whom there is no use in practical affairs. The men who arouse admiration are those who, like Edison or Ford, can apply with exceptional brilliance ideas that other men have conceived. The successful politician is, almost invariably, what Bagehot recognized in Sir Robert Peel as the "uncommon man of common opinions." Jefferson and Lincoln, no doubt, are partial exceptions to this rule; but both of them united to profound political insight a skill in the management of men which has a recognizable kinship with the executive type in great business enterprise.

Certain other features of this American tradition need to be emphasized. It has always been difficult to persuade Americans to take long views in matters of social constitution. The changes in the character of its economic life have been so swift that, until practically the other day, a long term plan was out of date almost before it sought acceptance from the people. What was the West in Jefferson's day was already a part of the East when Jackson entered the White House; and the West that Jackson knew had little relevance to the frontier by the time of the Civil War. Nor must we forget the layer upon layer of immigration, each with a new source in the Old World, and each bringing some new element into the tradition. The one constant feature of the social landscape is the virtually universal passion for physical prosperity. The speed with which this passion spread had never previously been equaled; and it was built at once upon the possession of massive physical resources and an inventiveness in their use which has made the idea of mass production a typically American conception. The character and extent of this idea has made the United States a civilization in essence different from anything known in the Old World until the Russian Revolution of 1917.

Its influence has been overwhelming. In the first place, it developed in almost every citizen the idea of a dynamic career. He could not believe that he would remain where he began. He could not escape, until some such time as the Great Depression of 1929, from the conviction that he would better his condition in a material way. The result has been that almost every element in American life has been shaped by this conviction. It has had enormous influence on all the forms of religious life; no church which urged the desirability of asceticism had any hope of influence or much hope of survival. It has been responsible for the amazing range of American philanthropy. Suffering, even in foreign countries, seemed like nothing so much as a contradiction of the American idea; and the price of success has always been the obligation of the man who has obtained it to find the ways and means of proving his goodwill to his fellow-creatures. It has enormously influenced the habits of American education; there have been few colleges which did not assume that the character of their training should be ultimately controlled by the successful business man. It is, indeed, tempting to argue that, the Negro and the sharecropper apart, all Americans regard themselves as middle class in character. That is why socialism has made such little progress in the United States; and it is perhaps the most solid reason for the absence of a doctrinal trade-unionism which found permanent expression in a political party. There are few Americans, in fact, who do not set great store on the chance of accumulating private property; and it is this attitude, more than any other, which explains why the revolutionary ideas of the European continent have found it so difficult to get a hold upon the American mind.

The zeal for accumulation by the individual sets the background for some important elements in the American tradition. It has been, at least since the Civil War, a whole-time job. The result has been that few American men could announce that they were functionless in the sense of an aristocrat in England or France or Tsarist Russia. They gave all their energies to work; they were, indeed, expected to do so. This has evolved an American ruling class with little knowledge of how to spend their leisure when they had it. In general, they were not certain that leisure was not a kind of sinful waste; and the great collectors, Morgan, or Frick, or Huntington, brought together their superb books and pictures and *objets d'art* not so much as amateurs to whom selection was a source of pleasure, but, rather, as professionals who sought, in the particular sphere they made their own, at once to outbid any rival who might appear upon the scene, and, after their death, to leave a permanent memorial which would satisfy the national passion for philanthropic effort.

The zeal for material well-being has had a profound effect, also, upon the American tradition in politics and literature. No foreign observer can watch the political process without noting how temporary and casual is, in general, the hold of the elected person on the constituents he represents. An occasional figure, like Senator Borah, may make a permanent career at Washington, but the real high road for the average member of a legislative assembly is less the quality of his contribution to the state or to the nation than his ability to gratify his supporters with a constant succession of small favours. That is, of course, the secret of the success of the machines like Tammany; its leaders bind their followers to them not by the doctrines they profess but by the favours they confer. No doubt there comes a time, after an interval, when some city boss steps beyond the permitted line and is replaced by a reform administration; but it rarely lasts for long simply because the reformers lack that gift of personal kindliness which no boss ever omits to display. And the average American, in the long run, finds it difficult not to believe that the bankers and financiers are merely doing for themselves on a great scale what the city boss and his henchmen do with relative moderation, accompanied by a kindly interest in the fortunes of their constituents, not least if these latter be the first generation of Americans.

And with, of course, remarkable exceptions, the same is true of literature in the American tradition. It is, unless it seeks deliberately to imitate some European exemplar, experimental rather than imitative in character. Its emphasis is usually on substance rather than on form. It is, above all, a middle-class literature in the important sense that it finds its power of appeal in its representation of ordinary American life as a vast and romantic adventure. Where, as with Henry James, the roots of its tradition lie in Europe rather than in America, the main impression one derives from reading it is that the author, in drawing his Americans, is remote from the mainstream American life. His American, man or woman, is divorced from the tradition that gives America its peculiar character; and he becomes a stranger to his native land who sees his fellow-countrymen through the eyes of one who has deliberately chosen a foreign mirror through which to look at them. But Emerson, Thoreau, Mark Twain, Hawthorne, and Melville, while they may be deeply influenced by the central stream of civilized intelligence, are always profoundly American, not least in the sense that, wherever their imagination may roam, it is always the American tradition that they put their ultimate allegiance. And once an American writer fails in that allegiance, it is difficult not to feel that the pseudo-European style through which he finds expression is really a mask which he wears like one who hides behind a domino at a ball.

At the centre of the American tradition is the idea of enlightened self-interest. It is assumed that with energy and determination every man can not only look after himself, but is part of a world in which the capacity to advance is universal. That outlook lies at the core of the thought of men so different in temperament and training as Abraham Lincoln and Woodrow Wilson; and there is an important sense in which it is the main principle of Franklin Roosevelt's policies. The consequence of this outlook is far-reaching. On the one hand, it creates a suspicion of all action taken by the government on behalf of the individual. It is argued that this limits his capacity for enterprise and responsibility, and it is widely held, sometimes in the most unexpected quarters, that what a man does for himself is almost certain to be better done than what is done on his behalf. Enlightened self-interest is regarded as the parent of experimentalism; and it is insisted that an accumulation of small acts of self-denial enables any energetic citizen to advance his fortunes. This is perhaps why it seems to take a great crisis—world war, for example— to evoke great sacrifices from Americans; the drama needs to be staged on a vast scale before the average man thinks far beyond the cultivation of his own garden. He can be kind and hospitable and friendly; but the limits of his imagination are more narrow than one would expect from the scale of the civilization in which he is involved. Nor do I think it is fanciful to connect this attitude with the priority of the practical man over the thinker.

Few Americans find it easy to be happy unless they are doing something. The gospel of hard work which they have inherited, in part from the impact of the physical environment and in part from the Puritan tradition, makes it difficult for them not to equate contemplation with laziness. That is why they find the creative use of leisure a more difficult art than any other nation with which I am acquainted. That is why, also, even when they play, there is a seriousness in the amenities of life which is unparalleled elsewhere. To the rich man, for instance, golf is less a game than a pursuit in which, with the aid of the club professional, he gives an almost religious attention to the reduction of his handicap. That is why, again, the intercollegiate athletic contests, whether they are baseball or track-running or even debating, make so important a difference to the status of an academic institution. I have heard a president of Princeton University address its football team before a game with Harvard in terms not very different from Haig's famous "Backs to the Wall" order of March 1918. And athletic eminence may easily result in the kind of solid career which brings the player comfort for the rest of his days. The American is rare who knows how to play merely for the pleasure of playing. He finds it hard to be lazy; so that even in a relatively small town an indifferent bridge-player will take lessons from a professional teacher rather than be looked upon as a failure. A surprising number of Americans do not think it strange that the author of a system of card-playing should turn his attention, in the grim years of the Second World War, to the development of methods by which permanent peace may be secured.

It may well be that so striking a change as the emergence of a specialist in bridge into a specialist in international affairs is merely one expression of that pioneering tradition which has made Americans so apt to specialize in omnicompetence. It may well be, also, that it is the Puritan element in the American tradition which makes them not only take their play so seriously, but assume that they will be open to criticism if their way of earning a livelihood is out of accord with the call of the times. For few peoples, save, possibly, the Japanese, are more sensitive to praise or blame than the Americans. They have none of the Englishman's capacity for assuming that his own judgment about himself is final. They have little of that power of moral and intellectual self-sufficiency which is rooted in the French habit of mind. They never seek, like the Germans since the era of Bismarck, to give a universal character to their national standard of conduct; and they cannot, like the Japanese, enfold themselves with a veil of mystery which the outsider is forbidden to penetrate. In a sense, the American outlook resembles that of the Russian to a remarkable degree. Each is eager to know what is thought about him; and each is as elevated by eulogy as he suffers from blame. This is why, I think, *The American Commonwealth* of Lord Bryce was a real event in the history of the relations between Great Britain and the United States. For Bryce's was the first book by a British writer in which the greatness of America was acknowledged in its due proportions. It atoned for the contempt and dislike which had been poured upon Americans by writers like Captain Basil Hall and Mrs. Trollope and even Charles Dickens. It was the recognition that the United States had reached its historic majority; and it is not, I think, unfair or inaccurate to date the decline of that "inferiority complex"—which emerges in the pages of N. P. Willis and was symbolized with genius by Dickens in the character of Jefferson Brick—from the publication of Bryce's book. And this is true even though, half a century before, Tocqueville had seen the significance of America far more profoundly than Bryce; for Tocqueville was really writing a book on French civilization, and the United States crept into its pages as a source of illustration rather than as the central theme.

Ever since its emergence as an independent political community America has been a political democracy; and the idea of majority rule through representative institutions has been deeply embedded in its tradition. But we must be careful not to embody in the idea of this political democracy more than it in fact implies. It is essentially a democracy of the middle class which assumes, though it does not announce, the authority of wealth, and has been careful, throughout its history, not to permit its informing idea to jeopardize the claims that men of property invariably put forward as the boundaries beyond which democracy may not pass. No one can scrutinize the political history of the democratic tradition in America without seeing that those boundaries are in fact more narrow than might be inferred either from a classic utterance like the Gettysburg speech or from the myriad orations which are evoked on each Fourth of July. They are restrained quite deliberately by the Constitution itself; they are still more restrained by the masterful construction John Marshall, and most of his colleagues and successors, have employed as their method of interpreting its purpose. They are restrained by the difficulty of absorbing into an effective unity the countless immigrants from so many nations of whom America is composed. And they are restrained by the fact that, despite passing phases of passionate anger, the effective organization of the working class into trade-unions began only in the eighties of the last century and has not yet begun to attain an adequate political expression.

But that is not all. There is an important sense in which the very vastness of the opportunity America offered its citizens was inimical to the fulfillment of what a democratic community implies. For, first, until the frontier was exhausted there were few Americans who expected to stay on the bottom rung of the ladder, and fewer still who ever expected that their children would stay there. They mostly took it for granted that the revised edition of Jeffersonian democracy which Woodrow Wilson called the "new freedom" was open to them; and, save in moments of panic or crisis, they rarely dreamed of attacking property, because they expected so soon to own it themselves. That the history of the United States would, despite everything, follow the general pattern of capitalist democracy in Europe occurred only to a few men of special insight like John Taylor of Caroline. In the result, until at least the outbreak of the Great Depression in 1929, the American was rare who recognized that the European pattern was emerging; and if he urged this conclusion in terms of socialism, it was relatively easy to push him aside on the ground that socialistic ideas were a European product with no relevance to the special conditions of American civilization.

So that, in the years, especially after the Civil War, the walls which protected property from democratic invasion grew increasingly high. The farmer was increasingly driven from ownership to tenantry. The worker in industry increasingly found that machine technology called for a scale of investment which only the great corporations could hope to attempt. The professional man, whether lawyer or doctor, engineer or architect, found that economic comfort was rarely attainable unless he was willing to be a dependent of the economic masters of America. And since the political parties were, in their turn, the means through which those masters did their will, it followed that the successful politician, whatever might be the rhetoric of his perorations, was successful because, somehow, he had come to an understanding with men like Mark Hanna or Nelson Aldrich, who were nothing so much as the agents of Wall Street and State Street. It seemed obvious to President Coolidge, whose mind was that of the average successful resident of Main Street, that Mr. Andrew Mellon should be his Secretary of the Treasury since few fortunes rivaled the Mellon fortune in the United States. It would have been interesting to hear the judgment of Jefferson or John Taylor upon that conclusion.

The American Constitution established a political democracy; and the circumstances in which it operated involved a large measure of social equality. The traditions which have been evoked by the history of the last three centuries have given opportunities for individual advancement which, save for Russia since 1917, have been unparalleled in their scale in modern times. It is, moreover, probably true to say that nowhere was the social ascent more easy nor the belief in its validity more profound. Until, at any rate, the Civil War, it would be broadly fair to argue that the proportion of immigrants who failed to better the position they had held in the Old World was relatively small. There are dramatic careers in the industrial field, as there are dramatic careers in the political. Men force their way to success by reason of their own energy and ability. The absence of barriers in their way made the individualism of the Gilded Age seem the mental climate most appropriate to achievement. If the battle was hard, the rewards were magnificent, and most of the social theorists of the time, from William Graham Sumner at Yale to John Bates Clark at Columbia, were emphatic in their conviction that a government which confines itself to police, defence, and the opportunity of education is doing not only most of what it may legitimately do, but is also assuring the survival of the fittest. There are, no doubt, real problems, like the railroads, the growth of trusts, depression among the farmers, the danger lest, as in the great forests of the Northwest, inadequate measures of conservation should be adopted to safeguard the interests of the future. But, in general, the faith in *laissez-faire* was widespread and profound; the growth in population and productive capacity not less than the rise in the standard of life seemed to suggest that the American system reproduced the order of nature. Certainly until the Great Depression of 1929, it did not seem to the vast majority of Americans that a positive state meant more than the protection of the lazy and the inefficient against the consequences of their own inadequacies.

Yet it may be argued, I think, without unfairness, that once the main incidence of American economic effort became industrial rather than agrarian in character, they were too few in the United States who realized that the complexity of relations in the great society made it urgent that there should be a rapid increase in the power of government to regulate. The forms of political democracy obscured, but did not conceal, the fact that they were being based on an economic foundation which was growingly oligarchical in character. The great business man of the eighteen forties and fifties became the great corporation of the eighties and nineties. Montana might display all the typical organs of a democratic state; but behind those organs the effective power which moved them was in the hands of the Anaconda Copper Mining Company. The electors of Delaware might send their two representatives to the Senate; but everyone knew that their real principal was the great Du Pont family. No doubt there are states, like New York and Massachusetts, or California and Washington, the population of which is too big to be dominated by a single interest; and, no doubt, also, there are epochs when the depth of national feeling has reached an intensity so great that, as in 1932, all habits of traditional allegiance are swept on one side. But it is important to note that in all normal circumstances no relation is more significant in American politics than that between the party machine, whether in state or city, and the great corporations, and that there are areas, like Imperial Valley in California, or Jersey City in New Jersey, in which the meaning of political democracy is hardly known. Nor is it irrelevant that when the first Senator La Follette was seeking to make Republicanism progressive in Wisconsin, he had to build up a machine to carry out his purpose. In the American tradition, in brief, the forces which bind men together generally are interests rather than ideas; and those who give their support to the successful candidate almost assume that they have made an implied contract enforceable by reason of the consideration upon which it is built.

To two other elements in the pattern of the political tradition I must draw attention. The first is the judicial element. It is, of course, true that the United States has had many great judges, whether in the federal courts, like Marshall and Holmes, Brandeis and Cardozo, or in the state courts, like Shaw of Massachusetts or Kent of New York. But it is also true that among their functions not the least the courts have performed is to act as a brake on the democratic habits of legislatures. Anyone who reads either the address to the court by Mr. Choate in the Income Tax cases, or the decision of the court itself, or examines some of the utterances of Mr. Justice McReynolds during the springtime of the New Deal, or analyses the injunctions granted against trade-unions in strike cases, will have no difficulty in understanding why Mr. Justice Holmes was insistent that judges do in fact legislate.[1] They are, in a word, a third chamber of the legislature in the area of their operation and it is difficult not to argue that in all major political matters they find it extremely difficult to avoid the temptation to substitute their own ideas of what is politically wise or reasonable for the conclusions at which the elected members of legislature have arrived. Certainly it is hard not to feel that the vital difference between the decision of the Supreme Court in *Abrams v. United States*,[2] and what would have been found by a court in Nazi Germany was less in the actual result arrived at than in the noble phrasing of the famous dissent of Mr. Justice Holmes. But when the courts in a political system cross the tenuous boundary which separates legal issues from political conclusions it will usually be found that they are acting, however unconsciously, as counsel against the purposes of democracy.

The other element of importance is that of the Civil Service. No doubt there are departments of the American government, the Geological Survey, for example, and the Bureau of Standards, which it would be very difficult to overpraise. No doubt, also, there are periods of great crisis when the Executive attracts to itself men and women of brilliant capacity and remarkable initiative. But I think it is broadly true to say that the American Civil Service, both in the federal and in the state governments, has been the Cinderella of the American democracy to which no prince appears at midnight with a glass slipper. For since the highest posts are political, it is rare to find among their occupants either men or women with the time to work out a great programme on an ample scale; there have been exceptions, of course, but it is rare to discover them. And when one moves down the hierarchy, it is difficult to find, outside exceptional men like Mr. Joseph B. Eastman of the Interstate Commerce Commission, or that Mr. Edward Mosely to whom the United States owes so much of the legislation that protects safety on the railroads, officials who have either the status or the authority to do creative work of the quality a democracy requires. It is true, indeed, that in the period of the New Deal there developed a new sense of the significance of government; it did much to restore that confidence in democratic principles which business men did so much to destroy in the first years of the Great Depression. But, apart from a small number of men in each Department, it is pretty true to say that the posts available were not likely to attract men of first-rate talent whose qualities had a marketable value elsewhere. And when to this difficulty there is added the continuous, often profound hostility of Congress to the idea of positive administration, it was pretty inevitable that, below the highest grade of officials, not many men of outstanding capacity would suffer the humiliation it was the special delight of Congress, both in the Senate and the House of Representatives, to inflict upon them. The abolition of the National Resources Planning Board, and the determined efforts made to arrest the development of the T.V.A., which is one of the outstanding American achievements of modern times, equal, if they do not surpass, the attempt of the State Department to bolster up the Vichy regime and to support, through men like Giraud and Peyrouton, the France which in the opinion of many people betrayed its own citizens in the summer of 1940. It is little short of amazing that the propertied interests of the United States, with all their heavy responsibility for the Great Depression, should have been able to depict creative administration as the equivalent of bureaucracy when it was by that creative administration that it was saved in 1933. The one objective of property was to maintain, in the second and third terms of President Roosevelt, the belief in a system of "free enterprise" which had long ceased to have relevance to the conditions of American economic life.

It is interesting to realize the methods by which this belief has been maintained. It is interesting because, alongside the political democracy so deeply rooted in the American tradition, most of the instruments through which the picture of the scene to be interpreted to the American is painted have become a branch of Big Business. That is true of the cinema; it is true of the radio, it is true of the overwhelming proportion of the press. Even if, here and there, a source of doubt whether the habits of Big Business fit into the habits of a democratic way of life, find means of expression, in some of Mr. Chaplin's films, for instance, in the remarkable use to which President Roosevelt put the radio, in a small number of weeklies whose total circulation does not add up to the influence of a single publication like the *Saturday Evening Post*, or in the occasional columns of an eminent though small-town journalist, like the late William Allen White, the incidence of the whole picture is enormously and continuously tilted towards the support of vested interests against the democratic tradition for which America came into being as an independent nation. And the immense influence of advertising moves in the same direction. In general, too, that is the end which the theatre serves; only an occasional play raises doubts about the validity of the "economic royalists'" claim to rule. If it is different with the printed book, as when Mr. Steinbeck's *Grapes of Wrath* brings home so vividly the tragedy of the migrant unemployed, or Mr. and Mrs. Lynd's remarkable studies in *Middletown* draw an impressive contrast between democracy as an idea and democracy in action, the number of Americans to whom these criticisms of the actual situation penetrate is gravely small compared to those who live by the ordinary newspaper, the ordinary film, or those trade journals which spend so much of their space in explaining that American democracy involves a government which leaves unfettered the activities of business men. It is not, I think, an exaggeration to say that Mr. Sinclair Lewis's *Babbitt* is an accurate composite photograph of the mind produced by instruments of propaganda.

Mr. Babbitt is kindly, he is hospitable, he has moments when he dreams that he can break away from the conventions by which he is mastered. He is an honorable husband and a father with an eager desire to spoil his children. He is proud of his house and his car, and he is anxious that his wife shall be at least his equal in spending power to any of her average neighbors. He rarely reads, and still more rarely thinks. Surrounding him is a vast miasma of what he thinks good fellowship, but which, in fact, hides from him the sight of that actuality he uncomfortably suspects is near at hand. He is capable of a temporary indignation. But as soon as he begins to count the cost of its translation into action, he realizes that he is in fact a prisoner who dare not take the risk of attempting to escape. So that he settles down to the acceptance of conventions which he is persuaded to identify with the American tradition even while he is oppressed by the uncomfortable suspicion that they are in fact its antithesis.

And to the immense weight of these influences must be added the power of Big Business in the educational world as well as in the realm of scientific research. The schools, where they are publicly controlled by the state governments, are almost wholly devoted to the exposition of a faith which makes "getting on in the world" practically an article in a religious creed; and where they are private, institutions, they do not even question the validity of the traditional economic system. In the field of higher education the power of wealth is almost overwhelming. Where the university or college is maintained by the state, it is difficult for radical theory to express itself in any subject which may endanger the rights of property; it is typical that the University of Montana should have dismissed a distinguished professor of economics for proving that, over long years, the great copper companies had evaded their fiscal obligations. The university or college which depends on private endowment is, in some ways, more liberal in outlook than the university or college dependent upon state funds; but in any field of study which raises the issue of property it is rare indeed to find that the challenging mind is sure of a welcome. It was, after all, a great New York newspaper which practically invited Columbia University to dismiss the eminent historian Charles Beard for examining in a realistic way the origins of the Federal Constitution; and when, in 1919, the police of Boston, under great provocation, went on strike, the immediate reaction of the president and corporation of Harvard University was to offer its services to the governor of Massachusetts though they were wholly unaware of the grievances through which the strike had arisen. Nor is it unimportant that the investigation has established the payment to professors of economics of not inconsiderable sums by trade associations to argue in their textbooks against the dangers of public ownership.

The simple fact is that the American educational system reflects the character of the economic system within which it functions. It could hardly, indeed, be otherwise. One could no more expect a capitalist society to permit its teachers generally to undermine the foundations of private property than one could expect the schools and universities of the Soviet Union to admit teachers whose energies are devoted to expounding the fallacies of Marxism, or the authorities in the academic institutions of Vatican City to exhibit an eager tolerance for scholars who think more highly of Strauss and of Bauer, of Loisy and of George Foot Moore, than of the representatives of the official outlook. No society ever permits the foundations of its system to be called into question unless it is certain that it will triumph overwhelmingly in the reply.

What is of interest in the working of the American educational system is less its subordination to the effective sources of sovereignty than the immense mythology it has contributed to the shaping of the American tradition. Few aspects of its life have done so much to persuade the masses not only to believe that the path from log cabin to White House is direct and universally open, but also to accept the faith that every man has a full opportunity to climb to the apex of the social pyramid. If Napoleon persuaded the common soldier to believe that he carried a marshal's baton in his knapsack, the American school has made it difficult for any able and ambitious boy not to dream of the day when his name will be mentioned with those of Rockefeller and Astor, of Vanderbilt and Henry Ford. And, after all, until quite recent times the chances in the economic field were so immense, the examples of remarkable achievement so numerous, that it was far from easy for the skeptic not to be doubtful about the validity of his own skepticism. The hope of the White House for the politically ambitious young man might, in truth, be far more imaginary than real. The innumerable books and speeches which have eulogized the almost self-educated Abraham Lincoln as the symbol of the common people of America have usually failed to note that Lincoln was that symbol essentially because he was a very extraordinary man. A vast legion, no doubt, has set out on the road to the White House, but it is only a small platoon that has ever had real hope of arriving there.

And yet, when this has been said, we are bound to remember that the political career has been more fully open to ordinary people in the United States than in any other country in the world right down to our own day. It has been easier for the poor and the humble to attain membership of either House of Congress or of the state legislatures than in any country save the Soviet Union. Nor is that all. The absence of a monarchical system has meant the absence of a court, and the absence of a court has meant the absence of that special atmosphere of "deference" which Bagehot noted in England as typical of the Victorian Age. There is no career that is closed to any American, save on the ground of color, and, perhaps, also, of creed. The embassies and legations of the United States are not what John Bright called the Foreign Office of Great Britain—the "outdoor relief department of the aristocracy." Lawyer, doctor, engineer, university professor, there is a wide highway along which the humblest may pass to the summit of professions such as these. While it is no doubt true that there are some half-dozen American universities in which the student has advantages either by reason of birth or wealth, there are scores of other universities in which there is no such advantage. Even the long years of depression and war have done relatively little to destroy that fundamental element in the American tradition—the belief that a man makes himself and that his best chance of self-fulfillment comes from opening to him as widely as possible the gates of education. There are, indeed, narrow boundaries set to his hopes if he is of Negro descent. The experience of Governor Smith, in 1928, makes it clear that the time has not yet come when a Roman Catholic may count on entering the White House. Save in the world of industry and finance, there are many invisible barriers to the upward progress of the Jew, universities where he may not teach, hospitals where he may not practice, clubs which he cannot join, even areas in cities where he cannot rent a house or spend a night in a hotel.

We must not underestimate the price that is paid by these minorities, whether on racial or religious grounds, for their exclusion from a full participation in the American tradition. It is a high price materially; that is shown by the wage differential in the South, to take one example only, as between white and colored labor. And, not less, it is a high price, spiritually, for the sense of psychological frustration imposed on these minorities is often as ugly and as brutal as the characteristic habits of Nazi or of Fascist. It breeds in large numbers of American citizens an unnecessary inferiority complex, and this, in its turn, finds expression in excessive arrogance or undue humility.

Yet even when this price is entered on the debit side of the American tradition—and it is a heavy addition to that side—what remains in amplitude of opportunity is remarkable. The ordinary man has the conviction that no gates may be barred to his entry. He feels that he has the right to experiment with himself. He feels the elbow-room that comes from membership in a community that is dynamic in quality. Not only can he lift up his eyes to the hills, the community expects him to lift them up. That he has made his way forward gives him a title to pride; there is no assumption that he is moving outside the boundaries to which, by his origins, he ought to be confined. For the ordinary American citizen no trace has remained of that feudal heritage which still has deep influence on the social relationships of most European countries. There is an equality between citizen and citizen which one finds widespread in France and Scandinavia, but very partially in England, and hardly at all in Central or Southeastern Europe. The English workman may speak frankly to his employer, but he stands, as it were, with his cap in his hand. He expects always to be a workman; he cannot forget his dependence on his employer. There is no such habit of deference in the American workman. He is aware of an economic distinction of class between himself and his employer. But he does not easily regard that economic distinction as entailing a social consequence; and he may well feel convinced, especially if he is young, that he will in any case transcend the economic distinction in course of time. I do not say that the conviction is likely to be realized; on the contrary, the development of the economic pattern in the age of giant industry reduces the likelihood in each decade. But it is important that the incentive to the conviction is inherent in the environment. It means that the static relations of the Old World have been banished from the new.

This difference in expectation is so vital to the understanding of the difference between the American tradition and that of Europe that it is worth while for a moment to illustrate its consequence. It is significant, for example, that it is difficult to find an American who can perform the duties of a butler or a valet as they are performed in a great English house by a trained English servant; indeed, the rich American who has arrived at the level where he desires to be conspicuous by domestic ostentation is likely to engage an English butler or valet, as his wife is likely to employ an English or a French maid. It is seen, again, in the relation between the officer class and the rank and file of the armies; the kind of disciplinary relationship which is imposed between the two grades in the historic European armies would provoke a riot if its imposition was sought in an American regiment. The European officer belongs to an organ which, historically, has usually been the instrument of aristocratic purposes; his regiment is the country in which he is a nobleman. But no such military tradition has ever existed in the United States, nor could it easily be formed. For though Washington was a Virginia gentleman and perhaps the richest American of his time, his army was built, like Cromwell's New Model, of small farmers and independent working men who enlisted, not because they were pressed, nor because they had no alternative means of life, but because they believed in the greatness of the cause for which they fought. And this has set the background of the American discipline in all branches of the service of defense. It has made impossible the growth of a caste spirit which could prevail against the notion that the soldier is in essence a civilian who, for temporary and democratic purposes, has taken up arms.

One final instance may be quoted. The Londoner is rare, the English citizen rarer still, who has been inside the palace of his king or knows the historic residence of the prime minister as more than a name. But few Americans visit Washington without going to see the White House, and there are days when it is crowded, not with some specially invited guests of high social status, but with ordinary citizens who wish to see for themselves how their president lives. And I have myself seen, in Albany, New York, and Olympia, Washington, a teacher taking in his class of boys and girls for a talk with the governor of the state after a visit to the legislative assembly. The psychological significance of all this is the absence it implies in the tradition of the hierarchical structure which surrounds so much of the process of government in Europe and Asia. Scandinavia and in a less degree Holland apart, there is nothing on either of those continents which can rival the decisive simplicity the American tradition has effected. It has not come without opposition; John Adams's conception of what the presidency should be in its public expression is sufficient proof of that. President or senator, governor or judge of the Supreme Court, the American has given his chosen representatives a stature of ample dignity without himself having to go down on his knees. That is an achievement of which the impact on the democratic idea is more profound than it is easy to recognize.

There is a religious element in the American tradition the nature of which it is obviously easy to mistake. The dramatic history of the colonies of New England in the seventeenth century, the almost theatrical exploits of the remarkable Mather dynasty in Massachusetts, the struggle between Puritan orthodoxy and the antinomianism of Anne Hutchinson, the defiant plea of Roger Williams for separation of state and church, the social prestige of the clergy until some such time as that of William Ellery Channing and Emerson, these factors, together with the admittedly great influence in forming the climate of the Revolution of ministers like Jonathan Mayhew and Charles Chauncy, has led, I think, to a misapprehension of the part played by this religious element. For perhaps fifty or sixty years after the landing of the Mayflower, there is no reason to doubt that the influence of Puritanism in New England was extensive and profound. There is no reason to doubt, either, that a considerable number of the early settlers left England for conscience sake, and that they approved the imposition of a rigorous code of conduct and belief upon all whom they were able to influence.

But it is important not to exaggerate either the influence of Puritanism on the American scene or the degree to which it expressed itself in a gloomy outlook even among the most faithful of its votaries. The full rigor of Puritan orthodoxy was, after all, challenged almost from the outset of the settlement of New England. What it contributed of importance to the life about it was far less a dogmatic theology than a sense of the urgency of effort and a will to be saved in heaven by attaining first to comfort and safety upon earth. That the party of theocracy was persistent and influential there is no reason at all to doubt; but it was already prepared to compromise by the middle of the seventeenth century, and, by its end, a liberal outlook had developed, as in the writings of John Wise, which was fatal to its claims. By the middle of the eighteenth century Puritan orthodoxy was already at a discount; and by the time when the obstinacy of George III and the folly of his ministers were preparing the ground for independence, it was already ceasing to be possible to make the profession of a Christian creed the basis of citizenship. That is why the separation of Church and State was so easily accomplished in 1787. The religious logic of Jonathan Edwards, and the passionate emotionalism of the Great Awakening, are far less authoritative than the demands of a life that is continually calling for experiment and makes the very concept of the frontier a perpetual source of the obligation to recognize novelty and adapt it to experience.

That is why what begins as a theocratic principle ends by becoming a tradition that it is not very easy to distinguish from utilitarianism. It may well be that there were many to whom this utilitarian outlook was framed in a religious background. To work hard, to live an orderly life, to have a name for integrity and fair dealing, not to spend one's substance in reckless display, to have the resolution to carry out the purposes you undertake—it is, roughly, to an ethic such as this that the religion of America had been shaped when the basic tradition was formed. Many who followed it, as in the case of Jefferson, were Deists; many others found it helpful to support this view by attaching divine sanction to its validity. What it is important to stress is the fact that, as so notably shown in both the life and the works of Benjamin Franklin, the environment of America shaped traditional religions to its needs much more than the traditional religions shaped the American environment to their claims.

And the outcome is, I think, not easily to be mistaken. The churches must aid men in their struggle to be citizens; religion is of social value as a means of keeping order and stirring men to make the exertions that life requires. That is what Nathaniel Hawthorne meant when he wrote that "the entire system of man's affairs, as at present established, is built up purposely to exclude the careless and happy soul. The very children would upbraid the wretched individual who should endeavor to take life and the world as what we might naturally suppose them meant for, a place and opportunity for enjoyment."[3] The vast continent needed men and women who had this faith if they were to subdue it to their purposes. And since to some of those whose faith was equaled by their capacity or their skill there came an immense reward, it became natural to think of that reward as God's favor to the man of grace; more, to think that worldly failure was the outcome of sin. The relation between man and his Maker then becomes an individual matter between them, interference with which is resented. This outlook at once encourages individualism in politics, since it urges a man to depend upon his own effort, and discourages the notion of churches as institutions with a part to play upon the political scene.

It is in its encouragement of individual effort that religion found its place in the American Tradition. And that power was intensified by the influence upon it of frontier conditions and frontier psychology. For these brought out all the drive to independence that was inherent in the Protestant idea. Mostly, the doctrines which developed were evangelical, and they emphasized the right of the individual to salvation. They were far more successful in terms of an emotional appeal than they were in terms of their intellectual content. They were in large part built upon the faith of their possessor in an inner light which it was beyond the power of scholarship even to reach, much less to destroy. For the dwellers of the frontier areas this inner light had the immense value of conferring upon them an unbreakable self-confidence which was easily capable of suffusing the whole of their personalities and thus provided them with armor against the physical and economic difficulties of frontier life. Not seldom, the character of the doctrines accepted seems to us to reproduce the wilder fanaticisms of the English Civil Wars, and a new Thomas Edwards would have had no difficulty in writing a new *Gangraena* about the Muggletonians, Come-Outers, Shakers, Rappites, and so on. It is true that a number of these sects, like the Moravians of Pennsylvania or the Brotherhood of Perfection, began with communist ideals; but it was rare for them to endure. The very nature of the physical environment made for individualism in economic matters. Outside the Mormons, indeed, and the Shakers, the persistence of the co-operative spirit in religion for any length of time and on any considerable scale was very exceptional.

The impact of this frontier religion was to intensify the idea of equality, and this, in its turn, had profound influence upon the idea of democracy in politics. It made for universal suffrage; it was impossible to exclude the self-confident pioneer of Kentucky or Tennessee from the right to determine how he would be governed. Nor must we forget that none of the emotional satisfaction which the multiplicity of religious sects afforded ever interfered with the growing secularization of American life. From the first third of the eighteenth century, at any rate, acceptance of the supernatural, often in the most fantastic forms, developed at an equal pace with an interest in science and philosophy. That secularization is shown, among other things, by the greater variety of the professions on which university graduates embarked between 1750 and

1800, as compared with 1700 to 1750, and the decrease in the proportion of those who desired the clerical career. It is shown by the widening interest in science and literature, and by the rapid growth of newspapers and pamphlets the basis of which was devotion to nonreligious matters.

By the time of the American Revolution a large part of the character which religion has contributed to the tradition had begun to take the form it has ever since assumed. Everywhere the established churches were losing ground, not least because colonies like Rhode Island and Pennsylvania where showing that religious toleration is closely connected with commercial prosperity. And it is significant that a propagandist of genius like Samuel Adams thought it worth his while to warn his correspondents against the dangers of prelacy. On the evidence, It seems clear beyond dispute that the experience of religious freedom begat an impatience of constraint in political matters. Perhaps that is one of the reasons why the prohibition of any religious test as a qualification for federal office went through so easily at Philadelphia in 1787. By 1833 even Massachusetts had accepted the separation of Church and State as part of its constitution. There still remained a small number of states in which a faith in the teachings of Christianity was necessary to public office; and Tocqueville was present in court when the testimony of a witness was refused on the ground of Atheism. The case of Abner Kneeland again shows that half a century after the making of the Federal Constitution a man could still be imprisoned for blasphemy, in the face of protest from men like Emerson, Theodore Parker, and Channing. And laws against blasphemy continue on the statute books of a number of states.

The tradition that has emerged has something of the character that Tocqueville predicted for it in the great classic that was the outcome of his famous visit to the United States. He had left a Europe in which it was broadly true that it was rare indeed to hold democratic and religious opinions at one and the same time. He had read in the literature of the French Age of Reason that faith would decline as understanding developed. He found, to his surprise, that Americans believed in the close connection between religion and democracy. When he sought for the cause of this unexpected conception, he believed that it was because, with the separation of Church and State, the clergy did not concern themselves with political issues. The inference has followed that religion, in itself, is a mainstay of the social order, with the result that with minor qualifications, all property devoted to religious purposes is exempt from taxation.

That inference is a living part, it may even be said, perhaps, a growing part, of the American tradition. Particular faiths may be unpopular at some given time, as the Roman Catholic Church was unpopular with the Know-Nothing party in the fifties of the last century, or the Ku Klux Klan after the First World War. On issues by which the country is passionately divided, as on slavery, for instance, or the treatment of the Negro people today, the Churches will, as a rule, be careful to insist that the issue is outside their competence. No politician would think of running for office on the basis of an announcement of his atheism; certainly he would not be elected if he did. And no party which is seeking to win elections in a great centre of population, like New York or Chicago or Boston, would think of adopting candidates without regard to the distribution of religious opinions among the voters. Congress has its chaplains, as have the armed forces of the republic; and it is, on the whole, unusual for the president or the governor of a state not to offer the historic courtesies to the Church into which he was born. And, on the whole again, it is pretty accurate to say that the main impact of the Churches is to show a vague interest in mild reforms, but a deep antagonism to any radical social philosophy. Certainly it would be true to argue that it is the combined influence of religious institutions, including Jewish, that has dug the main abyss between the United States and the Soviet Union. The constant insistence by President Roosevelt on the duty of the Soviet Government to make possible freedom of religious worship to its citizens has been of extraordinary interest. What it is not easy to discover is whether the power of religion in the American tradition is due to the individualism it clothed in garments of respectability in the past or to the hope in its ruling class that the leaders of the Churches will moderate any popular zeal for reform in the years to come.

The famous phrase of the Massachusetts Constitution which sought to establish "a government of laws and not of men" expresses a vital element in the American tradition which is of peculiar interest both for what it has achieved and for the crosscurrents it has encountered in the historic environment. Part of its strength is due, no doubt, to the fact that the maxims of popular government enshrined in the Common Law seemed, as indeed they were, a safeguard against tyranny whether in Church or State. The tyrant might be a monarch like George III, or a Tory governor like Andros or Hutchinson, or a vested interest like that of British mercantilists; one can detect in the growth of esteem for, and power among, the lawyers in the eighteenth, as compared with the seventeenth century, a sense of respect for objective rules which cannot be twisted to anyone's favor. Nor is it possible to mistake the enhanced prestige of the idea of law as soon as the debate began with Parliament which grew into the War of Independence. The need to state a case that was logically convincing against the claim of the House of Commons meant a new regard for the lawyer who could show from Coke and Locke and Blackstone the right of Americans to self government. And, once the Constitution had been ratified, the Supreme Court attained a status in public respect which not even the poorest of its members have permitted it to lose. For the Supreme Court has been, in a very especial sense, the guardian of property against the power of numbers. From the days when Chief Justice Marshall gave it this character—despite the presence of occasional members on the Court like Justices Holmes and Brandeis and Cardozo, with their view that legislative experiments "must be considered in the light of our whole experience and not merely in that of what was said a hundred years ago"—to protect the property of the few against the will of the people has remained the function of the lawyer in most American courts and, above all, on the Supreme Court of the United States. This has been, broadly speaking, clear beyond mistake.

That function has been to arrest the pace of the dynamism inherent in American society. It is not merely that it has arrested obvious techniques like the income tax or the prohibition of child labor. It is not merely that the courts have regarded "due process" not, as Judge Learned Hand so aptly described it, as an expression of "the English sporting idea of fair play," but rather as though the Fifth and the Fourteenth Amendments were, in Mr. Justice Holmes's famous jibe, the enactment of "Mr. Herbert Spencer's "*Social Statics*." The courts have been hostile to trade-unionism almost throughout its history. They have used the idea of liberty and contract to strike down measure after measure which a legislative assembly believed, after careful examination of the evidence, to be necessary to the social welfare. And, from the time of the Sedition Laws of 1798, they have not hesitated to admit appeals to freedom which were, in fact, what Mr. Justice Cardozo called "the masquerade of privilege or inequality seeking to entrench itself behind the catchword of a principle." Their hostility to the development of an effective administrative law has been nothing so much as a method by which they could strike into impotence the first efforts to develop in the great society of the United States the obvious implications of the positive State. American courts, in general, have used the power of judicial review to replace the experts inference from social and economic fact, which he examines in the spirit of scientific inquiry, by criteria which derive both their content and their standard from an America which hardly knew what the great society involved.

Yet, in general, the rule of law, as lawyers think of that rule, has seemed to Americans an essential part of their tradition and the outstanding guarantee of their freedom. Living under a written constitution, trained, therefore, to think of the lawyer, in his capacity of judge, as the natural source of its final interpretation, they did not easily see that, in general, the man appointed to the bench was fairly certain to be a successful lawyer, and that few people could be successful lawyers unless they possessed as clients the prosperous class in the American community. Or, alternatively, the men nominated to the bench were usually receiving the reward of service to their political party; and it was then at least equally unlikely that they would have opinions which differed at all widely from the party norm. It is only necessary to read the enormous volume in which the Judiciary Committee of the Senate reported its hearings on the fitness of Mr. Justice Brandeis for the Supreme Court, or, from a different angle, the correspondence between Theodore Roosevelt and Senator Henry Cabot Lodge on the desirability of nominating Mr. Justice Holmes to the court of which he was for a generation the greatest member, to realize that the normal criteria of judicial fitness have been an eager acceptance of the American past rather than an eager interest in the American Future.

And this attitude of acceptance of these criteria is, I suggest, remarkable because the American tradition is one in which veneration for law is at least equaled by the widespread habit of a violence which disregards the habits of law. Partly, that violence is the inevitable accompaniment of a frontier civilization; where the settled habits of law are absent, it is not surprising that men should take its making, as in the Gold Rush of 1849, into their own hands. Partly, also, the violence derives from the mixture of races and philosophies out of which, at so swift a pace, America has emerged. It is connected very directly with the fact that it was so easy, if the law was put aside, to make one's way to wealth on so immense a scale. That led to the corruption of courts and legislatures of a type comparable in intensity with the normal habits of Southeastern Europe. But it is important to remember that "graft" cannot become endemic in a society without creating a class of men who live by their power to flout the law. The business man who buys the political machine, whether he be big or small in his ambitions, is bound to beget the "boss"; and since the boss can survive only by his power to deliver to business the favors it is purchasing, gangsterism is the necessary corollary of the boss system. And once this technique is accepted at the apex of the economic pyramid, it is bound to be accepted at its base as well. Senator Penrose belongs to the same species as such a boss as Platt of New York or Pendergast of Kansas City; and their species is part of the same genus as that of which a gangster like Capone is likely to remain the supreme symbol for the first half of this century. For once men seek to by-pass the law, they are bound to call into being not merely those who will evade it if they can, but those who will break it with savage indifference if they know no other road to power and fortune.

Two other factors in this aspect of the American tradition require emphasis. There is a real sense in which the American respect for law has of itself begotten lawlessness. For the effort to control every field of human contact by statute—an obvious deposit of the Puritan Heritage—with the result that the sale of tobacco and liquor can be prohibited, meant that a group of men would arise to supply these wants to which the law refused satisfaction. The more widespread the want, the greater would be the profit in supplying it, and the more earnest would be the zeal of those responsible for applying the law to see that it was enforced. Out of this there developed quite naturally a sense of satisfaction in out-witting lawmakers. And once there is that kind of tension in the social environment, which this generation has witnessed in the conflict between those who regarded prohibition as almost an article of religious faith and those to whom it was a wanton interference with personal freedom, the stage is set for the breeding of violence by the attempt to compel obedience to the law. No one can read the history of the methods by which Mr. Rockefeller established his supremacy in the oil industry without seeing that the long trail of bribery and corruption, thuggery and suicide, that accompanied it gave birth inevitably to a world in which the law was not a principle to respect, but an obstacle to evade. And Mr. Rockefeller is only an outstanding figure in a vast procession of men prepared to hack their way to power remorselessly. The methods by which Texas became American, the domination of the farmers by the railroads, the habits of the lumber and the cattle millionaires—all these must be set in the framework of a community which wants at once the advantages of settled rules without allowing them to impede their march to fortune.

The other factor of importance is the need to realize that the primitive values of the pioneer, which loom so large in the American tradition, are psychological as well as geographical in character. It is not merely on the frontier that men seize the opportunity before their eyes; they seize it also in that settled realm where, in a new industry or a new method of organization, there is the big chance present for the taking. Capitalist industrialism presented to men like Astor and Vanderbilt, Jay Gould and Rockefeller, exactly the same chance in kind as virgin America presented to the Puritan settlers of the seventeenth century. Just as the Red Indian was the enemy in one generation, so was a strong trade-union in the later period; and the same satisfaction that was felt when an Indian attack was beaten off was felt when a strike was broken. The central ideal in the perspective of which all values are set is the lure of vast and sudden wealth. Its influence on every aspect of American life is hardly capable of over-estimation. It infects the politician, the lawyer, the priest, even the teacher. And it infects them while they are troubled in their consciences by that American dream of equal opportunity which is always challenging the values of a business civilization.

This, I think, is why so large a proportion of American millionaires have sought to achieve goodwill in the community by the generosity of their public gifts. The men whom Theodore Roosevelt attacked as "male-factors of great wealth" sought thereby to prove, perhaps as much to themselves as to their fellow citizens, that they followed a path which was not merely a selfish one. They might act in their business life with the remorseless cruelty of a Caesar Borgia; but like the latter they craved a reputation of being benefactors of the society they dominated. They erected great buildings, they founded universities, they bought rare pictures and manuscripts and books, they endowed great researches in science and medicine, in archaeology and exploration. The condition they exacted was the admission of their right to shape the power of the State to their own interests. But this condition made the idea of a rule of law which bore equally upon all citizens a myth by which they were hardly even themselves deceived. And it meant, also, that most of those who sought to challenge their supremacy had to fight their way to wealth by themselves insisting that the rule of law was a myth. Later, the newcomers, too, would pay the price of their insistence by a similar generosity. What all of them omitted to notice was that the habit of mind they engendered did profound and widespread injury to that respect for law upon which so much of the future of the American tradition depended.

The power of a tradition to endure depends upon its capacity to command a continuing faith; and this, in its turn, depends upon its power to evoke hope and exhilaration from the masses. A ruling class is usually safe so long as the system it controls is able to secure this evocation. For so long as men have the sense that the road is open, they do not feel that they must take to jungle paths. No student of American history can fail to observe that, the Negro problem alone apart, its mental climate, is one of discovery, expansion, optimism. There are periods, no doubt, of crisis; but the vitality of the scene is so abundant that it is rare for men to be unable to overcome them rapidly. The legend of America is of unlimited spaces, of endless opportunities, of resources which know no bounds. All that is valid in the Old World it has inherited; to that it has added a chance of personal fulfillment which the Old World has never known. And to these immense benefits there was added a virtual freedom, for over a century, from the dangers of military attack, the power, accordingly, to emphasize the primacy of civil life as the context in which political effort was set. If the successful soldier has been rewarded four times with the presidency of the United States, it is as a person in civil life that he has received his reward.

The United States, moreover, has been free from all the limitations of a feudal tradition. It has had no permanent ruling class either in a personal or in a geographical sense. If it has been essentially a bourgeois civilization, its middle class has never, as in Europe, had to share the possession of the state power with the survivors, whether the landowners or a military caste, of an earlier regime. No doubt it suffered the terrible anguish of a civil war, the marks of which can still be seen in the mind and habits of the South and in its relative place in the social economy of America; and it is even true that though the Civil War formally abolished Negro slavery, it did not solve the problem of the Negro's status in the social and economic life of the nation. But, apart from this exception, the hindrances of which in the Old World have stood in the way of the rise of the common man have been in principle absent. Nor is there any other nation with such natural resources to explore which has explored them so profoundly. No other nation, either, has been so little the prisoner of its past, or so apt to technological invention and its use to ease the burden of toil. No other nation has placed less emphasis upon birth, or regarded with greater honor the task of earning one's daily bread. No other nation has made the road to knowledge more accessible to the mass of its people. Nor is there any other nation in which the faith in progress has been more deep or universal, the confidence in the ability of the ordinary man to solve for himself the problems by which he is confronted more abiding.

For something over three hundred years after its emergence into world history these have been the elements out of which the American tradition was built. It was rarely called into question; and some of the outstanding figures in the American record, Jefferson, for example, and Walt Whitman, believed in it with a fervor that was almost religious in its intensity. If, on occasion, the tradition was challenged, if, sometimes, men feared for its preservation, or could not, like Henry James, accept the inference it implied, it is difficult to doubt that, until the end of the First World War, the acceptance of the framework it provided for life in the United States was the postulate on which the overwhelming majority of its citizens organized their daily activities. They might be poor; they would not remain poor. They might be out of work; a job was waiting around the corner. They might be half-literate; their children would go to college. They might be foreign born; in the fullest sense of the term their children born in America would inherit the tradition in all its amplitude. It may even be said that after 1919 the tradition enjoyed an Indian summer which lasted for a decade. It was as nothing so much as the fulfillment of the tradition that, in his inaugural address on March 4, 1929, President Hoover could announce to the world that the problem of poverty had been solved in the United States.

It was within eight months after that ardent declaration had been made that the United States was caught in the greatest depression of its history. The unemployed were counted by millions; men who had been accounted wealthy were bankrupt paupers; perhaps a third of the productive capacity of America remained unused; something between a quarter and a third of its population was dependent upon public relief; scores of thousands of farmers were in the hands of creditors; hundreds of banks were compelled to close their doors; and a dollar based on the largest gold reserve in the history of the world had to be revalued and cut loose from gold.

On that momentous day when President Franklin Roosevelt took office it was no longer possible to pretend that the American tradition held the same high place even among the citizens of the United States that it had held when President Hoover entered so confidently upon his task. New winds of doctrine were blowing from East and West, some of them cold winds, cheerless and harsh. If the next years were to show that Adam Smith was right indeed when he said that there "is a great deal of ruin in a nation," the three terms—this fact alone was a startling development of the tradition—were to open a new epoch in American history, to force its people to ask themselves new questions, even to compel them to answer some of the old in a new way. Americans became aware, in part, at least, to their chagrin, that they were, with all their power, still a unit only in a larger and more complicated whole from whose fate they could not separate themselves. A new meaning emerged for California and Oregon and Washington when Pearl Harbor emphasized the significance of being a Pacific power; and there was a portent of unmistakable urgency when it became obvious, with the fall of France, that the occupation of North Africa by a hostile power might challenge the safety of the United States from the Caribbean to the North Atlantic. Much that, until then, had been little more than rhetoric became almost overnight a stark reality; for the Japanese menace bound up the fate of the United States with Australia and Canada, as the German menace bound it up with that of Canada and Great Britain and the future of the Middle East. There is a sense in which the United States had taken the First World War almost in stride; there was hardly a moment in its course when American citizens felt that they had to think out afresh the historic principles by which they had prospered in the first century and a half of their existence as an independent national community.

But the epoch from March 4, 1933, down to the catastrophe of Pearl Harbor shook the United States to its foundations. Not only did it become obvious that its enemies were striking at the roots of its civilization; more important were the facts, first, that the organization of recovery and of victory would require a total mobilization of all its resources, for its own safety not less than for that of its allies, but it was clear, in the second place, that the validity of the American tradition would be tested not by the victory over its enemies so much as by the purposes that victory was made to serve when it was won. No doubt there were millions among the men and women called into national service by America's entrance into the Second World War who thought of little beyond the central fact of powerful enemies upon whose defeat depended on the independence of the United States in the future. But among those millions, and, not least, among the younger generations of Americans, there were many who had vital questions to ask to which they would demand an answer. Most of them were filled with a passionate devotion to the American Dream; but most of them also were going to insist that the time had come to make the dream come true. They had grown up with the clarion call of American promises ringing in their ears; and they had watched, in the years since 1929, a mass of misery and suffering and poverty which contrasted strangely with the tradition of which they had been told.

The years from the Great Depression to the liberation of civilized life from the threat of Nazism and the militarists of Japan were years in which Americans were perhaps more confused in their thinking than at any time since the Civil War. Though Franklin Roosevelt and his supporters strove hard to adapt the historic tradition to the new conditions it confronted, the antagonism he encountered went, perhaps, deeper than any president had met in the second seventy-five years of the republic's history. Property was everywhere on the defensive. The hatred of the Soviet Union was intense. Businessmen emphasized that adventure and security were antithetic ideals, and they sought to prove that where the federal government took the initiative, instead of leaving it in private hands, there was bound to be the decay of civilization. The little man sought everywhere for an escape from problems which he felt beyond his power to solve. Sometimes he took refuge in forms of religious revival which, like the Buchmanite movement, sought to liberate him from fear by an emotional revival of self-confidence. Sometimes he began to doubt the validity of the democratic idea; and he followed with enthusiasm the gospel of men like Father Coughlin who spoke to him, indeed, in a terminology that was formally Catholic, but upon the basis of an attitude not easily distinguishable from that of Hitlerism. The cinema became, with a mass of magazines whose reading matter sought to shut out the real world, a vital method of consolation. Though the tragedy of persecution in more than half of Europe brought to America a mass of refugees, some of them, like Einstein and Thomas Mann, among the outstanding intellectuals of the Old World, most Americans, save for a relatively small group of liberals, were too preoccupied with their domestic problems to appreciate the scale of the tragedy. And even the liberals were divided; for there were not a few who vigorously insisted that America could best help Europe by the fulfillment of democracy at home, while there were others who argued that, in essence, there was no real difference between the ends of Hitler and Japan, on the one hand, and those of the Soviet Union on the other. And when, from September 1939 to May 1940, the leaders in Europe rather maneuvered for position than fought on the scale of 1914 there was a growing tendency to think that the war abroad was nothing more than a new stage in the evil power politics of the Old World with which America need not concern itself.

The scene began to change with Hitler's conquest of the Low Countries, of Norway and of France; and the sight of Britain at bay alone in the summer of 1940 began to suggest that between the American tradition and Nazi totalitarianism there was an antithesis it was difficult to overlook. That suggestion was reinforced when Hitler struck at the Soviet Union; and inevitably, it became a living part of every citizen's thoughts after Pearl Harbor and the sweeping conquests of the Japanese forces. There were then few Americans who failed to understand how profound the challenge to all for which the United States stood was, how necessary was the decisive defeat of Nazism in all its forms, European or Asiatic, if the American dream was to possess reality in the history of the future.

The recognition that the challenge was profound did not, indeed, answer the central question of how much vitality the American tradition still retained. The United States showed courage and initiative, resolution in plan and skill in execution. In common with its allies, it moved forward, stage by stage, to a victory that was obviously bound to be formally overwhelming. But it was careful not to put to itself in the period of conflict the questions it was urgent to ask, much less attempt to answer them. No doubt all its leaders, from the president downwards, paid formal tribute to the ideas of democracy and freedom. No doubt, also, the United States displayed an unequalled power of organizing its resources for the struggle. Its youth went to their rendezvous with destiny in a mood of sublime courage which, if it was equaled in Britain and the Soviet Union, and in the marvelous endurance of a half-armed China, was nowhere surpassed. But the war was not, for the overwhelming mass of Americans, a renewal of faith in the historic tradition. Their mood was one of conviction that the enemy must be over thrown, but of doubt and hesitation about the consequence of his defeat. There was little sense, among those who planned the direction of the war, that they were engaged in a crusade for the renovation of the American tradition. On the contrary it was sometimes a little difficult not to question whether they were certain that it ought to be renewed. As almost always in a crisis, they showed a power of improvisation on a scale that it is legitimate to equate with genius. As always they made their war to win their war; they did not engage in its agonies for any end other than the complete overthrow of their opponents.

But they did not discuss what they were fighting for, nor how those ends could be achieved. They did not suddenly awaken to a renewed sense of the splendor of the American dream. Before they entered the war, indeed, President Roosevelt spoke with the impressive eloquence of the Four Freedoms and indicated with incisiveness that they could be fulfilled in our own generation. Mr. Henry Wallace, the vice president of the United States during Roosevelt's third term, made a series of addresses of which the main theme was the urgency of so using the victory over totalitarianism that the next age would become what he termed the "century of the common man"; but the significant thing about the impact of Mr. Wallace's approach is that he was not renominated by his party and was replaced by one of those professional politicians who was unlikely to disturb the voter who did not like the inconvenient questions to be posed.

So that I do not think it is unfair to argue that Americans have refused to ask themselves whether the historic principles of their tradition can be adapted to the environment of a new time. They had, and not least president Roosevelt had, a sense that their power was very great, that the influence they could exert would be greater, in the next generation, than that of any other people. In both these conclusions they were probably justified. But there were too few thoughtful Americans who were willing to inquire for what their power would be used, or what effect their influence would have upon a civilization that is in the melting pot. And, to the outsider, that refusal to inquire was something it was hard not to connect with the character of the answers they were suspicious they might receive. For they were deeply aware not only of the increasing tensions of our society; even more, they were aware that, when, in a period of crisis, increasing tensions demand new formulas, we must move from one set of social idealisms to another set, and adapt to the claims of these the form of economic and political organization which is proving obsolete, and even dangerous. For it is not less true today then it was when Lincoln was building his claim to the allegiance of all civilized men nearly ninety years ago that a house divided against itself cannot stand. They issue which the guardians of the American tradition today seem to me to be evading is whether there is that division, and, if so, what will be the outcome. Until that question is answered with the confidence of Jefferson and his followers, it seems to me quite certain that the historic American tradition, for all its great achievements, will be viewed with uncertainty and even suspicion by those who should be its beneficiaries.

Notes

1. *Southern Pacific Company v. Jensen*, 244 U.S. 205 (1916).
2. *Abrams v. United States*, 250 U.S. 616 (1919). See Z. Chafee, *Free Speech in the United States* (Cambridge: Harvard University Press, 1941), chapter 3.
3. Cf. Lloyd R. Morris, *The Rebellious Puritan* (New York: Harcourt, Brace, 1927), 331.

2

The War and the Intellectuals

Randolph S. Bourne

To those of us who still retain an irreconcilable animus against war, it has been a bitter experience to see the unanimity with which the American intellectuals have thrown their support to the use of war-technique in the crisis in which America found herself. Socialists, college professors, publicists, new-republicans, practitioners of literature, have vied with each other in confirming with their intellectual faith the collapse of neutrality and the riveting of the war-mind on a hundred million more of the world's people. And the intellectuals are not content with confirming our belligerent gesture. They are now complacently asserting that it was they who effectively willed it, against the hesitation and dim perceptions of the American democratic masses. A war made deliberately by the intellectuals! A calm moral verdict, arrived at after a penetrating study of inexorable facts! Sluggish masses, too remote from the world-conflict to be stirred, too lacking in intellect to perceive their danger! An alert intellectual class, saving the people in spite of themselves, biding their time with Fabian strategy until the nation could be moved into war without serious resistance! An intellectual class, gently guiding a nation through sheer force of ideas into what the other nations entered only through predatory craft or popular hysteria or militarist madness! A war free from any taint of self-seeking, a war that will secure the triumph of democracy and internationalize the world! This is the picture which the more self-conscious intellectuals have formed of themselves, and which they are slowly impressing upon a population which is being led no man knows whither by an indubitably intellectualized President. And they are right, in that the war certainly did not spring from either the ideals or the prejudices, from the national ambitions or hysterias, of the American people, however acquiescent the masses prove to be, and however clearly the intellectuals prove their putative intuition.

Those intellectuals who have felt themselves totally out of sympathy with this drag toward war will seek some explanation for this joyful leadership. They will want to understand this willingness of the American intellect to open the sluices and flood us with the sewage of the war spirit. We cannot forget the virtuous horror and stupefaction which filled our college professors when they read the famous manifesto of their ninety-three German colleagues in defence of their war.[1] To the American academic mind of 1914 defence of war was inconceivable. From Bernhardi[2] it recoiled as from a blasphemy, little dreaming that two years later would find it creating its own cleanly reasons for imposing military service on the country and for talking of the rough rude currents of health and regeneration that war would send through the American body politic. They would have thought anyone mad who talked of shipping American men by the hundreds of thousands—conscripts— to die on the fields of France. Such a spiritual change seems catastrophic when we shoot our minds back to those days when neutrality was a proud thing. But the intellectual progress has been so gradual that the country retains little sense of the irony. The war sentiment, begun so gradually but so perseveringly by the preparedness advocates who came from the ranks of big business, caught hold of one after another of the intellectual groups. With the aid of Roosevelt, the murmurs became a monotonous chant, and finally a chorus so mighty that to be out of it was at first to be disreputable and finally almost obscene. And slowly a strident rant was worked up against Germany which compared very creditably with the German fulminations against the greedy power of England. The nerve of the war-feeling centered, of course, in the richer and older classes of the Atlantic seaboard, and was keenest where there were French or English business and particularly social connections. The sentiment then spread over the country as a class-phenomenon, touching everywhere those upper-class elements in each section who identified themselves with this Eastern ruling group. It must never be forgotten that in every community it was the least liberal and least democratic elements among whom the preparedness and later the war sentiment was found. The farmers were apathetic, the small businessmen and workingmen are still apathetic towards the war. The election was a vote of confidence of these latter classes in a President who would keep the faith of neutrality.[3] The intellectuals, in other words, have identified themselves with the least democratic forces in American life. They have assumed the leadership for war of those very classes whom the American democracy has been immemorially fighting. Only in a world where irony was dead could an intellectual class enter war at the head of such illiberal cohorts in the avowed cause of world-liberalism and world-democracy. No one is left to point out the undemocratic nature of this war-liberalism. In a time of faith, skepticism is the most intolerable of all insults.

Our intellectual class might have been occupied, during the last two years of war, in studying and clarifying the ideals and aspirations of the American democracy, in discovering a true Americanism which would not have been merely nebulous but might have federated the different ethnic groups and traditions. They might have spent the time in endeavoring to clear the public mind of the cant of war, to get rid of old mystical notions that clog our thinking. We might have used the time for a great wave of education, for setting our house in spiritual order. We could at least have set the problem before ourselves. If our intellectuals were going to lead the administration, they might conceivably have tried to find some way of securing peace by making neutrality effective. They might have turned their intellectual energy not to the problem of jockeying the nation into war, but to the problem of using our vast neutral power to attain democratic ends for the rest of the world and ourselves without the use of the malevolent technique of war. They might have failed. The point is that they scarcely tried. The time was spent not in clarification and education, but in a mulling over of nebulous ideals of democracy and liberalism and civilization which had never meant anything fruitful to those ruling classes who now so glibly used them, and in giving free rein to the elementary instinct of self-defence. The whole era has been spiritually wasted. The outstanding feature has been not its Americanism but its intense colonialism. The offence of our intellectuals was not so much that they were colonial—for what could we expect of a nation composed of so many national elements?—but that it was so one-sidedly and partisanly colonial. The official, reputable expression of the intellectual class has been that of the English colonial. Certain portions of it have been even more loyalist than the King, more British even than Australia. Other colonial attitudes have been vulgar. The colonialism of the other American stocks was denied a hearing from the start. America might have been made a meeting-ground for the different national attitudes. An intellectual class, cultural colonists of the different European nations, might have threshed out the issues here as they could not be threshed out in Europe. Instead of this, the English colonials in university and press took command at the start, and we became an intellectual Hungary where thought was subject to an effective process of Magyarization. The reputable opinion of the American intellectuals became more and more either what could be read pleasantly in London, or what was written in an earnest effort to put Englishmen straight on their war-aims and war-technique. This Magyarization of thought produced as a counter-reaction a peculiarly offensive and inept German apologetic, and the two partisans divided the field between them. The great masses, the other ethnic groups, were inarticulate. American public opinion was almost as little prepared for war in 1917 as it was in 1914.

The sterile results of such an intellectual policy are inevitable. During the war the American intellectual class has produced almost nothing in the way of original and illuminating interpretation. Veblen's "Imperial Germany"; Patten's "Culture and War," and addresses; Dewey's "German Philosophy and Politics"; a chapter or two in Weyl's "American Foreign Policies"—is there much else of creative value in the intellectual repercussion of the war? It is true that the shock of war put the American intellectual to an unusual strain. He had to sit idle and think as spectator not as actor. There was no government to which he could docilely and loyally tender his mind as did the Oxford professors to justify England in her own eyes. The American's training was such as to make the fact of war almost incredible. Both in his reading of history and in his lack of economic perspective he was badly prepared for it. He had to explain to himself something which was too colossal for the modern mind, which outran any language or terms which we had to interpret it in. He had to expand his sympathies to the breaking-point, while pulling the past and present into some sort of interpretative order. The intellectuals in the fighting countries had only to rationalize and justify what their country was already doing. Their task was easy. A neutral, however, had really to search out the truth. Perhaps perspective was too much to ask of any mind. Certainly the older colonials among our college professors let their prejudices at once dictate their thought. They have been comfortable ever since. The war has taught them nothing and will teach them nothing. And they have had the satisfaction, under the rigor of events, of seeing prejudice submerge the intellects of their younger colleagues. And they have lived to see almost their entire class, pacifists and democrats too, join them as apologists for the "gigantic irrelevance" of war.

We have had to watch, therefore, in this country the same process which so shocked us abroad—the coalescence of the intellectual classes in support of the military programme. In this country, indeed, the socialist intellectuals did not even have the grace of their German brothers and wait for the declaration of war before they broke for cover. And when they declared for war they showed how thin was the intellectual veneer of their socialism. For they called us in terms that might have emanated from any bourgeois journal to defend democracy and civilization, just as if it was not exactly against those very bourgeois democracies and capitalist civilizations that socialists had been fighting for decades. But so subtle is the spiritual chemistry of the "inside" that all this intellectual cohesion—herd-instinct become herd-intellect— which seemed abroad so hysterical and so servile, comes to us here in highly rational terms. We go to war to save the world from subjugation! But the German intellectuals went to war to save their culture from barbarization! And the French went to war to save their beautiful France! And the English to save international honor! And Russia, most altruistic and self-sacrificing of all, to save a small State from destruction! Whence is our miraculous intuition of our moral spotlessness? Whence our confidence that history will not unravel huge economic and imperialist forces upon which our rationalizations float like bubbles? The Jew often marvels that his race alone should have been chosen as the true people of the cosmic God. Are not our intellectuals equally fatuous when they tell us that our war of all wars is stainless and thrillingly achieving for good?

An intellectual class that was wholly rational would have called insistently for peace and not for war. For months the crying need has been for a negotiated peace, in order to avoid the ruin of a deadlock. Would not the same amount of resolute statesmanship thrown into intervention have secured a peace that would have been a subjugation for neither side? Was the terrific bargaining power of a great neutral ever really used? Our war followed, as all wars follow, a monstrous failure of diplomacy. Shamefacedness should now be our intellectuals' attitude, because the American play for peace was made so little more than a polite play. The intellectuals have still to explain why, willing as they now are to use force to continue the war to absolute exhaustion, they were not willing to use force to coerce the world to a speedy peace.

Their forward vision is no more convincing than their past rationality. We go to war now to internationalize the world! But surely their League to Enforce Peace[4] is only a palpable apocalyptic myth, like the syndicalists' myth of the "general strike." It is not a rational programme so much as a glowing symbol for the purpose of focusing belief, of setting enthusiasm on fire for international order. As far as it does this it has pragmatic value, but as far as it provides a certain radiant mirage of idealism for this war and for a world-order founded on mutual fear, it is dangerous and obnoxious. Idealism should be kept for what is ideal. It is depressing to think that the prospect of a world so strong that none dare challenge it should be the immediate ideal of the American intellectual. If the League is only a makeshift, a coalition into which we enter to restore order, then it is only a description of existing fact, and the idea should be treated as such. But if it is an actually prospective outcome of the settlement, the keystone of American policy, it is neither realizable nor desirable. For the programme of such a League contains no provision for dynamic national growth or for international economic justice. In a world which requires recognition of economic internationalism far more than of political internationalism, an idea is reactionary which proposes to petrify and federate the nations as political and economic units. Such a scheme for international order is a dubious justification for American policy. And if American policy had been sincere in its belief that our participation would achieve international beatitude, would we not have made our entrance into the war conditional upon a solemn general agreement to respect in the final settlement these principles of international order? Could we have afforded, if our war was to end war by the establishment of a league of honor, to risk the defeat of our vision and our betrayal in the settlement? Yet we are in the war, and no such solemn agreement was made, nor has it even been suggested.[5]

The case of the intellectuals seems, therefore, only very speciously rational. They could have used their energy to force a just peace or at least to devise other means than war for carrying through American policy. They could have used their intellectual energy to ensure that our participation in the war meant the international order which they wish. Intellect was not so used. It was used to lead an apathetic nation into an irresponsible war, without guarantees from those belligerents whose cause we were saving. The American intellectual, therefore, has been rational neither in his hindsight nor his foresight. To explain him we must look beneath the intellectual reasons to the emotional disposition. It is not so much what they thought as how they felt that explains our intellectual class. Allowing for colonial sympathy, there was still the personal shock in a world-war which outraged all our preconceived notions of the way the world was tending. It reduced to rubbish most of the humanitarian internationalism and democratic nationalism which had been the emotional thread of our intellectuals' life. We had suddenly to make a new orientation. There were mental conflicts. Our latent colonialism strove with our longing for American unity. Our desire for peace strove with our desire for national responsibility in the world. That first lofty and remote and not altogether un-sound feeling of our spiritual isolation from the conflict could not last. There was the itch to be in the great experience which the rest of the world was having. Numbers of intelligent people who had never been stirred by the horrors of capitalistic peace at home were shaken out of their slumber by the horrors of war in Belgium. Never having felt responsibility for labor wars and oppressed masses and excluded races at home, they had a large fund of idle emotional capital to invest in the oppressed nationalities and ravaged villages of Europe. Hearts that had felt only ugly contempt for democratic strivings at home beat in tune with the struggle for freedom abroad. All this was natural, but it tended to over-emphasize our responsibility. And it threw our thinking out of gear. The task of making our own country detailedly fit for peace was abandoned in favor of a feverish concern for the management of the war, advice to the fighting governments on all matters, military, social and political, and a gradual working up of the conviction that we were ordained as a nation to lead all erring brothers towards the light of liberty and democracy. The failure of the American intellectual class to erect a creative attitude toward the war can be explained by these sterile mental conflicts which the shock to our ideals sent raging through us.

Mental conflicts end either in a new and higher synthesis or adjustment, or else in a reversion to more primitive ideas which have been outgrown but to which we drop when jolted out of our attained position. The war caused in America a recrudescence of nebulous ideals which a younger generation was fast outgrowing because it had passed the wistful stage and was discovering concrete ways of getting them incarnated in actual institutions. The shock of the war threw us back from this pragmatic work into an emotional bath of these old ideals. There was even a somewhat rarefied revival of our primitive Yankee boastfulness, the reversion of senility to that republican childhood when we expected the whole world to copy our republican institutions. We amusingly ignored the fact that it was just that Imperial German regime, to whom we are to teach the art of self-government, which our own Federal structure, with its executive irresponsible in foreign policy and with its absence of parliamentary control, most resembles. And we are missing the exquisite irony of the unaffected homage paid by the American democratic intellectuals to the last and most detested of Britain's tory premiers as the representative of a "liberal" ally, as well as the irony of the selection of the best hated of America's bourbon "old guard" as the missionary of American democracy to Russia.[6]

The intellectual state that could produce such things is one where reversion has taken place to more primitive ways of thinking. Simple syllogisms are substituted for analysis, things are known by their labels, our heart's desire dictates what we shall see. The American intellectual class, having failed to make the higher syntheses, regresses to ideas that can issue in quick, simplified action. Thought becomes any easy rationalization of what is actually going on or what is to happen inevitably tomorrow. It is true that certain groups did rationalize their colonialism and attach the doctrine of the inviolability of British sea-power to the doctrine of a League of Peace. But this agile resolution of the mental conflict did not become a higher synthesis, to be creatively developed. It gradually merged into a justification for our going to war. It petrified into a dogma to be propagated. Criticism flagged and emotional propaganda began. Most of the socialists, the college professors and the practitioners of literature, however, have not even reached this high-water mark of synthesis. Their mental conflicts have been resolved much more simply. War in the interests of democracy! This was almost the sum of their philosophy. The primitive idea to which they regressed became almost insensibly translated into a craving for action. War was seen as the crowning relief of their indecision. At last action, irresponsibility, the end of anxious and torturing attempts to reconcile peace-ideals with the drag of the world towards Hell. An end to the pain of trying to adjust the facts to what they ought to be! Let us consecrate the facts as ideal! Let us join the greased slide towards war! The momentum increased. Hesitations, ironies, consciences, considerations— all were drowned in the elemental blare of doing something aggressive, colossal. The new-found Sabbath "peacefulness of being at war"! The thankfulness with which so many intellectuals lay down and floated with the current betrays the hesitation and suspense through which they had been. The American university is a brisk and happy place these days. Simple, unquestioning action has superseded the knots of thought. The thinker dances with reality.

With how many of the acceptors of war has it been mostly a dread of intellectual suspense? It is a mistake to suppose that intellectuality necessarily makes for suspended judgments. The intellect craves certitude. It takes effort to keep it supple and pliable. In a time of danger and disaster we jump desperately for some dogma to cling to. The time comes, if we try to hold out, when our nerves are sick with fatigue, and we seize in a great healing wave of release some doctrine that can be immediately translated into action. Neutrality meant suspense, and so it became the object of loathing to frayed nerves. The vital myth of the League of Peace provides a dogma to jump to. With war the world becomes motor again and speculation is brushed aside like cobwebs. The blessed emotion of self-defense intervenes too, which focused millions in Europe. A few keep up a critical pose after war is begun, but since they usually advise action which is in one-to-one correspondence with what the mass is already doing, their criticism is little more than a rationalization of the common emotional drive.

The results of war on the intellectual class are already apparent. Their thought becomes little more than a description and justification of what is going on. They turn upon any rash one who continues idly to speculate. Once the war is on, the conviction spreads that individual thought is helpless, that the only way one can count is as a cog in the great wheel. There is no good holding back. We are told to dry our unnoticed and ineffective tears and plunge into the great work. Not only is everyone forced into line, but the new certitude becomes idealized. It is a noble realism which opposes itself to futile obstruction and the cowardly refusal to face facts. This realistic boast is so loud and sonorous that one wonders whether realism is always a stern and intelligent grappling with realities. May it not be sometimes a mere surrender to the actual, an abdication of the ideal through a sheer fatigue from intellectual suspense? The pacifist is roundly scolded for refusing to face the facts, and for retiring into his own world of sentimental desire. But is the realist, who refuses to challenge or criticize facts, entitled to any more credit than that which comes from following the line of least resistance? The realist thinks he at least can control events by linking himself to the forces that are moving. Perhaps he can. But if it is a question of controlling war, it is difficult to see how the child on the back of a mad elephant is to be any more effective in stopping the beast than is the child who tries to stop him from the ground. The ex-humanitarian, turned realist, sneers at the snobbish neutrality, colossal conceit, crooked thinking, dazed sensibilities, of those who are still unable to find any balm of consolation for this war. We manufacture consolations here in America while there are probably not a dozen men fighting in Europe who did not long ago give up every reason for their being there except that nobody knew how to get them away.

But the intellectuals whom the crisis has crystallized into an acceptance of war have put themselves into a terrifyingly strategic position. It is only on the craft, in the stream, they say, that one has any chance of controlling the current forces for liberal purposes. If we obstruct, we surrender all power for influence. If we responsibly approve, we then retain our power for guiding. We will be listened to as responsible thinkers, while those who obstructed the coming of war have committed intellectual suicide and shall be cast into outer darkness. Criticism by the ruling powers will only be accepted from those intellectuals who are in sympathy with the general tendency of the war. Well, it is true that they may guide, but if their stream leads to disaster and the frustration of national life, is their guiding any more than a preference whether they shall go over the right-hand or the left-hand side of the precipice? Meanwhile, however, there is comfort on board. Be with us, they call, or be negligible, irrelevant. Dissenters are already excommunicated. Irreconcilable radicals, wringing their hands among the debris, become the most despicable and impotent of men. There seems no choice for the intellectual but to join the mass of acceptance. But again the terrible dilemma arises—either support what is going on, in which case you count for nothing because you are swallowed in the mass and great incalculable forces bear you on; or remain aloof, passively resistant, in which case you count for nothing because you are outside the machinery of reality.

Is there no place left, then, for the intellectual who cannot yet crystallize, who does not dread suspense, and is not yet drugged with fatigue? The American intellectuals, in their preoccupation with reality, seem to have forgotten that the real enemy is War rather than imperial Germany. There is work to be done to prevent this war of ours from passing into popular mythology as a holy crusade. What shall we do with leaders who tell us that we go to war in moral spotlessness, or who make "democracy" synonymous with a republican form of government? There is work to be done in still shouting that all the revolutionary by-products will not justify the war, or make war anything else than the most noxious complex of all the evils that afflict men. There must be some to find no consolation whatever, and some to sneer at those who buy the cheap emotion of sacrifice. There must be some irreconcilables left who will not even accept the war with walrus tears. There must be some to call unceasingly for peace, and some to insist that the terms of settlement shall be not only liberal but democratic. There must be some intellectuals who are not willing to use the old discredited counters again and to support a peace which would leave all the old inflammable materials of armament lying about the world. There must still be opposition to any contemplated "liberal" world-order founded on military coalitions. The "irreconcilable" need not be disloyal. He need not even be "impossibilist." His apathy towards war should take the form of a heightened energy and enthusiasm for the education, the art, the interpretation that make for life in the midst of the world of death. The intellectual who retains his animus against war will push out more boldly than ever to make his case solid against it. The old ideals crumble; new ideals must be forged. His mind will continue to roam widely and ceaselessly. The thing he will fear most is premature crystallization. If the American intellectual class rivets itself to a "liberal" philosophy that perpetuates the old errors, there will then be need for "democrats" whose task will be to divide, confuse, disturb, keep the intellectual waters constantly in motion to prevent any such ice from ever forming.

Notes

1. In October 1914 ninety-three German writers and teachers published an "Appeal to the Civilized World" in which they praised the military establishment and defended Germany's war effort.
2. Friedrich von Bernhardi, German general and military historian. His book, *Germany and the Next War* (1912), advocated a war of conquest for Germany and was used by the allies for propaganda purposes.
3. In the 1916 campaign Woodrow Wilson pledged himself to non-intervention in the European war.
4. Organized in 1915 as a non-partisan group, The League to Enforce Peace espoused a post-war league of nations that would use economic sanctions or military force against any member waging war.
5. In an earlier, unpublished manuscript Bourne wrote, "In the first place, would not a League that provided for the armed enforcement of peace by the whole League upon any member who broke the peace before submitting the dispute to arbitration, be virtually an alliance of all against each, and would not the United States be compelled, under these terms, to enter a war in which we perhaps had no concern whatever? If the League is formed on the basis of the present Entente, with the addition of a sobered Germany, would such a League be essentially different from the armed truce which existed in Europe from 1871–1914? . . . Such a League under any circumstances, would be little more than a mutual guarantee of the status quo." ("Doubts About Enforcing Peace," Bourne MSS, Columbia University Libraries.)
6. The references are to Lord Balfour, British Foreign Secretary and former prime minister who headed the British war mission to the United States in April 1917, and to Elihu Root, appointed in the same month to head an American mission to revolutionary Russia.

3

Sanctions and the Security of Nations

John Dewey

From *Are Sanctions Necessary to International Organization?*—a discussion between Mr. R. L. Buell and Mr. Dewey, published as a pamphlet by Foreign Policy Association, June 1932. Mr. Dewey's contribution is here published entire. Editorial changes in text (enclosed in brackets) consist in substituting "it is sometimes urged" etc., for "Mr Buell urges" etc.

The problem of the use of sanctions to achieve a peaceful international organization involves many questions. But two great principles run through the complexity of details and reduce them to clarity and order. The first of these principles is that the use of sanctions is impracticable, so much so that any attempt in that direction is sure to make international relations worse instead of better. Even the attempt to push it to the front in the discussion is ill-advised, for it distracts attention from the measures likely to be of efficacy in improving the relations among nations. The second principle is that even if the use of coercive force by joint agreement were possible it would be undesirable, since resort to force fastens upon us the war system as the ultimate means of settling international controversies. "Enforcement of peace" is a phrase which combines two contradictory ideas.

In spite of Articles X and XVI in the Covenant of the League, the latter has consistently refused to invoke the use of sanctions. Its record in this respect is without a flaw.[1] This fact is of itself evidence that the notion of applying sanctions is utopian. If the idea is capable of practicable application, how is the policy of the League to be accounted for? If the blame is put on the nations outside the League, it only becomes the clearer that nations are still so divided among themselves that the idea of combined joint action is utopian. If the claim is simply that the Council of the League has failed in its duty, this alternative only proves that even those nations which are most united among themselves are incapable of uniting to employ coercive force.

The statement that the failure of the League is due to the non-adherence of the United States deserves, however, particular attention. As I see the matter, the actual case stands almost at the opposite pole. As a matter of fact it is Americans, those advocating that we join the League, who are most active in urging the policy of sanctions. France is committed to the use of sanctions under especial conditions connected with maintaining the sanctity of the Versailles treaty, and with the added qualification of either an international force with its own staff, or military and naval guarantees from Great Britain and the United States. Some of the smaller nations that are satisfied with the *status quo* think sanctions would strengthen their security against the imperialistic tendencies of the greater powers. But in general the great powers are so much opposed to the invocation of sanctions that their attitude is represented by the statement of MacDonald that reference to them in Article XVI is "dead wood" and should be cut out of the Covenant.

The evidence of the steadfast refusal of the powers to resort to sanctions is found in the history of the League at every emergency which has arisen. Sober students and historians who believe thoroughly in the League have praised it on the special ground that it has resorted only to publicity, to conciliation, to the building up of harmonious public opinion and sentiment. Strangely enough it is only advocates of the League on this side of the ocean who criticize the League for failing to use coercive measures—possibly because of their remoteness from the factors which actually control European action in international matters. I can think of nothing more unrealistic than urging the impossible—in spite of the appearance of realism which is said to attend the "implementing" by force of the conduct of the League.

Since I cannot go over the whole history of the League, I shall select one case which to me is typical. In connection with Locarno, Great Britain agreed to guarantee the Franco-German frontier, while refusing to guarantee the Polish-German settlement. It was everywhere admitted that Great Britain's attitude was dictated in part by the realization that in the latter case she could not carry the other members of the British Commonwealth of Nations with her. What then is the prospect of Britain's signing a blank check in favor of forcible guarantees to be applied all over the world?

And of course there are other causes for the abstinence of Great Britain. Europe is not a united happy family. Even the nations which were allies in the World War have opposed interests. It would be impossible for Great Britain to surrender her traditional foreign policy to the extent of actually promoting France's hegemony on the continent, such as would be effected if Great Britain cordially assented to sanctions in order to guarantee the war settlements in Eastern Europe. The rivalries of nationalistic interests, the sore spots, the resentments, suspicions, and jealousies which exist among the great powers make the execution of united coercive measures impossible; to try to use them would only increase existing antagonisms and fan a dormant flame into a blaze.

The particular point which has been mentioned is of course but one aspect of France's unceasing demand for a guaranteed security of the perpetual force of the Versailles treaties. As Walter Lippmann wrote in the *New York World* in 1927: "Substitute the word 'revision' for the word 'aggression' and the words 'maintenance of the Paris Treaties' for the word 'security' and you have the real meaning of this interminable debate." Aside from the question of right and justice, conflict of interests will continue to forbid that effective unanimity which is required for the use of sanctions. So far as Great Britain and France especially are concerned, the situation was well stated by a writer in the *Round Table* for June 1928: "When the English-speaking world uses the word peace it thinks of a state of things in which not only there is no war, but in which the political structure is the result of general acceptance and is not merely acquiesced in because there is *force majeure* behind it. When France talks about *la paix*, she means rather the political situation created by the treaties of peace. It is a legal rather than a moral situation."

Suppose a case, apart from any reference to the peace treaties, in which Great Britain, France or the United States was pronounced in such default in meeting an international obligation as to justify, under the terms of the Covenant, an appeal to sanctions. Does anybody believe that they would be put into operation? And what would be the effect upon public sentiment in this country if an effort were made to set them in motion? Would the effect be favorable to the promotion of international organization for peace? If one will face in his thought the picture of the reaction that would occur here, the inevitable inflammation of nationalistic sentiment, he will appreciate the effect on any other strong nation of the invocation of sanctions against it. And why limit the scope of the nations which might be affected by it? In the minds of American advocates of sanctions there seems to exist always an unexpressed premise as to just what nation is to be the guilty party.

Let us take a less hypothetical case. Suppose that in 1929 Russia in her dispute with China in Manchuria had gone as far as Japan went in the same province in 1931–32. The feeling against Russia was, on grounds quite aside from her supposed action in Manchuria, such that sanctions might possibly have been invoked against her. But would it have been possible to convince Soviet Russia or her sympathizers in the rest of the world that the real ground for action was the alleged one? And how could the sanctions have been executed? How could they have been made effective? Is it not obvious that nothing but an old-fashioned bigger and better war would have served that purpose? And is it not highly probable, practically certain, that there would have been enough domestic opposition in various nations to prevent punitive action? Could labor in Great Britain have been brought to the use of sanctions?

For we are not on speculative grounds in dealing with the case of Russia. There was an economic "quarantine" of Russia attempted at the height of the hostility to and fear of her communism. Russia suffered undoubtedly; many persons were added to the roll of those who starved to death. But in the end it was unsuccessful except in embittering all Russians, independent of their economic philosophy, against the rest of the world. Even nations much weaker than Russia have the power of withdrawing into themselves and enduring until the storm is spent. During the storm, however, old resentments are renewed and the temper which makes for future war is fostered.

I can only conclude that those who mourn and who rebuke the League because it has not chosen to employ the sanction provided for on paper assume a decadence of nationalistic rivalries and ambitions which does not accord with facts. They assume a harmony in the various Chancelleries of the world which is non-existent. If the assumption of the existence of this harmony were acted upon, the action would merely accentuate the disagreements which already exist. There may not be the most elevated diplomacy in Europe which is conceivable. But its foreign offices are at least wise enough to realize the danger attending an appeal to sanctions, and hence agree to allow the clauses relating to it in the Covenant to become a dead letter. I can but believe then that the League has been well advised in putting up with rebuffs rather than to adopt the sensational and striking course of resort to coercive measures. That which is academic in American discussions would be fatal in Europe. Nor is the matter wholly academic here. Appeal to sanctions keeps alive and invigorates all the attitudes and convictions which have caused us to remain outside the League. Worse than that, it stimulates the activities of the extreme isolationists; it provides them with ammunition, and all in a cause which is hopelessly utopian.

In what I have thus far said I have ignored the distinction drawn by [some] between economic and military sanctions, in behalf of the former and against the latter. Is this distinction practicable in fact? Certainly it is not authorized by anything in the Covenant of the League. Article X declares that nations agree not only to respect but to "*preserve*" territorial integrity. There is no limit set to the means to be employed; to "preserve" means to preserve. Article XVI states the means to be used. Section one specifies economic and financial measures. But the impression that this section stands complete in itself so that invocation of economic sanctions may or may *not* be followed up by military measures has no warrant in the document. It is opposed to its express terms. The two following sections are integral with the first. For the second section begins, "It shall be the duty of the Council in *such* case to recommend to the several Governments concerned what *effective military, naval and air forces, etc.*," while the third section obligates member-states to permit passage of troops. From the standpoint of the Covenant, economic sanctions are not a possible substitute for war; they are one of the instruments of war.

Those who make the distinction between economic and military sanctions may at least have something in common with the opponents of sanctions: They should strive to modify radically Articles X and XVI of the Covenant. Even then the question remains how far the separation is practicable, and whether the framers of the League were not sufficiently realistic in combining the two so that if reference to military sanctions is eliminated, economic sanctions should go too.

First let me say something, about the prevailing use of the term "boycott" by the adherents of economic sanctions. Its use is not only loose but is actually misleading. A boycott is a private individual or group affair, non-political in nature: a refusal to economic patronage either to a particular firm or corporation or to business representatives of a particular nation. Its nature is indicated by the conditions of its origin in Ireland, and by Indian and Chinese boycotts. Neither the word nor the idea has any application in international affairs.[2] *There* we can have only embargoes and blockades. In the Covenant there is of course no such loose and irrelevant term as boycott. There is "*severance* of all trade or financial relations"; "*prohibition*" of intercourse among nationals, and "*prevention*" of all intercourse between nationals, financial, commercial and even personal. The terms are sweeping enough to remind one of a medieval interdict. In any case, severance and prohibition mean embargoes, while prevention is meaningless without a blockade.

The question then comes up whether economic sanctions can be *successfully* applied without a blockade by land or sea: a recourse to war measures. I doubt if an answer can be given applicable to all cases. In the case of sanctions applied to a weak nation with the practically unanimous and earnest support of all other nations the threat of them might operate. But it seems to me clear that even with a nation which is weak (the case of Russia has already been mentioned) there is no assurance that the threat would be successful unless followed by war-measures, while it seems quite certain that the effect upon public sentiment would be to create resentment and to foster militarism. The nation against which sanctions are used would feel that it had yielded not to the claims of justice but to superior force, quite as much as if it had been defeated in war.

In many cases, all the precedents go to show that a purely economic boycott would not be successful even against weak nations. I think of Turkey in its war of liberation with Greece. Turkey had constant clandestine French support against the help given by Great Britain to Greece; both the French and Italians joined in smuggling arms and munitions through even a blockade for the sake of profit. I can think of but few cases in which desire for profit and political rivalries would not go far to render a so-called economic boycott ineffective. Even in the World War, with all the military and naval resources of the Allies, the blockade of Germany, openly an act of war, was not completely successful.

There is a great deal of talk of a rather irresponsible sort, intellectually speaking, about putting "teeth" into the League and into the Paris Pact. Everything goes to show that *merely* economic sanctions would be a set of poorly made, easily broken, crockery teeth. Teeth in international affairs mean *teeth*–blockades and other war measures. The case of Japan is crucial. It is argued that if the League and the United States had made an early demonstration of the intention to apply economic sanctions in case China and Japan did not submit their dispute to some kind of adjudication, the Mukden incident would probably have been quickly settled and the Shanghai campaign prevented.[3] It is of course extremely difficult to deal with historic cases in which it is alleged that if something had happened which did not happen, something else would have, or would not have happened. The speculative character of the proposition is not reduced when [it is sometimes] urged that the peaceful settlement would have been brought about not only by economic sanctions alone, but that a blockade would not have been necessary for the successful operation of the economic sanction. All that was required, according to [this], was legislation prohibiting the clearance of exports to the "aggressor" state and the entrance of imports from it.

Speculative hypothesis for speculation, mere "prohibition" without "prevention" would not have been successful in deterring Japan from her course, while it would have created resentments most detrimental to the development of a world order and would have played into the hands of the military. We can be pretty sure that Japan would have withdrawn from the League; that, since the United States is the chief importer of her goods, she would have laid up a resentment against us highly provocative of war, ulterior if not immediate, and that the outcome would have strengthened the powerful party in Japan which desires Japan definitely "to go Asiatic."

A realistic appraisal of the probable action of Japan will have to take into account her peculiar position and traditions. Westerners are likely to forget that Japan is not only an island separated from America and Europe but also from Asia, and that for centuries she pursued a deliberate policy of seclusion and exclusion. It is impossible to exaggerate the effect of these conditions upon Japanese mentality. The late war taught us how comparatively easy it is in any case for a government to control public opinion by propaganda and by shutting out all news and information contrary to its case. The task is immensely easier to accomplish in Japan. Since the Japanese public believed with intensity of ardor that its cause against China was just and a matter of national self-preservation, it is unrealistic to suppose that merely passing laws, without a blockade and other show of force, would have altered the policy of Japan, or that its effect would have been other than to increase resentment and add to the prestige of the military party.[4]

The belief that this would have been the case is not a mere matter of speculation. One hundred and thirty-five American missionaries on the ground in Japan signed, without trying to excuse the action of Japan, a statement in which the following sentence is included: "Without necessarily renouncing the use of economic pressure by all the nations against an aggressor as provided in the Covenant of the League we believe in the present circumstances that the threat of an embargo against Japan only serves more fully to unify Japanese public opinion in support of the military policies"—a statement whose moderation makes it the more worthy of credence.

The conception that fear of economic loss will deter any nation whose emotions are inflamed from conducting warfare is disproved by all recent history. Japan is probably the only country in the whole world on whom such fear would have the least deterrent effect. The dread of economic sanctions may be expected to have the most force in those countries in which industrial interests are paramount and in which they have the most weight in civilian government. In Japan the situation is reversed. Prestige lies with the military because of the strength of the feudal tradition, and the military elements are superior to the civilian in the cabinet. All facts go contrary to the belief that a mere legalistic gesture would suffice to swerve the policy of a country where the military have taken the bit in their teeth in a runaway race and have the support of public opinion. To argue for sanctions and "teeth" and then to stop short in their use is as impossible in fact as it is inconsistent in logic.

By retracing what actually did happen in Manchuria one can reconstruct what probably would have happened if there had been the threat by all the powers of economic coercion of Japan—supposing, that is for the moment, that all the powers had had sufficient unanimity of opinion and policy to make the threat. Day after day there were inquiries and protests. Day after day, the civil authorities made explanations, and gave certain conditional assurances about future actions. Day after day the military went ahead with their foreordained plan of campaign, leaving the civilian authorities blandly to explain that the conditions upon which their promises had been based had not been fulfilled. Events moved rapidly. There is no reason to suppose that Japan would not have followed the same course with a threat of economic sanctions impending until she confronted the world with her *fait accompli* in Manchuria. It is not a pleasant spectacle but nothing is gained by concealing from ourselves that this is the kind of world in which we live.

The retort that all this could not happen if the Paris Pact were implemented with force, or if the teeth in the Covenant were used, merely sets before us the original dilemma. Teeth that are not mere false teeth, only paper teeth, signify a blockade and a readiness to go as far as events make necessary in further use of armed force. If successful, it is the kind of "success" which any war brings with it, a success which events have demonstrated is *not* conducive to an organized world order, and which, in the case of Japan would have left intense resentment behind and strengthened the supremacy of the military. Without the use of armed force, the show of economic teeth would have produced resentment without any practical effect in Manchuria, and would have left recourse to purely pacific measures in a position more ridiculous than at present. There is one fact that is now assured and not merely speculative. Japan is actually withdrawing her forces from Shanghai, and an official spokesman admits this is done because Japan incurred the "odium" of the rest of world. Even if she had withdrawn under a threat of coercion (which with a proud nation like Japan is hardly likely), I submit that the after-effect in Japan would have been a much sorer and more bellicose attitude than now exists.

It should be added that if international economic sanctions had been adopted, China could not have held aloof; she would have been compelled by forces within and without, to be a party to them. Japan has claimed that the non-official boycott in China was sufficient justification for her Shanghai adventure. Obviously if China joined in an official boycott, the alleged excuse of Japan would have been greatly reinforced. Her intensified sense of provocation would have been the basis for carrying her campaign against China as far as she wished. In all probability, her campaign would have extended up the Yangtse valley to Hankow; to Tientsin and Peiping, possibly to Amoy and Canton. All that China gained by refraining from a declaration of war would have been lost.

I turn from the point that economic sanctions cannot be severed from military and still be successful, to another point which bears upon their practicability. Before economic sanctions can be put in operation there must be a determination of the state against which they are to be employed. The term "aggressor nation" is currently employed to describe this state, and it is employed as if it had a recognized standing in the Covenant. In fact it does not appear there, the nearest approach being "covenant-breaking state." But whatever the term, the guilty nation must be settled upon. What is the basis upon which it is assumed that Japan could have been held guilty in time to arrest the Manchurian expedition and prevent the one in Shanghai, even if the rest of the argument for the efficacy of economic sanctions be accepted? The investigating commission to determine the facts of the case has only just arrived in Shanghai—in

April, 1932. This fact is a sufficient commentary on the assumption that it is a simple and easy matter to determine the nature and residence of the guilt which justifies the use of sanctions. Doubtless the inquiry might have been expedited; that it could have moved as rapidly as the Japanese army moved, I take the liberty of doubting. And it would have been faced at every step by Japan's claim that the Chinese were the real aggressors, and by the claim that since Japan was being attacked she could not postpone positive action.

There is another special feature complicating the determination of the covenant-breaking state. In its exact form, it belongs only to the Sino-Japanese situation, but something corresponding would be found in every complicated dispute between important nations. Japan's claim that China was the real "aggressor" is bound up with the Chinese claim that the treaties ensuing upon the Twenty-One Demands are not valid, because they were secured under duress—and also, as Chinese civilians unanimously believe, by bribery of Chinese officials. Anyway China served notice as soon as she could that she did not regard them as binding. What a fine situation in which to determine which nation is responsible! Imagine the enthusiasm with which France would greet a decision that treaties obtained under duress are invalid! Even as it is, the international commission will, I imagine, skirt this question, contenting itself with scolding China for neglect in observing her treaty duties. What it would have done if the imposition of economic sanctions and the outbreak of a general war had been dependent upon its decision, I will leave the believers in sanctions to pass upon.

It is asserted that the failure to check Japan in her course has strengthened the idea that reliance must be placed on armed force, has weakened the peace movement and the desire for disarmament, and has set back the prospects of world organization. Specifically, it is urged that non-resistance by force has intensified Japan's faith in armed force as an instrument of national policy; has furthered the belief in China that international agencies cannot be depended upon; has aroused fear in Russia which finds outlet in increased dependence upon armed force, and has created unrest and fear of the consequences of disarmament all over the world.

There is sufficient truth in these statements so that I have no desire to deny them. I agree fully with the statement that "had the League and the United States successfully curbed Japanese militarism and secured a peaceful settlement of the difficulties between China and Japan, the international consciousness of the great powers, especially, would have been immeasurably strengthened, a fact which would have greatly facilitated the solution of other pressing international problems." But what does such a statement signify in and of itself save that *if* peaceful measures had achieved a peaceful solution, the state of the world would now be much more pacific than it actually is? So far as it is implied that appeal to sanctions would have "curbed" Japanese militarism (even if we go so far as to hold that the military would have been scared off from their adventure), or more generally still would have secured a peaceful settlement, the statement is either a *non sequitur* or a begging of the question at issue.

It is quite true that pacific means have not up to date been highly successful in restraining Japanese militarism—although it is probable that there has been an arrest[5] since it is likely that original plans went much further than Shanghai. But the assumption that threats of coercive force would have really restrained her militarism sounds to me much like the pleas we gave way to during the World War, that militaristic opposition to and conquest of German militarism would sound the death knell of all militarism. Instead we have a world more completely armed than in 1914. I submit that by this time we ought to have got beyond the notion that resort to coercive force is going to weaken the tendency to resort to coercive force; it only shifts its focus.

Of course the answer which is constantly made to this point is that there is a great difference between national and international force, between war as an instrument of national policy and international war; that what is now argued for is "international defense and international sanctions." I do not see that the analogy with the World War is at all weakened by this retort. Nations from the five continents outside of Europe were in arms against the Central powers. That seems to mark a fair approach to international war and international sanctions. In retrospect, however, matters look very much like an old-fashioned alliance for various ends of nationalistic defense and nationalistic aggrandizement. Although there was a "sacred union," the Allied nations do not seem now united even secularly, to say nothing of sacredly. The world has had its lesson as to the power of a union for the exercise of coercive force to create a real harmony of interest and purpose. A coercive combination against Japan might accomplish a decisive victory more quickly than did the combination against the Germanic powers, and with less suffering and destruction. That it would promote genuine world organization for peace seems to me as illusory in one case as in the other.

Since personally I do not think the argument that economic sanctions would cause suffering to the innocent is at all a conclusive argument against employing sanctions (provided there were assurance that they would really be successful in creating an international order of and for peaceful international relations), I shall only make one remark on this. There are plenty of innocent people in the world suffering at the present time. There can be no justification for adding to their number unless it is clear beyond all reasonable doubt that the addition will really be a factor in promoting a genuine harmony of interests among the nations of the world. And that is just the point to be proved and which has not been proved.

There are certain other points [which are sometimes made] which seem to be irrelevant to the main issue, but which I shall touch upon for the sake of completeness.

I do not agree with those who urge that resort at present to sanctions is a European idea and opposition to it is an American idea. As I have already said, it seems to me that at present Europeans are altogether too realistic to believe in invocation of sanctions, while it is American advocates of the League who urge their use and who urge us to join with Europe in imposing them. In this attitude these Americans are faithful to the role of Wilson in insisting that this factor be made a part of the Covenant. But it can be said with truth that American opposition to the idea of sanctions was a chief factor in keeping the United States out of the League, and that opposition on *principle* as well as on grounds of practicability was a decided factor in generating the American idea of outlawry of the institution of war—that is of war as a juridical means of settling international disputes. In so far, opposition is an American idea.

It is argued that it is inconsistent for those who oppose international sanctions to join in a *private* boycott of Japanese goods. On the contrary, except for those extreme pacifists who believe that any overt act which may inflict suffering on anyone else is wrong, such a boycott is the only form that economic action against Japan can consistently take. It *is* a boycott, not a blockade. It does not involve even a suggestion of political force. It expresses moral disapproval in a way which it is hoped will arouse attention. The assertion that a private boycott runs on all fours with a political, financial and commercial interdict logically implies that Japan is correct in her contention that a Chinese boycott of Japanese goods is justification for armed retaliation on the part of Japan, and that Gandhi's boycott of British goods justifies armed retaliation on the part of Great Britain—a position which even the British party of coercive force has not taken in defence of its action.

My discussion would not be wholly ingenuous if I passed in silence over a phase of the argument which holds that as a matter of fact the great nations did not hesitate to send military and naval forces to Japan in defence of their own national interests. Probably there are some who, independently of their views on the topic of sanctions, would deny this statement. I am not among them. Persons who support the intervention of the United States in Latin America have frequently justified our nationalistic action there on the grounds that under the Monroe Doctrine we are really acting as a kind of trustee for European powers. There is another possibility: abstinence from *all* armed interventions. The same is true as to China. The sole alternative to conjoint coercive action is *not* individualistic national action; it is cessation of the policy of protecting, by means of armed force, persons and property voluntarily placed within a jurisdiction where they are endangered. If two great European powers were at war, the United States would not regard it as a hostile act if American property were destroyed when it happened to be located on a field of battle. The same principle can be applied in "backward" countries. All nations might suitably have joined in sending ships to evacuate all nationals endangered by local warfare, but such action as that, while appropriate and desirable, has nothing to do with imposition of sanctions; it is not "defensive" war, national *or* international.

The main positive contention for the use of sanctions is that the creation of a "successful international organization" is dependent upon assurance that there is a force at the disposal of cooperative action which can bring the peacebreaker to terms, and that nations will not disarm nor trust themselves to the adoption of exclusively peaceful measures unless there is assurance that an international force will undertake their defense. Short of an international force devoted to keeping the peace it is said that nations will rely upon their own force.

The argument appears to surrender the restriction to economic sanctions. But much more important than this fact is that in as far as it is admitted to have weight, it points straight to the French proposal for an international army and navy under the control of a general staff, while it rests upon the French premise that security is the all important thing, and that security can be guaranteed only by force. If security is the main thing, and if an international army will achieve it and if nothing else will, the conclusion seems to be the necessity of an international army. All the arguments which can be brought against the latter weigh against the premises from which it follows. The argument that international order and a coercive force to enforce peace are so nearly synonymous that we cannot have one without the other proves, if it proves anything, the necessity for a superstate with its own army and navy.

But even so, the argument that the use of sanctions under conditions which now exist is a prerequisite for the creation of an international order puts the cart before the horse. *If* there existed a general concert of interests and harmony of purposes, a specific international organization would at least be practicable of attainment, whether or not it were desirable; and its force be directed against a recalcitrant nation. But to suppose that the use of combined coercive force is a means of promoting the formation of such an organization—to say nothing of it being the best or only means—is like supposing that individuals can be clubbed into loving each other. It reminds one of the statement given out by the Japanese that they were fighting the Chinese at Shanghai in order to promote friendly relations of the two nations.

In connection with the argument that organization for coercive purposes (that is, the use of sanctions) is a necessary pre-condition of an internal order [it is sometimes] assumed that the opponents of sanctions believe that "good faith" will *suffice* to create such an order. I do not know who these optimists are, and I regret that I cannot share their optimism.

It is well-known that conditions can be indispensable without being sufficient. I do not see how world organization of and for peace can be brought into existence without the growth of harmony of interests and community of values along many different lines. I do not know of any single device which will bring it automatically into being. But I can think of no one thing more hostile to the development of this needed harmony and community than the overhanging menace of coercive force. All who oppose the invocation of sanctions in international affairs believe that reliance on informed public opinion and good faith is a *sine qua non*. They also believe that it is a power favorable to the growth of stable peace, while the use of force is by its very consequences hostile to such a growth. This brings us to the other basic principle: the undesirability of recourse to coercive force in order to accomplish international ends, of peace, even if it were practicable.

While I sympathize heartily with criticisms of the dangerously exaggerated nationalism which afflicts the world today and agree with those who hold that it constitutes a situation close to international anarchy, I get the feeling in reading some proposals for remedying the situation that the attributes and activities of national states have been merely transfered over to some bigger substitute organization. It is extremely difficult to get away from concepts and modes of thinking which are sanctified by long tradition. It is much easier to seek improvement by setting up some rearrangement of them in a new pattern than it is to develop new concepts and to think in terms of them.

So in reading about "international war," "international defense," and an international order equipped with coercive powers I cannot escape the impression that policies are being framed and plans formed on the basis of an imagination still in thrall to nationalism, at least to that aspect of nationalism which enthrones force as the ultimate arbiter. I realize that this feeling or impression is no argument, but I record it for what it is worth. In grandiose plans for the world-state, it is certainly clear that the start is made with the idea of the state as at present organized, which is then magnified till all states are absorbed into one. I cannot think that emancipation from the evils of nationalism will be obtained by any manipulation of the elements which constitute the nationalistic state, but only by development of that sort of interaction between social units and groupings that is exemplified in the intellectual, industrial, commercial relations of the states of the Union with one another. It is these interactions operating to effect reciprocal advantage for all concerned that holds the states together in unity, not any political entity superimposed upon them and exercising coercive force upon them.

I do not claim the analogy is perfect, but I think no reasonable person will hold that the coercive force of the federal government is chiefly or in any large degree that which keeps the various states together; or that it is a factor of any great importance as compared with the bonds of common tradition, habits of mind, beliefs, information, intercommunication, commerce, etc., which tie the people of the states together. Nor can I imagine any sensible person today who, when he looks at rivalries of interest and latent frictions between sections which still exist, would urge as a remedy the strengthening of coercive force exercised from above upon them (We tried "force bills" after the Civil War.). I cannot imagine such a person proposing anything but means which will positively intensify the bonds of common interest and purpose which exist among sections. If civil war were finally resorted to it certainly would not be as a desirable remedial measure but as an awful evil which had to be endured.

Coming to definite arguments, that in regard to the analogy of international coercive power with domestic police power in the enforcement of law seems to have reached a deadlock; the reasons put forth by each side do not seem to have much effect on the other. I cannot refrain however from summarizing the reasons which actuate those which deny the justice of the analogy, since they bear directly upon the fact that international coercive force is a form of war—something admitted by both sides to be undesirable.

The most obvious, but at the same time the least fundamental, reason why the proposed analogy breaks down is that, with respect to the internal affairs of the state, there already exists a body of laws (common and statute) which determines both the material and the manner of the use of force; which decides, that is, both the objects for which public force shall be employed and the exact ways in which it shall be used. There is no provision that force may be used for any purpose which a court at any particular time thinks desirable. There is a large body of regulations and precedents which determine as narrowly as possible the circumstances in which and the ends for which public authority will employ force for purposes of execution and restraint. Police, sheriffs, and so forth, are so far from being allowed to employ any kind of force which they judge may be effective that they themselves act under laws which prescribe and limit their use of force. All of these precedent conditions are notoriously lacking in the case of the so-called police application of international sanctions.

I remarked that this particular defective analogy was not so fundamental as others. It points, however, to one which is fundamental. The reasons why there are laws regulating both substance and procedure in the use of police force is because, within each state where the laws run, there is substantial agreement as to important social interests and values. In other words, the laws do not exist because there is the possibility of the use of coercion for their enforcement, but force can be used because the "laws" apart from coercion are the customs, the agreed upon modes of life, of the community; or else they are declarations of the recognized will of the community by *methods* which in the main are self-enforcing in the life of the community. Laws that are enforced are enforced because there is a community consensus behind them. The threat of force does not bring about the consensus. So at this point the analogy between the domestic police force and the use of sanctions as an agency for promoting the formation of a stable and peaceful international order breaks down completely.

The considerations just adduced bring us to the third element of difference. How can the employment of police force against individuals or at most small gangs be thought to have any similarity to the use of force against an entire nation? Not only would the domestic criminal, if known, be reprehended by all about him, but he is, if the force against him is successful, only an insignificant fraction of the population. If the population of New York State were practically unanimous in refusing to obey a federal law, it would not be police which would be called out if it were decided to use coercion, but the army and navy. The result would be civil war, not the ordinary processes of courts and sheriffs. There may be circumstances in which civil war is practically unavoidable. But I cannot imagine anyone saying that it is intrinsically desirable or that it should be provided for in advance because such provision is a necessary means of promoting a peaceful order.

Although I am compelled to believe that the use of police force in executing decisions of courts and other legal bodies is necessary in every stage of human civilization so far attained, I confess I cannot understand the satisfaction which upholders of sanctions find in seeking justification for international force in the fact of police force. I am not such an extreme non-resistant that I believe we can dispense with coercion in domestic matters. But that the use of coercive force in domestic force does an immense amount of harm, that at times it is doubtful whether it accomplishes enough good to offset the evil it does, seems to me clear. Ex-Justice Holmes is on record, if I recall correctly, in expressing a doubt on this very point. Doubtless there are still some persons who cling to the abstract notion of vindictive justice. But most civilized persons today are convinced that coercive and punitive forces are last resorts; that the necessity for appealing to them is itself proof that something is wrong in normal social processes, and that the social ideal is to find the measures which will change the causes which make the invocation of force necessary in particular cases. It is a strange thing to me that in the very country and at the very time when it is so tragically apparent that reliance upon coercive force in domestic matters is a broken reed, there should be an active agitation for treating appeal to coercion as the important and necessary condition of good international relations.

We come now to comparison of the value of sanctions with that of other measures which may be used. First, and with respect to the Paris Pact, I want to say a few words about the subject of "defensive" war. I quite agree with those who hold that "defensive" war logically implies "aggressive" warfare, and the need for some criterion for distinguishing between them. The original idea of the outlawry of war was to outlaw the institution of war and not just some special brand of war. It was pointed out that nothing could destroy the right of self-defense—the same right that an individual has, when violently assailed, to protect himself. This latter right does not depend upon making a distinction between offensive and defense assault and battery; this is completely outlawed. So with war.

Unfortunately, however, there was not an adequate education of the public in the meaning of the idea of outlawry before its official adoption. Still more unfortunately, there were believers in the necessity of military force among the politicians of the world who strove to give the idea an innocuous meaning, and who tried to turn the fact of self-defense, which is neither a product of law nor capable of being abrogated by law, into the concept of the legality of defensive war. Influential statesmen anxious for the speedy adoption of the Pact indulged in ambiguities. Either M. Briand himself never fully grasped the idea or he was interested in mitigating its force.[6] For in his speech of August 27, 1928, he limited the idea of renunciation of war in a way which left room for introducing the idea of two kinds of war, one of which was not outlawed. He said that it was "war as a means of arbitrary and selfish action" which was outlawed. And several times, as if for the sake of emphasis, he limited the significance of the Pact to "selfish and willful" war, thus giving ground to those persons who claim that even under the Pact, there is a place for a kind of war which is noble and disinterested. Moreover, a number of Americans who had previously ridiculed and opposed the idea of outlawry, and who were devoted to the idea of sanctions, seized upon this loophole and making it central in their interpretation of the Pact, brought forward the notion of "international" defensive war.

Consequently there is still an ambiguity in the Pact which can be taken advantage of to sustain the contention that the Pact itself demands international sanctions and war, unless the "defensive war" it permits is to become purely nationalistic. However, there is another and better alternative. That is to clarify international law so that the distinction between the right of self-defense and the concept of "defensive war" is made clear. Had this been done before Japan's incursion into Manchuria, every pretence on her part that she was fighting a defensive war and therefore had not broken the Pact would have been swept away.

The argument is made that the refusal of other nations to admit the legality of accessions of territory, or other gains, resulting from violation of the Paris Pact will not be adequate; that it is a half-way sanction, but *only* a half-way one. The argument is supported on the ground that past non-recognitions have not operated to prevent nations from enjoying the fruits of their aggression. The argument from precedents overlooks one important difference. The cases cited are refusals of recognition by *particular* nations, as of Great Britain's seizure of Egypt by France, of various undertakings of the United States with respect to Latin American countries. The refusal which is contemplated by the "peace-sanction"(originally suggested by Mr. S. O. Levinson, the author of the Outlawry idea) is one to be exercised by all nations in common, and one which, through the influence of Secretary Stimson, has been officially acted upon by the Assembly of the League. If there is no difference in results to be expected from isolated national action and organized international action, what becomes of the argument regarding the difference between national and international defense, national and international war? The logic of the argument from the failure of national non-recognition to the necessary failure of present and future international non-recognition compels us to conclude that the *only* merit of international sanctions is that it represents a stronger economic and military coercive force.

The argument that non-recognition of say Japan's position in Manchuria will not lessen the ability of Japan to establish herself there so solidly that non-recognition will mean nothing raises hypothetical questions. It ignores to my mind the slow but effective operation of imponderables. But speculative matters aside, it raises the question: Upon what shall those who desire a world organized for peace depend: upon force and the threat of force, or upon peaceful measures in the development of common interests and purposes?

"Peace-sanctions" are not "half-way" sanctions because they are not sanctions at all in the sense of those who argue for economic and military sanctions. For they do not involve the application of coercive force. They are sanctions simply in the sense in which undesirable consequences which flow intrinsically from the performance of an act are sanctions. If a nation obtains territory by means which are juridically banned, then juridically those gains are null and void. To some it will seem unrealistic to put faith on strictly moral agencies and influences. But it would seem as if the history of war, the history of the consequences of the use of physical and coercive force, were enough to convince reasonable persons who want peace of the unrealistic character of any other means.

We do not insist that good faith and moral pressure are *sure* to operate, that they are bound to be sufficient. But we do say that the measures which can be taken in their name are more promising roads to stable and enduring peace than is to recourse to coercion, actual or veiled. It is now necessary to argue that the possibility of using the latter rests back upon the former, since the pledge to use coercive force depends for fulfillment upon the good faith of the national making it. You cannot employ coercion in an endless regress against those who do not observe good faith, Mr. Buell [writes]. "Admittedly all international obligations in the last resort must rest upon good faith and the force of public opinion."[7] Since this is fact and since it must be the fact, we hold that consistent action upon the basis of the fact is the best way to promote the positive influence of good faith and public opinion, while the habit of continuing to think and act in terms of coercion perpetuates the ideas and emotions which sustain the institution of war. It correspondingly weakens the operation of the good faith and public opinion which are admitted to be the ultimate reliance.

Any one of us can sympathize with those who are impatient with the present relations of nations and who are indignant with those nations that, after professing a love of peace and promising to forego the use of warlike measures to settle their disputes, fail to live up to their good word. Their breach of good faith has the psychological effect of causing us to doubt the efficacy of all good faith and to imagine that the use of coercion is the only thing which nations will respect. But in spite of a reaction in this direction that is natural because of desire for speedy results, all history and understanding of human nature tell us, I believe, that the view is shortsighted and in the end defeats its own purpose. I am not convinced beyond every peradventure of a doubt that the Outlawry of War will rid the world finally of the war system. If nations insist upon fighting they will do so, just as individuals commit suicide.

But I am sure of two things: First, that if the peoples of nations *want* to have done with war, the Outlawry idea is the best method for giving expression to that desire which has yet been discovered, and secondly, that it is fatal for those who welcome the Outlawry idea and who believe in it to play, even in thought, with the idea of sanctions or coercive force. In so doing they, however, unintentionally, reinstate the idea of war and undermine their own position. Devotion to sanctions comes naturally and logically only from those who believe that wars are the inevitable way of settling disputes between nations, and who do not believe that the traditional policies of balance of power and alliances can be done away with. For, in effect, the enforcement of sanctions signifies only that at a given time and for the time being there is an alliance of nations which thinks itself sufficiently strong to restrain by coercion some nation from going to war or else to conquer and penalize that nation if it does go to war. Were it not for the fear that someone would think that I was recommending the idea, I would say that the conception of a *Pax Romana* can be realized more readily by a thoroughgoing alliance, economic, financial, military and naval, of the British Commonwealth of Nations and the United States than by any scheme of "international defense and war" yet devised.

In the long run, the efficacy of the Paris Pact, of the Outlawry idea in general, depends upon the growth of community of interests and purposes among the nations of the world. The Outlawry agreement, like any jural arrangement, is protective of interests that exist; it reinforces them with the power of pledged good faith. But there are definite measures which can be adopted that will add to the efficacy of dependence upon good faith and public opinion as expressed in the Paris Pact. I believe that if the energies of those who want peace were united to promote these measures, immensely more would be accomplished for peace than will be effected by keeping discussion and thought fastened upon the use of coercion.

1. The Covenant of the League, by modification of Articles X, XV and XVI, can be brought into harmony with the Pact of Paris. Unless this is done, opposition to the adherence of the United States will continue. The one thing most certain in our foreign policy is that we shall not assign to any group of foreign powers a disposition of our own decision as to our future course of action in matters involving war and the threat of war. Quite aside from the attitude of the United States, such action will prevent different methods and measures from assuring peace from interfering with each other and virtually encouraging warlike action— an interference which unfortunately took place in the Sino-Japanese embroglio.

2. There can be formally adopted as a part of international law the principle that all occupations, privileges, possessions that are effected in violation of the Peace Pact, that is by acts which are not consonant with the pledge to use peaceful measures in settlement of disputes, shall be juridically null and void. The principle has been endorsed by the Assembly of the League and can and should be officially incorporated into international law.

3. There should be adopted into international law the principle that any dispute or controversy not brought to settlement by the ordinary processes of diplomacy, or by mediation, conciliation, arbitration, etc., shall remain in *status quo*.[8] Doubtless this idea is implied in the Paris Pact but if it were made explicit and nations were to pledge themselves to it, a given violation of the Pact would stand out more clearly and the response of public opinion would be quicker and more pronounced.

4. The fundamental distinction between the right of self-defense and the concept of defensive war should be established in international law.

5. The United States should adhere promptly to the World Court to which should be referred, with a view to the enlightenment of public opinion and the unification of the moral judgment of the world, any and every case in which there is a claim that the terms of the Pact have been violated, when the question is not settled by the ordinary means of negotiation among nations.

Finally, it should go without saying that these measures are additional to and not substitutes for the increased use of all possible means of consultation, conference, mediation, arbitration, and all other possible agencies of peaceful settlement. Let us throw our energies into strengthening them and not, because they and the Pact have not as yet been completely successful, fall back upon the continued use of coercive force.

Editor's Note. (p. 567 "The League has consistently refused to invoke the use of sanctions.")

In 1935, the League *seemed* to break its record for consistency by voting sanctions against Italy; in *reality,* however, the case was quite otherwise: the only thing the League consistently preserved was its basic policy of *appearing* to be a League of Nations, while *being* and *acting* as a Combination of Great Powers. The Government of Great Britain assumed the role of leader in the League movement to impose sanctions; the actual record of the Government of Great Britain, acting through, with and for the League, is therefore conclusive evidence as to what *really* transpired in 1935:

Norman Angell, in his book *The Defence of the Empire,* goes into the whole matter at some length. For the purposes here, a few quotations will suffice.

"*At Italy's* request we imposed an embargo upon the export of arms to Abyssinia. Thus, at a time when Italy was feverishly pouring armies into Africa for the purpose of conquering Abyssinia, we showed our 'impartiality' by applying an embargo 'to both parties', an embargo which, while it did not even embarrass Italy: made it impossible for Abyssinia to acquire the means of defence.

"The *Italian demand* that we should refuse licences for the export of arms to Abyssinia *happened to be a breach of our obligation* in the 1930 arms traffic treaty with Abyssinia to allow the Abyssinian Emperor to supply himself with the arms he needed in self-defence. Italy manufactures her own munitions and Abyssinia does not possess a single munitions factory. The argument was that by denying Abyssinia arms 'conciliation' was more likely to succeed." (pp. 144–145; italics mine.)

Again: "The spokesmen of the British Government announced with pride that whatever else it did it would take *no course in the matter of sanctions* which might provoke war with Italy. From that moment the conversation might just as well have ceased. Italy had only to say that in the event of any specified sanction being employed she would fight, for that sanction to go into the 'inapplicable' list. An eminent Italian professor has pointed out that from the moment the British Cabinet announced *'it would be no party to a policy involving war'* the *real* chairmanship of the Sanctions Committee passed to Signor Mussolini." (p. 146; italics mine.)

In support of the Italian professor's conclusion, writes Angell, "There is one supreme piece of evidence which settles the last point. In M. Laval's account of his meeting with Sir Samuel Hoare and Mr. Eden on Sept. 10, 1935, occurs this statement: 'We agreed that hostilities were about to begin almost immediately and . . . we found ourselves *instantaneously* in agreement upon ruling out military measures, not adopting any measure of naval blockade, never contemplating the closure of the Suez Canal—*in a word, ruling out everything that might lead to war.*'" (p. 147; italics mine.)

Further: "Mr. Churchill, who has examined the internal evidence as to whether our sanctions policy was 'real or sham,' writes that from first to last the committee charged with devising sanctions 'conformed docilely to the limitations prescribed by the aggressor. They proceeded to the rescue of Abyssinia on the basis that nothing must be done to hamper the invading Italian armies.' (p. 148).

"Mr. Winston Churchill has summarised the position thus: 'First the Prime Minister had declared that sanctions meant war; secondly he was resolved that there must be no war; and thirdly, he decided upon sanctions.' (p. 146.)

And continuing to quote Mr. Churchill: "'It is true that included in the sanctions were many measures, *especially financial* measures, which in the long run would have destroyed the Italian financial power to purchase necessities in foreign countries, and that these would have eventually affected their war-making capacity.

"'But the chief of these, the financial sanctions, *did not require Geneva* to impose them. The credit of Italy had already fallen, and was bound to fall, so low that the ordinary market factors would have been *as valid as the League decision.*'

"'Thus the sanctions which we have been pressing with so great a parade were not real sanctions to paralyze the invader, but merely such half-hearted sanctions *as the invader would tolerate, because in fact they stimulated Italian war spirit.*'" (pp. 147-148; italics mine.)

The above are cited from Mr. Angell's book simply for their bearing on the *question of fact* involved in Mr. Dewey's statements in the text to which this is a note. As for their bearing on the *issue* of the use of sanctions, it is only fair to Mr. Angell (who is an advocate of the use sanctions) to say that he uses these citations and other evidences to prove that sanctions have never *really* been imposed. (Which proof is also not irrelevant to Mr. Dewey's argument.)

To conclude this note: In 1935 the Governments of Great Britain and France happened to use the League of Nations as their stalking-horse. But that they really did not need to do so has since been amply demonstrated. Great Britain's Committee for Non-Intervention in Spain serves their purposes just as effectively, if not better.

Notes

1. See note at end of Chapter—Ed.
2. The statement in this sentence is elliptical or truncated; the succeeding sentences fill it out. Clearly "neither the word nor the idea [boycott] has any application in international affairs" *as those affairs are conducted by governments.*—Ed.
3. See Note at end of Chapter—Ed.
4. A concrete illustration in point is Mussolini's establishment of the day "sanctions" were imposed by the League as a National (Roman) Holiday devoted to glorifying the Invincible Military Spirit and Power of Italy—Ed.
5. That it was *only* "an arrest" is now evident.—Ed.
6. This was and is far too generous a concession to M. Briand—Ed.
7. In Mr. Buell's contribution, printed in the same pamphlet.—Ed.
8. This suggestion like the one in the preceding paragraph is due to Mr. S.O. Levinson and was first made public in the *Christian Century* for February 3, 1932 [Author's note in original.].

4

Future Peace

The Remaking of Scientists and Soldiers

Chris Hables Gray

THE POLITICS OF SCIENCE

Science is the most prestigious worldview today in both the developed and the undeveloped worlds. Marxist or capitalist, Shiite or Sunni, Protestant or Catholic, all pay a certain homage to science. Many people, especially scientists, give it the role of their personal defining ideology or religion. Therapies, policies, and countless other systems seek its mantle, from astrology to psychiatry to Stalinism to UFOlogy. Whether or not they are indeed sciences depends on one's definition of a science, but they wish to be.

The legitimizing power of science has been claimed by many political viewpoints. This is certainly true of most variations of capitalist ideology. Whether sympathetic to the state or not, from Democratic liberals to free-market libertarians, the vast majority of the ideological supporters of capitalism give science a central role in their cosmology.

But this is just as true of almost all of the Western alternatives to capitalism, such as early anarchism and almost all brands of Marxism. Peter Kropotkin, a world-famous geographer in his own right, argued that science supported anarchism and anarchism was scientific (1970). While Mikhail Bakunin also felt undistorted science supported anarchism, he was less naïve about the possible misuse of science's material and moral power. He warned against the authoritarian tendencies of scientists and the misuse of science by governments. Most importantly, he validated the importance of unscientific abstractions, such as passion and justice, for analyzing and changing the social system (1953). Postmodern anarchists are very skeptical of science, and many have fully taken up the critique of the postmodern feminists and anarchist theorists such as Paul Goodman, who even in the 1950s disputed science's claims to normative truth and disinterested good (1964).

On the other hand, most Marxists still argue that Marxism is scientific, although there are exceptions (see Fee, 1986). Marxism-as-science is a claim that has even convinced some scientists. Between the World Wars many prominent British scientists were Marxists, such as J. B. Haldane and J. D. Bernal, and they even went so far as to argue that future science could only be communist. Stalinist science policy, as exemplified by the Lysenko affair, eventually dissuaded them of this particular delusion. But, in general, it seems illusions about science's total applicability led these ex-Stalinist scientists to continue their arguments for the scientific management of society and for the expansion of science into politics in all its forms, especially warmaking.

Ironically, the well-organized antimilitarist groups of scientists, such as the Cambridge Scientists' Anti-War Group and the Association of Scientific Workers (ASW) in Britain, were led by Bernal and others into the heart of the British war effort in the late 1930s. The leadership of the ASW even collected a list of scientists willing to do war work, despite numerous protests from scientists with more consistent anti-war politics. Finally, the ASW came to the contradictory conclusion that while "war [is] the supreme perversion of science" the danger of "anti-democratic movements" which were a threat to "the very existence of science" meant that "we are prepared to organize for defence" (McGucken, 1984, p. 159). For them, a perverted science is better than no science at all.

Many U.S. scientists also campaigned for a greater role in government decision making, especially on military issues. Along with access to policy making, the scientists usually proposed scientist-controlled institutions to hand out government money. They wanted money without accountability, which didn't happen except in limited cases such as the National Science Foundation. Usually scientists did get lots of money, but at the price of becoming accountable to the military.

Is it any wonder that science has survived, indeed triumphed, in today's perverse form? Well-meaning radical scientists played a major role in the creation of the postmodern war system through the application of scientific methods to social and military processes (Hales, 1974). It was under the mistaken impression that the Nazis were close to developing atomic bombs that a number of antimilitarist, even pacifist, scientists conceived and created the first atomic bombs, unleashing the possibility of annihilation upon the world. That the advances of science and the developments of war may have led to our present situation anyway does not lessen the guilt of the physicists, as many freely admitted. Even J. Robert Oppenheimer said, "Physicists have now known sin."

Still, he didn't feel that guilty. Witness his postwar advocacy of tactical nuclear weapons as a counterweight to development of the hydrogen bomb being pushed by

Edward Teller and John von Neumann. Oppenheimer's general evasion of responsibility, famous public quotations such as the one above notwithstanding, can be seen in this letter in 1946 to Vannevar Bush defending the general amnesty given to German scientists and their recruitment into the U.S. military-research apparatus (while a similar integration was taking place on the Soviet side of the Iron Curtain with the scientists they had captured):

> You and I both know that it is not primarily men of science who are danger-
> ous, but the policies of Governments which lead to aggression and to war.
> You and I both know that is the German scientists are treated as enemies
> of society, the scientists of this country will soon be so regarded (quoted in
> Keyles, 1987, p. 338).

This begs the question: sure, atomic bombs don't kill people, people kill people, but do you give atomic bombs to killers?

By the end of World War II many scientists congratulated themselves on science's integration into government. Some, such as the technocrat physicist Arthur Holly Compton, a Nobel laureate, thought that all of culture should be subordinated to science. He argued that "Only those features of society can survive which adapt men to life under the conditions of growing science and technology" (quoted in Sherry, 1977, p. 128).

Scientists also began pushing for a more worldwide policy role for scientists through the World Federation of Scientific Workers, founded in 1946, and UNESCO, whose first director was Julian Huxley, a leading British liberal. Most capitalist and communist scientists were equally enthusiastic about this alliance. Since 1946 there has been an unprecedented number of scientists in public policy positions. What's seldom discussed about these scientist-politicians is that one of the main reasons they have a voice in public affairs is because of their ability to make weapons. But this is not surprising. In many ways war is the dirty secret of science.

Consider how brief the treatment of this relationship is in philosophy. Such famous philosophers of science as Thomas Kuhn, Hilary Putnum, and even the dada-anarchist Paul Feyerabend hardly ever confronted it. In computer science, a discipline mothered and fathered by war and the military, philosophical works like Margaret Boden's ignore this genealogy altogether; which is all the more startling when one considers how open and debated it is among computer scientists themselves. But there are exceptions. David Dickson's *The New Politics of Science* (1984) is an excellent overview of U.S. Cold War science. Not only does he always keep the militarized context of late-twentieth-century U.S. science clear, but he also situates it within an intense capitalistic discourse that turns individual scientists, government agencies, and non-profit universities into profit-seeking organizations for all intents and purposes.

SCIENTISTS AND WAR

The relationship between scientific discovery, technological invention and war has varied, as even a quick-and-dirty history shows. In ancient times Archimedes refused to reveal the details of the engines of war he invented to defend his mother city, Syracuse, from the Romans. Earlier, the wheel was used on toys for hundreds of years before it was used on chariots. In China, gunpowder was for fireworks, not killing (Mumford, 1934, p. 84). War was only indirectly affected by discovery and innovation, except at those times when a new weapon or technology would revolutionize warfare completely. The Bronze Age became Iron as the stronger metal bested the earlier one. Chariots swept the ancient Middle East; Sun Tzu's subtle and codified insights into war allowed the State of Wu to dominate the Middle Kingdom; and English long bows cut down French knights in the Middle Ages. But after each innovation stability would quickly return. New methods often took hundreds of years before they were even applied to war.

In large part this is because war is such a strong cultural force. It often resisted the introduction of effective killing technologies for many years because they didn't fit the war discourse of the time. Even as recently as the seventeenth century in Japan, the warrior caste (samurai) succeeded in banning guns from 1637 to 1867 (Perrin, 1979).

Some have even argued that war and progress (technological and scientific) have been inexorably linked through the ages. There is much evidence to contradict this as a historical analysis, as John Nef shows in his book *War and Human Progress,* but the relationship of "progress" (technological and scientific) and war today is almost symbiotic. Perhaps as many as half of all engineers and scientists in the United States work for the military and in accord with military priorities (Nef, 1963; D. Dickson, 1984). Worldwide there are probably half a million scientists and engineers working on military problems (D. Dickson, 1984, p. 108).

The recent militarization of science is quite a change from the earlier relationship. Greek philosophy disdained war or anything practical. Roman engineering certainly focused on the needs of empire, but what we now call science (then still called philosophy) was hardly militarized. It was at the beginning of the modern era that this began to change significantly. The physics of cannonballs framed many of Galileo's questions, and the first major commercial product of optics was military telescopes.

Still, science was not focused on war even as war began to focus on science. Only 10 percent of the members of the early Royal Society, did war work. The number is at least four times higher now (Ziman, 1976, p.11). And today's technoscience is much more powerful than the earlier alliance of engineering brotherhoods, mechanics, alchemists, natural philosophers, and mathematicians who founded modern science.

There have always been objections to linking what many described as a quest for knowledge with improving the killing of fellow humans. Although he served Cesare Borgia and later King Louis XII of France as a military engineer, Leonardo da Vinci explained that he wouldn't even describe his ideas for submarines in his secret notebooks because "of the evil nature of men, who would practice assassination at the bottom of the seas by breaking the ships in their lowest parts and sinking them together with the crews who are in them" (quoted in Brodie, 1973, p. 239). Niccolò Tartaglia, the author of the first scientific study of gunnery, called simply enough *Nuova Scienzia* (1537), claimed that he was going to keep his work secret because "it was a thing blameworthy, shameful and barbarous, worthy of severe punishment before God and man, to wish to bring to perfection an art damageable to one's neighbor and destructive of the human race" (quoted in Brodie, 1973, p. 240). But later he changed his mind. He asserted that was because Italy was being menaced by Turkey, but why did he do the study in the first place?

John Napier, the Scottish inventor of logarithms in the early seventeenth century, feared a Catholic invasion of Britain, so he designed a tank and a gigantic cannon. However, he never revealed the details of his inventions because there were already too many "devices" for "the ruin and overthrow of man" (p. 243).

Even in 1945 such reservations were still heard, but to little effect.

SOCIAL RESPONSIBILITY AND COMPUTER SCIENTISTS

Within weeks of the obliteration of Hiroshima, scientists from the Manhattan Project were organizing "to promote the attainment and use of scientific and technological advances in the best interest of humanity." They formed the Federation of Atomic Scientists (FAS) with other newly established scientists' groups and began publishing the *Bulletin of the Atomic Scientists* (Heims, 1980, p. 233). They also initiated the Pugwash Conferences, named after the town in Nova Scotia where they first met. In 1995 the Pugwash group was awarded the Nobel Peace Prize. But over the years scientist have been far from united.

The political divisions among physicists in the post-World War II period are well known: they ranged from Albert Einstein's pacifism to Edward Teller's militarism, and included the uproar over Oppenheimer's losing battle with McCarthyism. However, physics wasn't the only discipline where this drama took place. Computer science had its own martyr in Alan Turing, probably hounded to suicide by the British authorities because of his homosexuality.[1] And computer science has had its warlords as well, such as the analog expert Vannevar Bush, who directed the Office of Scientific Research and Development.

Bush is particularly interesting because he was directly and philosophically interested in the effect of science on war. He began his book *Modern Arms and Free Men*, an impassioned call for preparedness, with the statement that "Modern science has utterly changed the nature of war and is still changing it" (1949, pp. 2–3). Bush pointed out that it was Abraham Lincoln who first established official government science by setting up the Academy of Sciences during the Civil War. President Woodrow Wilson authorized the National Research Council for World War I. But in World War II with the National Defense Research Committee and the Office of Scientific Research and Development (employing over 30,000 people) a new level of science-war integration was achieved (p. 6).

This "new Era" as Bush calls it, actually started with World War I. He cites two factors: first, mass production and precision manufacture; second, the internal-combustion engine. "Between them," he says, "they made mechanized war possible, and the world will never be the same again." Submarines, airplanes, complex fire-control computing systems for gunnery on surface ships, and high-speed machine guns, all meant that war now required "a new kind of courage and endurance, a skill at operating machines under stress, and for the first time the factory behind the lines became a dominant element in the whole paraphernalia of war" (pp. 10–11). Two important concepts began here:

> First was the idea of reliable complexity in intricate devices, in masses of electrical and mechanical parts interconnected to function in a precisely predetermined manner, and dependable in spite of their intricacy because of the contribution of standardized mass-production methods. The second idea was that of relegating to a machine functions of computation and judgment formerly performed by men, because the machine could work more rapidly, more accurately, and more surely under stress. (p. 13)

Bush concludes, "When the First World War ended there were thus in existence nearly all the elements for scientific warfare." Also, in his view, "The long process of applying scientific results, all the way from the original academic theory or experiment to the finished device, had become ordered" (p. 16).

A key part of Bush's work, once scientists were integrated into policy making, was protecting young scientists from the actual fighting. In fact, he felt that "the problem of keeping young scientists in the laboratories was one of the toughest and most irritating problems we faced in the war" (p. 99). They needed to be protected because "armed prosperity" meant permanent mobilization. Scientists couldn't risk getting killed in battle because they were needed to constantly prepare for war:

When war became total the armament race took on a new form. It is now a race not merely for the quick possession of a few battleships or other weapons that might decide an issue, but to attain immense strength of every sort, such strength that the appalling costs of preparation can be paid without wrecking the system that produces them, such mounting strength that armed prosperity can proceed to more arms and more prosperity. (p. 120)

Bush became a central proponent of preparedness and militarized science, although with many reservations. His was probably the mainstream response, but not all computer scientists agreed with him. Two the most important "fathers" of computation, John von Neumann and Norbert Wiener, both of Hungarian-Jewish descent, took substantially different positions from Bush toward science and war, Wiener was almost a pacifist while von Neumann was particularly prowar. Comparing their postwar careers we can see how antiwar scientists have been marginalized politically even as their discoveries were applied militarily whereas prowar scientists have been integrated into the highest levels of political power while claiming to be nothing more than objective experts without politics.[2]

When von Neumann was invited to join the FAS board he declined, claiming to have avoided "all participation in public activities, which are not of a purely technical nature." When invited again he wrote, "I do not want to appear in public in a not primarily technical context" (quoted in Heims, 1980, p. 235). This is the man who in arguing for the hydrogen bomb the year before had said, "I don't think any weapon can be too large" (p. 236). Even as early as 1946 he went out of his way to view the first postwar atomic tests, Operation Crossroad, which FAS objected strenuously to. He was hardly adverse to shaping military-political policy either: he met with Teller "immediately after they learned the news of the Soviet [atomic] bomb and discussed not whether but how to get political backing for an accelerated superbomb program" (pp. 240–47).

Norbert Wiener, the founder of the field of cybernetics, did substantial war work at MIT, but by the end World War II he had decided that he would refrain from any further research with military applications. At the end of 1946 he said, "I do not expect to publish any future work of mine which may do damage in the hands of irresponsible militarists" (p. 208).

By 1950 von Neumann was advocating preventive war. "If you say why not bomb them tomorrow, I say why not today? If you say today at five o'clock, I say why not one o'clock?" (p. 247) In the early 1950s he chaired the committee that justified the development of intercontinental ballistic missiles (ICBMs), starting with the Atlas.

Steven Heims, whose fascinating double biography of Wiener and von Neumann is subtitled *From Mathematics to the Technologies of Life and Death*, concludes that this was a "deep failure":

On their own terms, the Atlas missile and its successors were greatly successful, like the hydrogen bomb before them. But when one recognizes, with Einstein, that the implication of the nuclear armaments race is that "in the end, there beckons more and more clearly general annihilation," this achievement on a deeper level represents a horrendous failure of Western civilization in its use of science and technology. (pp. 274–75)

Wiener's resistance to war science was as thoughtful as von Neumann's support of it was thoughtless. Wiener argued that science was a limited knowledge system that needed ethics and moral philosophy if it wasn't going to contribute to the destruction of humanity.

Yet, Heims reports:

In the years 1968–1972 I asked a considerable number of mathematicians and scientists about their opinions of Wiener's social concerns and his preoccupation with the uses of technology. The typical answer went something like this: "Wiener was a great mathematician, but he was also eccentric. When he began talking about society and the responsibility of scientists, a topic outside of his area of expertise, well I just couldn't take him seriously." (p. 343)

Von Neumann died young, of cancer, in great fear. A man who made death for so many possible became psychotic in the face of death. Wiener died old and happy. Perhaps their deaths don't reflect their lives, or maybe they do, but there certainly is evidence that their politics influenced their science. In his book Heims contrasts their science in crucial ways. According to Heims, von Neumann believed in mathematics totally; through the power of numbers and calculations he felt every important problem could be solved. Wiener argued that mathematics was limited, so he put forward ecological, interactive theories creating the discipline of cybernetics, and then spent his last years working on prosthetics and similar projects. The military has found many uses for both of their work. Of their politics and philosophies, von Neumann, who claimed to have none, became a powerful political figure while Wiener was marginalized. Von Neumann's politics of no politics was just right for postmodern war.

The reasons for this go right to the heart of science as we know it. Heims points to two "pillars" that "hold up the practice of science." The first pillar is "value neutrality" institutionalized, in his view, in the Royal Society. In return for royal protection and encouragement the society "outlawed the subjects of theology and politics from its meetings." The second pillar is the idea of the inevitable progress of science.

"In the seventeenth century," he goes on to point out:

The rhetoric of value neutrality tended to obscure the fact that the new science was the beginning of a radical subversion of the status quo through a scientific-technological-industrial revolution. In the twentieth century, however, the claim of value neutrality has . . . tended . . . to hide . . . [the fact] that scientific work has . . . strengthened the hand of the already dominant centers of economic or political power. (pp. 261–62)

Von Neumann agreed that science is neutral and that it is progress. These two claims are metarules, in that they pretend to be givens by the very definition of science most scientists ascribe to. Just as significantly, von Neumann was, according to Heims, "himself emotionally in tune with men of power." Hans Morgenthau, a friend of von Neumann, concluded in his own work on the political systems that there is "in the great political masters a demonic and frantic striving for ever more power . . . which will be satisfied only when the last living man has been subjected to the master's will." He claimed this power lust was a form of love, and he saw this desire for power as intrinsic to humans and as the very basis for "power politics" (p. 323).

Some have argued that this "love" includes more base instincts among the individual scientists. As the repentant nuclear bomb designer Theodore Taylor admitted, "There is much to be learned by looking at the personal lives of the weaponers." He went on to elaborate on the intense personal pressures to develop new weapons: "There is the equivalent of an addiction . . . like drug abuse . . . power." In summarizing the relationship between science and the military he remarked, "We told the military what they wanted."[3] Many other observers have noticed this "hubris" factor in the technological push for new weapons (Broad, 1988; Vitale, 1985).

This dynamic has not changed. At ADS (Advanced Decision Systems), a military AI firm, a number of computer scientists admitted that they treated the generals and admirals they worked for like children. As Walter Bender, a scientist at MIT's Media Lab put it, "We cater to kindergarten children and admirals—people with very short attention spans" (Brand, 1987, p. 140). Other scientists, however, developed grave doubts. Susan Rosenbaum, for example, quit after ADS applied for a military contract she couldn't justify to herself:

I had always rationalized it as, "Well, we only do defensive work; we're just defending the country." Then we started going after a military contract that was offensive. We didn't get it, ultimately, but just the decision to pursue that kind of work pushed me over the edge. I couldn't rationalize it anymore. (Faludi, 1987, p. 13)

Jeff Dan, another ex-ADS researcher, designed the software program PeaceNet that allows thousand of peace groups to communicate electronically around the world. He admits, "I'm kind of surprised more people haven't left ADS. It's depressing to think all those people are still there" (p. 13).

In the early 1980s, the resistance within computer science to its own militarization led to the founding of Computer Professionals for Social Responsibility (CPSR), which had grown in the 1990s to dozens of chapters and thousands of members. CPSR led the critiques of the SDI program and it has played a leading role in raising questions about military computing in general. CRSR has also been very concerned about the threat to privacy posed by the lack of constitutional protection for the information transmitted and stored via electronic media.

Most members of CPSR feel that science is a social process, albeit a very powerful one, and that scientists must take some responsibility for the social consequences of their work, just as Wiener and FAS argued. As scientists must take responsibility for what they do, they also must admit that they don't and can't know everything. The central argument against military computing, for example, is that computer science can never be perfected. It is ontologically and epistemologically limited and incomplete. It can never be as complex as nature, including human intelligence. This is certainly not a view shared by all scientists, but it is a guiding principle for some, such as Charles Schwartz, a physics professor at the University of California at Berkeley, who refuses to teach graduate students physics anymore (Schwartz, 1988). Or Prof. Joseph Weizenbaum of MIT, who has called on computer scientists not to do vision research since it is framed by military priorities. There are also less established scientists, such as a recent PhD in AI from the University of California who refuses to publish any of her research because the military could use it. In 1995, the student Pugwash movement, an offshoot of the scientist's group founded after World War II, started circulating a pledge among science students to forgo war work.

On the other hand, mainstream science, with its emphasis on experimentation and materialism, is still generally oblivious to its role in postmodern war. As powerful as establishment science is, it is important to note that alternative visions of science continue to flourish in many surprising places, sustained by the obvious contradictions of postmodern science.

These contradictions have had an equal impact in a very surprising place—the military. Just as many scientists are trying to redefine what a scientist is, so are many military people redefining their own role.

SOLDIERS AND GENERALS FOR THE END OF WAR

Abolish war in all its forms!
—*Position statement of Veterans for Peace*

Since the first days of modern war military men and others have been arguing that new weapons would make war impossible. The poet John Donne was one of the many who claimed that artillery made war too horrible to fight (Brodie and Brodie, 1973, p. 70). Benjamin Franklin, on seeing the first balloon flight, predicted that balloons might make war obsolete (Sherry, 1987, p. 92). John Hay, Abraham Lincoln's personal secretary and later Theodore Roosevelt's secretary of state, assumed it to be "the plain lesson of history that the periods of peace have been longer protracted as the cost of destructiveness of war have increased" (Sherry, 1987, p. 92). Victor Hugo had a similar prediction regarding flying machines. He thought they would make armies "vanish, and with them the whole business of war, exploitation and subjugation" (Clarke, 1966, p. 3). Jack London said that "the marvelous and awful machinery of warfare . . . today defeats its own end. Made preeminently to kill, its chief effect is to make killing quite the unusual thing" (Sherry, 1987, p. 92). This has been quite the popular theory among inventors: Robert Fulton, Alfred Nobel, and Thomas A. Edison are among those who assumed their new technologies would make war unfightable (C. H. Gray, 1994). Henry Adams and H. G. Wells predicted either human suicide or the end of war. As R. Buckminster Fuller put it, "Either war is obsolete, or we are" (Sherry, 1987, p. 92). But why hasn't everyone accepted that war is obsolete?

It is true, and important, that war is no longer universally considered necessary, inevitable, or even good, as John Mueller notes:

> Many of the most fervent war supporters seemed beyond logical or practical appeal because they were so intensely romantic about their subject. Others were attracted to war because they believed it to be beneficial and progressive, and many, including some who loathed war, considered it to be natural and inevitable. Most of these views, particularly the romantic ones, were encouraged by the widespread assumption that war in the developed world would be short and cheap . . . None of these lines of thinking has serious advocates today, particularly as far as they pertain to international war in the developed world. (1989, p. 39)

Mueller is too optimistic. War obviously has its supporters to this day, but now they are on the defensive. While there have always been those who argued war was insane, lately the number has been growing. During World War I this became a mass movement among soldiers. The British antiwar soldier poets and the Russian, French, and German mutinies were all reflections of the terrible lesson of trench warfare: war is now inhuman.

This idea became broadly held in the United States during the Vietnam War. Widespread draft resistance, desertion, and mutinies in the field, at sea, and even in Guam and California shook the U.S. military. Only American English has a special word, "fragging" (from fragmentation grenades), for soldiers' killing of their own officers. Once back in "the World" (the United States) vets formed a number of antiwar groups, most notably Vietnam Veterans Against the War (VVAW). Today such activism continues within the mainstream veterans organizations and in special veterans groups, such as the Veteran Action Teams that have gone to Central America and the Veterans' Peace Convoys that managed to take humanitarian aid to Nicaragua despite U.S. government obstructions. In the early 1990s, veterans from the United States and Canada formed a group to abolish war by the year 2000. There are also several important peace-oriented think tanks founded by retired military men. The most important is the Center for Defense Information, whose leaders have included Adm. Gene La Roque, Rear Adm. Eugene Caroll Jr., Capt. James Bush, Col. James Donovan, and Maj. Gen. Jack Kidd. There is also the Institute for Space and Security Studies, founded by Lt. Col. Robert Bowman, who once was in charge of military space research for the Air Force. Even a dozen NATO and Warsaw Treaty Organization generals met and drafted statements saying that soldiers now must prevent war and that the first principle of military virtue is "to serve peace." They claim high technology has made war impossible (Generals [Brig. M. Harbottle et al.], 1984, p. 23): "In a nuclear age, the soldier's commitment can only be to the prevention of war. The first principle of military virtues must be therefore: 'A soldier has to serve peace'" (p. 23).

Many other military leaders have reached the same conclusion, including Dwight D. Eisenhower, Adm. Lord Louis Mountbattan, and Gen. Omar Bradley. Gen. Douglas MacArthur, of all people, said on September 2, 1945, after accepting the Japanese surrender that

> Military alliances, balances of power, leagues of nations, all in turn failed, leaving the only path to be by way of the crucible of war. The utter destructiveness of war now blocks out this alternative. We have had our last chance. If we will not devise some greater and more equitable solution, Armageddon will be at our door. (quoted in Meistrich, 1991, p. 102)

Of course, a few years later, he was demanding the right to invade China. This follows a familiar pattern. Commanders at war seldom see war as impossible. Adm. Hyman Rickover, the "father" of the U.S. nuclear Navy, served until he was over 80 years old. Soon after retirement he denounced his own career. As with the vast majority of the military repentants, he waited until his career was finished to renounce war and preparation for war. John F. Kennedy warned that "Mankind must put an end to war or war will put an end to mankind," a year later the world was brought to the brink during the Cuban missile crisis (p. 102).

Dissent is, of course, only a part of postmodern military culture. The dominant discourse is still controlled by believers in war. They will find wars or make them. They will also rearticulate the military's role so as to recoup the fear of total war into more military power. The slogan of the Strategic Air Command (Minutemen and MX missiles; B-52 and B-1 bombers) is "Peace is our Profession." The justification for Star Wars is framed in the same way, as were the invasion of Grenada, the kidnapping of Noriega (in the search for drug "peace"), and the war for Kuwait.

The recent upsurge in UN and NATO peace missions discussed in Chapter 1 represents something new, both qualitatively and quantitatively. Whether or not it means the military can convert to peacekeeping we don't know yet, but the growing dissatisfaction with war has clearly spread to the warriors themselves, and that is reason for hope.

But even as military culture struggles with whether or not war will continue, others from outside have sought to redefine what being a warrior means as well.

NEW TYPES OF WARRIORS

This very refusal of war might be the next step in the evolution of warriors. It is not a new idea. Through the ages soldiers have become nonviolent, and nonviolent activists such as Mohandas K. Gandhi have called for pacifist warriors. This can lead to bitter irony.

Brian Wilson, who served as an Air Force intelligence officer in Vietnam, later lost his legs trying to block a weapons shipment from the Concord Naval Air Station in California to Central America. Being a peace activist was much more dangerous to Wilson than serving as a soldier.

This is a paradox. Many peace activists around the world, even in Western countries, have had friends murdered by the state; they have seen people killed; they have been chased by cars, trucks, police, soldiers; and they have been captured, beaten, and locked up. These nonviolent activists have seen more violence than most military people. Their emotional experience can be quite similar to men and women in combat. Only their refusal to kill makes them different from warriors in the commonly accepted sense.

So, unsurprisingly, there are also strong currents in the peace movement proper that are trying to remake the warrior metaphor and claim it for themselves. Sometimes they look back to premodern versions of war. Native Americans and their supporters have often referred to themselves as rainbow warriors, a title also taken up by the Greenpeace eco-activists. Within grass-roots antiwar and peace groups there have been proposals for activists to make a commitment of several years to a peace army (from the First Strike Project)[4] or to work for peace (Beyond War). Established pacifists have an international peace brigade program that inserts peace "soldiers" into war zones as varied as Guatemala, Kuwait, and Sri Lanka, as the religious Witness for Peace and the Veterans Action Teams are doing in Latin America.

While most peace people, as they often call themselves, still manifest an open aversion to militarism and military metaphors, the influence of the warrior image is quite powerful, being used by draft resisters, veterans, feminists, Christians, and non-Christians. Even some neopagan peace activists are putting forward "The Path of the Pagan Warrior as Revolutionary Activism Today . . . [in] . . . Defense of Mother Earth & the Web of Life."

This highlights an intriguing aspect of this development: these peaceful warriors are quite often women. Of course, in the official U.S. military many of the soldiers are also women, although strict (and ineffective) divisions are made between warrior specialties and technical ones, and women are underrepresented in the higher ranks. In the peace movement it is almost the reverse. A majority of activists are women, as is an even larger proportion of the leadership.[5] In the mid-1990s women took the lead in waging peace in Yugoslavia, Angola, Russia, Nicaragua, Ireland, the Philippines. It is a social phenomenon even Pope John Paul II has noticed (Lederer, 1995).

So the very definitions of science and war, scientists and warriors, are being contested. If postmodernism means anything in relation to war and science it is the inevitability of change. Modern war was certainly never stable as an institution, but before it became suicidal it at least made limited sense. Postmodern war is much less sensible.

War has become so dangerous it threatens everything. Perhaps it can be ended or changed enough so we can survive. What it means to the future/present is in part already determined, reified in institutions, fixed in artifacts, and inscribed on our bodies. But there is that other part that has yet to be formed. Empires fall. Icons are shattered and reformed. Definitions change. New metaphors are forged. French philosopher Michel Foucault pointed out how important this can be:

> The successes of history belong to those who are capable of seizing these rules, to replace those who had used them, to disguise themselves so as to pervert them, invert their meanings, and redirect them against those who had initially imposed them; controlling this complex mechanism, they will make it function so as to overcome the rulers through their own rules. (1977, p. 86)

Foucault claims we can always have a say, even if it is disguised, perverted, or inverted at times. And to such deceptions go "the successes of history." True as this is, some things are better not said, or done, at all. The ends are not separate from the means. Which must serve as a warning to anyone who wants to co-opt one of the central tropes of the informatics of domination, the warrior, or the idea of pure information. Still, there do seem to be real possibilities in rejecting the role of victim (of science, of the warrior ethos) to embrace instead whatever moral possibilities there are to be active shapers of these cultural constructions. Perhaps deconstructing the warrior ethos and inverting it can be complementary. Maybe we don't have to do away totally with warriors (and how can we resist being cyborgs?), but cyborg-soldiers, autonomous weapons, war managers, and technobureaucrats seem much less inevitable.

These are times of great change, so there are possibilities. They are just not simple.

Notes

1. To this day the story persists among radical computer scientists that Turing was murdered by the British (or American) secret agents, although there is no direct evidence for this. The supposed method of death, a poisoned apple, is evocative though. Andrew Hodges has written a moving biography, *Alan Turing: The Enigma* (1983), about this brilliant and tragic scientist.

2. My thinking on von Neumann and Weiner, and on much else, has been strongly influenced by Eglash (1989).

3. All quotations by Theodore Taylor here are from public discussions at the University of California at Santa Cruz on April 28 and 29, 1986.

4. The peace army was endorsed by the National Mobilization for Survival and numerous other activist groups in the United States but never really got off the ground.

5. This is based on my 20 years as a participant-observer in various peace organizations and campaigns. It is true that generally the more formalized and bureaucratic an organization gets the fewer women are in it, but this isn't always the case, witness the Nuclear Freeze Campaign. For a moving and extended discussion of the warrior metaphor as it applies to women, see the issue of *Woman of Power* magazine dedicated to the "Woman as Warrior," 3, Winter/Spring, 1986.

References

Bakunin, Mikhail. (1953). *The Political Philosophy of Bakunin*. G. Maximoff, ed. Free Press.

Brand, Stewart. (1987). *The Media Lab: Inventing the Future at MIT*. Viking.

Broad, William. (1988). *Star Warriors*. Simon & Schuster.

Brodie, Bernard, and Brodie, Fawn. (1973). *From Crossbow to H-Bomb*. Bloomington: Indiana University Press.

Bush, Vannevar. (1949). *Modern Arms and Free Men*. Simon & Schuster.

Clarke, I. F. (1966). *Voices Prophesying War: 1763–1984*. London: Oxford University Press.

Dickson, David. (1984). *The New Politics of Science*. Pantheon.

Faludi, Susan. (1986). "The Billion Dollar Toy Box." *West Magazine, Sunday San Jose Mercury*, November 21: 12–18.

Fee, Elizabeth. (1986). "Critiques of Modern Science: The Relationship of Feminism to Other Radical Epistemologies." R. Bleier, ed. *Feminist Approaches to Science*. Pergamon Press.

Foucault, Michael. (1977). *Discipline and Punish: The Birth of the Prison*. P. Sheridan, trans. Vintage.

Goodman, Paul. (1964). *Utopian Essays and Practical Proposals*. Vintage.

Gray, C. H. (1994). "'There Will Be War!' Future War Fantasies and Militaristic Science Fiction in the 1980s," *Science Fiction Studies*, 21, no. 64, pt. 3. November: 302–14.

Hales, Mike. (1974). "Management Science and 'The Second Industrial Revolution.'" *Radical Science Journal* 1, January: 5–28.

Heims, Steven. (1980). *Jon von Neumann and Norbert Weiner: From Mathematics to the Technologies of Life and Death*. Cambridge, Mass: MIT Press.

Kevles, Daniel. (1987). *The Physicists: The History of a Scientific Community in Modern America*. Cambridge, Mass: Harvard University Press.

Kropotkin, Peter. (1970). *Kropotkin's Revolutionary Pamphlets*. R. Baldwin, ed. Dover.

Lederer, Edith M. (1995). "From Angola to Yugoslavia, Women are Waging Peace." *Oregonian*. August 28, pp. A1, A6.

McGucken, William. (1984). *Scientists, Society, and the State: The Social Relations of Science Movement in Great Britain 1931–1947*. Columbus: Ohio State University Press.

Meistrich, Ira. (1991). "The View Toward Armageddon." *MHQ: The Quarterly Journal of Military History*, 3. Spring: 94–103.

Mueller-Vollmer, Kurt. (1985). "Language, Mind, and Artifact: An Outline of Hermeneutic Theory Since the Enlightenment." K. Mueller-Vollmer ed., *The Hermeneutic Reader*. Continuum.

Mumford, Lewis. (1934). *Technics and Civilization*. Harcourt Brace Jovanovich.

Nef, John. (1963). *War and Human Progress*. Norton.

Perrin, Noel. (1979). *Giving Up The Gun: Japan's Reversion to The Sword, 1543–1879*. Berkeley, Cal.: Shambala Press.

Schwartz, Charles. (1988). "Scientists: Villains and Victims in the Arms Race: An Appraisal and a Plan of Action." *Bulletin of Peace Proposals* 19, nos. 3–4: 399–409.

Sherry, Michael. (1977). *Preparing for the Next War: American Plans for Postwar Defense 1941–1945*. New Haven, Conn.: Yale University Press.

———. (1987). *The Rise of American Air Power: The Creation of Armageddon*. New Haven, Conn.: Yale University Press.

Vitale, Bruno. (1985). "Scientists as Military Hustlers, in Radical Science Collective." *Issues in Radical Science*. London: Free Association Press.

Ziman, John. (1976). *The Force of Knowledge: The Scientific Dimension of Society*. Cambridge, England: Cambridge University Press.

5

Peace and Realpolitik

Marcus G. Raskin

Machiavelli teaches that to have a weak defense is to lose control over national sovereignty and freedom whether by the ruler or by the people. Indeed, to provide for the common defense is one of the critical aspects of governing. In the twenty-first century the meaning of common defense will change, and I will advert to a few of those changes that do not fit easily into a particular political boundary but that touch upon the character and quality of life throughout the planet. In other words, common defense is linked to the mutual sovereignty of humanity beyond boundaries.

The reality humanity faces is that even if its respective governments are humane and farseeing, and even if the proper frameworks are finally chosen by governments and assented to by the United States, life will remain fragile given the damage already done to the environment. Further, even as moral affections become central to public decisions, the transition from the practice of war, economic injustice, and authoritarian control will require great skill in sustaining. This is understandable. For thousands of years the submerged have believed that there is no other way to live in the world except by being dominated. Even in a world where conflict is at a minimum as a result of the adoption and effectuation of general disarmament; even if global corporations would surrender to an international system of monitoring, adopting environmental, economic, and social rights standards; even if there are credible means of dissolving political disputes into legal ones capable of judicial resolution; even if citizen groups would help in the disarmament inspection process; and even if anarcratic groups emerge that scorn the nation-state and attempts at world or regional domination, serious conflicts would continue. Third-stage liberalism is not a rose garden. But it can result in decent conditions for humanity.

What is clear is that the present dominant policies of the United States are dystopian. They require strutting dominance over others and paradoxically a fear of others, continuous war, ever-ballooning defense expenditures and massive self-deception about our motives and who and what we are. They require managers of superhuman capacities in bureaucracies that are infallible. These capacities do not seem to be present in politicians or bureaucrats, for such features require the coldness of a computer that makes no accidents, mistakes, or miscalculations. And of course computers are also fallible.

On a propaganda level the Bush imperialists must gather sufficient domestic political power to be believed while seducing or coercing other nations into accepting American leadership and good intentions. As part of its self-deception the United States must trumpet a very old philosophy that negates knowledge of peaceful purposes and affections among people. In American-style machtpolitik all citizens must believe that the good flows out of power and violence even as their leaders attempt to convince other nations that the United States is pacific and has The Way, if others would just accept the pyramid of authority the United States fashions. In an Orwellian sense America must argue against weapons of mass destruction while building up its own, adding to its nuclear arsenal with small bombs aimed at the people and land of the wretched. It must use disarmament rhetoric as a war-making instrument. And it must teach in the schools that this is the only way for a free nation to live in the world, especially one whose leaders and global corporations see no immediate counterforce to them but whose way of life is dependent on such ideas. The government must teach the polity the idea of asymmetry and double standards for the same actions. (Freedom fighters are not terrorists.) Its education system in subtle and overt ways must support this way of looking and acting in the world.

A nation that holds such views believes that it has found the key to world power and world empire. But in reality history suggests that no nation can speak for all of humankind, nor can any one economic system. When a nation tries, conflict turns into a series of unmanageable explosions leading to feelings of hatred and revenge that multiply, including the demise of republican institutions. Surely that was the case in the Roman Empire, where a large slave class, an overtaxed middle class who paid for wars, and continuous wars joined to dictate its demise. Of course, we should not forget that the Roman Empire lasted for several hundred years in agony and despised.

History is strewn with failed empires that placed their faith in war and conquest. The result was dystopia. The liberal hope of integrating the wretched and the working class into a world system of manageable decency, as Immanuel Wallerstein put it, will have failed.

History is cruel, for it forces on us the immediate and urgent problem that seems to require immediate action and answers. Old answers are used and are invariably disappointing in results. The American response to the 2001 attack on the United States was a classic case of the wrong response to the zealot gangs that killed three thousand people and destroyed billions of dollars of property. The second Bush administration, with its rhetoric of war without end, had no intention of changing any policy it thought would surrender the United States' invulnerable status and the power to decide disputes and intervene at will for one side or another in international affairs. It wanted the power to make, use, and break other leaders and nations. And it intended to use the laws domestically to ensure that the populace would be either passive or avid participants in war imperialism. But American society is unruly, and certainly democracy is not always enamored of unity, especially where the "better" classes and elites are split. Anger at the zealot attack papered over the class disparity in the United States in favor of class unity and patriotism. In fairness to the second Bush administration, it is not likely that any sovereign state with a military force would have responded by using legal means to resolve differences. But the question was how military force was to be used and to what end. Unfortunately, it is only the weak who seek international legal decisions. And even if the weak win their case on the merits, the powerful state is not likely to listen.

Perhaps in the grand sweep of history venality, corruption, and favoritism are to be taken for granted. They are the cost of politics in all political systems. Perhaps it does not matter what President Bush knew or didn't know, or that the ruling elites had relationships with the bin Laden family, as did Harvard University and the premium defense and intelligence investor, the Carlisle Group, whose early investors were the bin Laden family (until September 12, 2001). And perhaps it does not matter that the first President Bush was a consultant to the Carlisle Group or that after the September 11 crime the eleven bin Laden family members who were in the United States were flown out of the United States without being detained or questioned. Such matters might cause some wonder among the skeptically minded. After all, it is taken for granted that such privileges should be granted to the very rich and powerful. But there is a far more important lesson in September 11 than such connections and machinations. It has to do with the new distribution of power in the world.

The Soviet Union, seemingly invincible from the outside with its nuclear weapons and claims that it held the secret to historical progress, fell to pieces as a result of its own contradictions and decay. The United States learned in a particularly gruesome way that it is not impregnable; that it is not outside of history, and that all of humanity cannot escape peeing and shitting. What is a nation with worldwide responsibilities (pretensions) to do? Be less Machiavellian and more like Machiavelli—be less like General Patton and adopt the principles of Martin Luther King Jr. Machiavelli understood that long-term or strategic purposes should never be sacrificed for short-term gain. Machiavellians, on the other hand, believe only in policies for the short term: That is crisis management.

Machiavelli was not a Machiavellian, perhaps because he had suffered prison and exile at the hands of the powerful throughout much of his life. Extrapolating without doing violence to his own views, Machiavelli would have had a great deal to say about the American situation at the beginning of the twenty-first century. He had hoped for the unification of Italy, and he would hope for a world civilization in our epoch. But to get anywhere near that goal is to surrender the hubris of world empire. A nation may claim total power, but the result is that other nations will undertake to form a balance of power against the "superpower," with atrocious weapons if necessary. This is certainly the case at the beginning of the twenty-first century. When one nation announces itself as king of the hill, that nation is a target, a situation that can result in world disaster. So what is called for?

Leaders must look beyond their seeming invincibility and that of their state and the trappings of power. That is to say, they must devise different standards to measure and comprehend in the social, political, and economic space a reconstructive framework of inclusivity. Leaders need to secure the UN just because in its ethos it accounts primarily for population rather than capital or weaponry. For all of its flaws, the most glaring being the makeup of the permanent members of the Security Council, the UN, because of its ideals and universality, opens the door to a different understanding of how freedom is to be extended and how liberation is to be supported. It rejects the unilateral warrior imperialist model. In a world body we can learn that freedom is not a concept limited to those who own Lexuses, nor is it limited to the religious fanatic or the warriors of dominance and genocide. It is for those whose lives are smashed by poverty, disease, starvation, fear, and exploitation, that is, most of the world's population. Without addressing their needs there is no possibility of world civilization. Instead, its degradation, world empire (machtpolitik, American style), would dominate. Machiavelli would be sure to point out that the meaning of common defense and common security requires the transformation and surrender of sole sovereignty by *all* states to a new political body yet to be born. This does not exclude the most powerful nations, which, barring the use of a veto, are charged with the responsibility of *living within* the confines of international law. With the blessings of Franklin Roosevelt, left New Dealers sought the establishment of the United Nations. Attention was to be paid to problems that are mutual among the classes as well as those that emanate from poverty and wealth. This is not, I dare say, world imperialism directed from Washington, D.C. For most classes in America this is a difficult lesson to learn, for the United States, even after September 11, appears to be sitting on top of the world; therefore there is no reason to change, unless one examines the decay of public education (for example, in New York City); the increasing number of poor, victims of modern-day imperialism, globalization, greed, and domestic pauperization; and all the other services of dignity that life needs.

Machiavelli would have said there is no escape from the human condition, yet, there is the possibility of better and worse: if not happiness itself, then at least its promise. This is the importance of social movements, for they force onto stability a radical change or recalibration. This is what rationality linked to empathy must do. This is what King understood in his political action when he sought to bring together antiracism (racial justice), anti-imperialism, and antiwar:

> To crave security through domination as the major purpose of social exis-
> tence is to misunderstand our present condition. There are not enough guns
> and atomic weapons in the world to allow any portion of humanity to feel
> secure when it retains old conceptions of security based on separateness
> from the Other, military force, and passion for weaponry rather than people.
> Security defined through force, and being closed, is a retreat into our own
> ego shells. It is constantly staking out and using physical spaces and prop-
> erty against the Other, denying any other group its self-dignity except a
> deformed kind that does not exercise the human affections of caring and
> empathy. Self-interest and egoism enshrined in present concepts of security
> lead to a world that is brutish to the weak, nasty and frightening for every-
> one. Corporate self-interest and attendant irresponsibility to others require
> the destruction of the environment and the organizing of social relationships
> so that the strong will dominate the weak. It reinforces the mutual unhappi-
> ness and dependence of the colonizer over the colonized. Hubris becomes
> the coin of the realm and patriotism is defined as being a war lover and
> power imperialist.[1]

PREPARING PEACEFUL MEANS FOR PEACE:
THE REALPOLITIK OF THE POSTWAR ERA

Just as modern war is a product of intentional and unintentional acts of groups and individuals that in fact constitute a system of hubris, misplaced idealism, bureaucra-tization, and violence, so it is true that abolishing the war system will also appear (to the observer) as a system of intentional and unintentional acts that can be brought together and codified to reflect a change of consciousness and then of practice.

The September 11 bombings, which yielded a general consensus of retaliation against the Taliban, brought into question the war system. First, asymmetrical or sublimited war, either by nonstate actors or poor states subsidized by nonstate actors for military purposes, has finally reached the United States in a devastating way. The result caused the executive and Congress to adopt measures they thought necessary to protect "security." Together they joined in the establishment of a "homeland" defense force, increased surveillance of citizens, increased wiretaps, the authority to rummage through files of citizens, greater control of immigrants, de facto racial profiling, stringent surveillance at airports and ports, and greatly increased defense and intelligence budgets. Congress passed language allowing the executive to detain suspects or people purportedly with information about anything, without the benefit of being charged, having a proper legal defense, or standing trial.

There is an irony about homeland defense as it is construed. Its aim is protection against terror. Concentrating on terror may have the effect of dispensing with concern for ongoing institutional and structural issues whose damage on a yearly basis is very great. Judged in terms of mortality rates, defense would require a far different meaning than that given by the politicians in the 107th Congress and the second Bush administration. For example, ninety-eight thousand Americans die in hospitals because of hospital error each year; thirty-five thousand are killed on the highways every year, often as a result of poor roads or defective cars; and there are five thousand fatal industrial accidents yearly. Disease and starvation have reached pandemic proportions. Compared to the deaths of three thousand people and the astonishing pain that will stay with family and friends, a horror story in and of itself, one must wonder why other tragedies do not qualify as part of "homeland defense" or national security and international security.

The second change elicited by the bombings of the United States was the infelicitous idea that the American people are in a war without end. Antagonists can be other nations, either individually or as a group, that appear to challenge American hegemony. This hegemony, it is thought, protects the standard of living of the American people by ensuring access to the world's resources and guaranteeing markets for American goods on a profitable basis for the United States. In the case of AIDS it is understood by the international drug companies that AIDS is an expanding market. With U.S. pharmaceutical corporations holding the patents to drugs' production, AIDS is an assured market, guaranteed where necessary by U.S. government subsidy. Further, diseases allow for the expansion of Western medicine and Western nongovernmental organizations as exercises in knowledge philanthropy, that is, domination in a different guise. Whether AIDS will become the social force to end economic, social, and political disparity between classes, races, and genders is dubious. Influenza did not have that effect after the First World War.

The third concern is that of antagonists obtaining weapons of mass destruction and employing those nuclear weapons, missiles, and chemical, biological, and radiological weapons. On the other hand, it is assumed that the United States needs these weapons to keep the peace around the world, which also includes the U.S. use of force in low-intensity warfare. It needs weapons of mass destruction to ensure free markets and retain its paramount position. And it is prepared to use low-yield nuclear weapons in a preventive manner against non-nuclear states. But surely it would be obvious to any college student majoring in international relations or psychology that attempts will be made to find ways of becoming secure from the United States. Thus, the world becomes a self-fulfilling prophecy in which the United States is hated and feared. This surely need not be if efforts were made to link ending the war system to human rights.

The fourth change is more ambiguous. It concerns the value of the United Nations in the face of nationalism. NATO, that white man's club, is preferred by the United States and the West generally to the UN, where "non-whites" outnumber NATO in terms of population. Preferences aside, the great powers, and especially the United States, see the UN as an instrument of their own foreign and national security policies. The UN is not seen as an entity that can move nations in a direction more in keeping with ending the war system and promulgating symmetrical international law. Nevertheless, there was a nagging doubt from the standpoint of unilateral machtpolitik that the UN as a collective enterprise or through the veto could checkmate some policies of individual states. Leading members of the Department of Defense and the Heritage Foundation since the 1980s have held the Right's conventional belief that the UN is an unnecessary appendage that could be sloughed off in favor of unilateral strategies vis-à-vis arms control, the environment, and other issues. This policy laid the basis for imperial law, in which the United States would set the terms of reference for the world because of its high ideals, the good judgment of its leaders, and its commitment to open markets and democracies oriented to elections, whether sham or real. Pax Americana would be protected by the vast preponderance of military, economic, and technological power. Such policies are to be built on the idea of the American state as the collective Superman, running here, going there, and being fueled by patriotic fervor, which reinforces extreme nationalism and conceals better alternatives.[2] The existence of terrorists, whether of the clerical fascist nature or political criminals, is the complement to American hegemony, for neither offered a threat to the United States as the dominant nation, yet, they serve as the rationalization for misguided policies.

Leaders are in a quandary we might describe as social neurosis or tragedy. They want to expand the nation's reach for resources such as oil because they fear taking a chance on shifting individual preferences that have become embedded in social values, as in the case of the wanton use of cars. Few would argue against limiting their production. Similarly, few would argue that television should be turned off at "study hours," promulgating this as a law that television stations would have to abide by if they intended to retain their licenses. Few would argue in the two major political parties that the United States has reached the stage of wolfish capitalism. Yet, there is an even deeper reality that must be faced.

There is evidence of species decline, perhaps even suicide, given the destruction of the environment, starvation, the killing off of whole continents, diseases such as AIDS, and selfishness that detracts from the possibilities of universal, even local responsibility.

So this chapter is burdened with a subtext: There is a world to be protected and nurtured. Rationality is not the enemy of affections, and supermen exist only in comic books, the dreams of madmen such as Hitler, the obscurantist work of Heidegger, the inane chattering of columnists and TV commentators, and the dreams of bellicose civilians eager to be remembered in history as warrior liberators whose definition of democracy is mass manipulation for war. The tragedy is that people pay dearly for the Superman illusion, as they did in World War II and even in events leading up to September 11. What about revolutions? They are not tea parties. And according to conservatives, they are also illusions.

FEARING AND FAVORING REVOLUTION

Since the time of Jefferson, when radicals and what I would term reconstruction liberals favored the French Revolution in its early stages, Americans have been torn about revolutionary and liberation struggles. This sentiment was one of the strands of American history. Even the Monroe Doctrine was more than a balance of power attempt to keep the Holy Alliance out of Latin America. It reflected an attempt to stand with nascent republics at a time when the United States had little power to do so. The same sentiment can be found in Woodrow Wilson's rhetorical emphasis on self-determination (except for blacks, Latin Americans, Mexicans, and Africans). The second Bush administration holds tightly to the Wilsonian and Jacksonian fig leaf as justification for its triumphal policies. Although they may be difficult to assess, rhetorical claims come to be thought of as actual reasons for policies. They also create a body politic as a whole, a consciousness for self-deception, masking naked military and economic imperialism.

After the First World War American liberals favored, in an abstract way, nationalist movements because they believed that colonized people deserved their own place as subject actors in history rather than as objects of others. Americans mediated freedom through one leader who was the symbol of each new nation. In virtually all cases, Americans knew nothing about the colonized people except the name of the leader, who stood in for knowledge and familiarity with the decolonizing or oppressed group. The neoliberal model of step-by-step enfranchisement served as the guide for the Western enlightened position, although not in all cases.[3]

By the mid-twentieth century political colonialism no longer fit with the anti-imperialist sensibility that gripped millions of people. Revolutionary violence presented itself as an ongoing reality to be yoked to liberation and ideas of justice and nationalism. While the West used such language as rhetorical tools, it was out of the ordinary for leaders of colonial nations to think that *justice* and *peace* were linked to one another.

President Franklin Roosevelt used such language during the Second World War, giving every indication that he meant his talk of justice and his unwillingness to restore the British Empire. But for Winston Churchill and Josef Stalin, the issue was not justice; it was to repel and destroy the Nazi war machine. For Churchill the fruits of war would be to keep Germany as a balance against the East, while retaining the British Empire and securing a "special relationship" with the United States in which it would act as tutor and mentor to the "country cousins." For Stalin the war meant a return of a sphere of influence in East Europe (uneasy as it was), which the Russians had before the First World War. It was taken for granted by British Tories that those with state power could use various instruments, from military force to bribery, persuasion, and intimidation, to achieve their ends. Great Britain intended to hold on to India and "guide" the politics of Greece, Turkey, and the Middle East. To the chagrin of Churchill, Roosevelt's brand of liberalism demanded that a new world order be recognized resulting in its reconstitution, thereby ending Western imperialism.

The British took Roosevelt's rhetoric as an exercise in American cynicism in which the United States would inherit the British, French, and Dutch empires for its own purposes. Further, the United States and its oil corporations would wrest dominance from the British in the Middle East. A condominium emerged between the sheiks and shahs, who sold the oil deposits of their respective "nations" at low prices to American banking and oil companies in exchange for guaranteeing their rule against nationalist and radical upstarts. However, before the Cold War began in earnest, Harry Truman stated the liberal position toward colonialism. On the surface it had nothing to do with capitalism or American expansion, nor did it target the Soviet Union or communism as an unalterable enemy even though Western leaders such as Churchill and Truman never wavered in their hostility to the Soviet Union (Africa and the Middle East remained part of the sphere of influence of Western powers.):

> We believe that all people who are prepared for self-government should be permitted to choose their own form of government by their own freely expressed choice, without interference from any foreign source. That is true in Europe, in Asia, as well as the Western Hemisphere. . . . By the combined and cooperative action of or our war time Allies . . . [W]e shall try to attain a world in which Nazism, Fascism, and military aggression cannot exist.[4]

In practice, how was justice to be achieved in a world that hardly recognized that term, except during revolutionary moments? Third World revolutionaries were by no means comfortable with the presumptuous idea that nations had to be "prepared" for self-government, and certainly not by the colonial powers. It was hardly surprising that for them, as had been true for the revolutionaries of the eighteenth century, national liberation and violence were intimately linked. Furthermore, revolutionaries believed that they should obtain aid for their cause from any quarter. They sought first violent decolonization (proof of manhood), as Frantz Fanon, the psychiatrist revolutionary, claimed in *Wretched of the Earth*, and then reconciliation.[5] Fanon thought violence necessary because the colonial powers would never give up imperialism unless they were confronted by violence, and therefore the colonized would remain trapped in submission.

The international system, which called for peaceful resolution of disputes according to the terms of the UN charter, for all practical purposes exempted the permanent members of the Security Council. The leaders of the great powers paid little attention to the decisions of international institutions unless the decisions that were made followed their own interests and policies. This was especially true of the United States and the Soviet Union during the Cold War, and then of the United States alone after the Soviet demise. Thus, more than forty years after the establishment of the International Court of Justice, its ability to turn political disputes into law that sovereign great powers would accept was negligible. For example, the United States lost before the International Court of Justice in a case in which Nicaragua claimed that the United States was prosecuting a covert war of terror against a sovereign nation. Having lost the case, the United States made clear that it would not recognize the judgment of the court. The second Bush administration rejected the establishment of the International Criminal Court, fearing it would have jurisdiction over American soldiers as they carried out imperial peacemaking missions in different parts of the world. By September 2002 the second Bush national security document had made clear that "preemptive" war should be expected from the United States, and international law did not apply to American actions. The United States was not only sovereign for itself; it would be sovereign for others, deciding when they needed war to protect or uplift them.

Another puzzling legacy of the Second World War was the question of removing limits and restraints on new levels of technology and the technology of organization, as evidenced by the construction of nuclear weapons and the Nazi project of genocide. Violence had become more than a test of manliness. By 1945 all restraints were removed, from bombing civilian targets to killing prisoners, to destroying people in gas ovens and atomic blasts. Planning for future warfare contemplated that wars would be fought with demonic weapons, although tens of millions of people still lost their lives in "small" regional and civil wars.

Yet, warfare did not happen on a worldwide scale after 1945. Some argue that the very ferocity of weapons on both sides acted as a deterrent against general war between the United States and the Soviet Union. War was limited to the Third World and the construction of an expensive and shameless alliance system. The proxies the superpowers chose fell into different categories. The United States had no admission requirements to its worldwide alliances save allegiance to anticommunism. Its members could be tactical allies, freebooting gangs that served their versions of God, ideological zealots, or the cynics who corrupted themselves and plundered others.[6] But the United States on most important diplomatic and economic matters expected the smaller nations to ask permission. Without "asking" the less-developed nation was in mortal danger of suffering a coup or civil war (Brazil, Venezuela, and Iran, as examples). The Soviets were less creative in their allies, often being stuck with national liberation movements that turned out to be nightmarish in practice (Ethiopia) or economically costly to sustain (Cuba).

There is nothing in the Cold War record to suggest that the Soviets wanted a war with the United States or would have courted such a war even if neither side had nuclear weapons. Soviet diplomatic leadership under Stalin was always cautious, seeking deals with the West at the expense of local communist parties. This attitude did not change with his successors. Conversely, there is nothing in the record to suggest that the Soviet leadership inhibited itself from supporting nations for ideological or geopolitical purposes because of nuclear weapons and possible nuclear war, as in the case of Cuba.

Another question might have been taken seriously, at least since the Second World War. Were there ever moments in the twentieth century that could have been turned into a framework to avoid wars and arms races? In *The Arms Race*, Philip Noel-Baker, the British arms expert, pointed out that, had the British not pulled out of the disarmament conference of 1935, the Germans would have disarmed. Such judgments cannot be proved, although they were used by the peace movement to legitimize those who argued that a basis always exists for ending the war system. Peace must be more than the interval between wars. Wars, to use Gabriel Kolko's apt phrase, are the very meaning of socially accepted blindness. Humanity deserves pity because wars bring about shifts and surprises that cannot be calculated once war begins. Yet, no nation wants to give up its "arms." Sometimes this is out of fear, but often a country's unwillingness stems from those institutions of the state that are caught in ideological and economic blindness.

The Cold War brought a somewhat different meaning to the U.S. state and ideas of internationalism that seemed embedded in the idealistic foundational documents of the UN, UNESCO, and regional economic programs under the aegis of the UN. Limited agreements were reached between the United States and Soviet Union in the Cold War on arms, troop placements, and strategic weaponry. Similar limited arrangements could have been made with the Soviets that would have helped to control the nuclear arms race. It would have been possible for the United States to reject the idea of building the H-bomb in 1952 had the advice of Enrico Fermi and Isidor Rabi (both men were Nobel prize winners who worked on the atomic bomb's development) been followed; they called for a solemn pledge not to go forward with the development and construction of the H-bomb. The implicit notion was that the Soviets would follow suit. It should be noted that by 1953 in the Soviet Union Stalin was replaced by Georgi Malenkov, who pursued a number of initiatives to end the Cold War. The Fermi-Rabi proposal would have inhibited the arms race just as George Kennan's idea of mutual disengagement would have resulted in the independence of Eastern Europe from the Soviet Union. The result would have been cuts in military budgets, policies spelled out in resolutions of the United Nations, and planning papers prepared by Vassily Leontieff, a Nobel Prize winner in economics. Such ideas were hardly farfetched. The United States concluded an agreement with the Soviet Union for both sides to withdraw their forces from Austria, a treaty arrangement that held throughout the Cold War and allowed for the independence of Austria.

ENDING THE WAR SYSTEM: SOME FORGOTTEN BACKGROUND

In a famous document that UNESCO published in 1949, the authors claimed that war begins in the minds of men.[7] There is no question that there is a psychological aspect to war that must be taken into account when considering alternatives to the war system. There may be an element of boredom that encourages young men to accept siren calls of older men to fight in aggressive wars. They take advantage of patriotic conflicts to escape the humdrum of family, job, and school. Certainly war is a form of regimented and chaotic play, a violent bacchanal, as William James implied in his famous essay on alternatives to war.[8] And war is a means of avoiding domestic class conflict in times of distress. Hitler understood this point and brought together a nightmarish brew for the world by mixing together the fears of the lower middle class, the starvation of the poor and working class, a national building program, anti-Semitism, and revanchism for the Versailles treaty.

Leaders and nations are inclined to expand their authority and power through war if there are no countervailing rules of behavior. If they are careful, leaders need not risk very much, instead proving themselves by risking the lives of others, although leaders can be targets for assassins.[9] Those who practice nonviolent resistance as an activist strategy are prepared to risk much more than are the leaders of warrior nations.

Unless conscious and continuous efforts are made to control the psychological, biological, and institutional pressures that favor aggression or the idea that force of arms is the only instrument for resolution of conflict and imperial exploitation, the institutional process of war making may never end. Given that war institutions are the "cultural" furniture of nation-states and subnational groups, war appears as a natural and necessary function of the state. Indeed, anarchist thinkers such as Simone Weil (also an axialist) argued that the sole business of the state is war itself, the protection and expansion of territorial holdings through war or warlike means. In the American tradition, the nineteenth-century American anarchist Benjamin Tucker claimed that the state should be delegitimated because it was solely an instrument of aggression. Similarly, liberal statecraft emphasized mediation, conciliation, arbitration, law, and even appeasement and population exchanges. But none of the seemingly rational alternatives to "organized murder" seemed to work, even when the pacifists William Jennings Bryan and Newton Baker became, respectively, Secretary of State and Secretary of War under Woodrow Wilson. Anarcrats might say that states are doomed to making war, especially where transnational relationships are weak, science is an instrument of state power, and patriotism is tied only to a particular place without similar bonds to humanity as a whole.

On the other hand, in the twentieth century the emergence of total war, which erases boundaries between combatants and noncombatants, made it more important than ever that citizens' movements concentrate on and confront war as an institutional system. Whatever war had been in the past, with its emphasis on heroism and the glorification of suffering, in the twentieth century it revealed itself for all to see as an exercise in political pathology and criminality. It created hopeless despair on the part of the oppressed.[10]

The politics of nations and war are invariably foggy. As demonstrated by John Dewey's life, the role of war in human progress—and defense of liberal values—caused consternation and contradiction for those who were anti-imperialist in their understanding of history. Norman Thomas's Socialist Party, which voted against economic and military intervention on the side of the French and British in 1940, was hardly wrong when it claimed that these two nations were colonizers that oppressed Indochina, Africa, and India through their respective forms of imperialism. Furthermore, in 1940 there was sufficient evidence to suggest that it was not only Vichy France that was collaborationist. French and German thought of the time preached and practiced anti-Semitism, a rapprochement with the European upper classes, and a federated Europe under German tutelage as a bulwark against communism.[11] Many in the British upper class also favored Italian fascism and were prepared to collaborate with Hitler.[12] And in the United States anti-Semitism and racism were practiced in business, the universities, and social life.

However, in the United States some on the Left joined with the Right, fearing alliances that would supposedly interrupt the American experiment of freedom. The competing alliance system before the First World War taught American isolationists and most conservatives in 1940 to heed George Washington's plea that the nation should never enter into entangling alliances.[13] Except for the Wilsonians such as James Shotwell and Quincy Wright, whose emphasis was on international organization rather than alliances, the prevailing scholarship of the time was that antagonistic alliances led directly to war just because of the interlocked arrangements within alliances that trigger the military engagement of each party. This domino effect was the reality of the alliance system that led to the First World War. Indeed, the French and British alliance with Poland triggered their direct engagement against the Germans, thereby becoming the diplomatic match that lit the Second World War. The match was an expensive one.

The costs of the Second World War were great in terms of human suffering, and indeed the nation that suffered the most, the Soviet Union, was never able to recover. On the other hand, in material terms that war was a boon to the United States.[14] The major powers, with the United States as the acknowledged leader, integrated military policy, organization, and technology into an ideology of mass murder, clothed as defense. People and democratic governments became obsessed with security and arms as the solution to society's multiple problems, much the way a neurotic might fixate on a real problem with an irrational solution that increases his or her problem. The enemy was thought to be the other modernism, communism, whose proponents claimed that they were the wave of the future because communism was the necessary stage for human freedom and economic progress.

It should be noted that clerical fascism was wrongly understood by modernists as the residue of a time gone by. Where it existed in the Catholic Church it had lost much of its power except among sects such as Opus Dei, which certainly has more political power than liberation theologians. In the Middle East, for example Saudi Arabia, clerical fascism was thought of by the West and the cynical princes as a quaint tool that could be used against leftist troublemakers. Among American leaders, to be imperial requires a full panoply of weaponry, including an Orwellian attitude toward words. Both are required to compensate for the foolishness born of arrogance.

War preparations are not abstract enterprises in which bureaucracies play war games according to international rules of just war. Indeed, except as window dressing, international law and just war theory or other theories of proportionality have little or nothing to do with weapons acquisition or wars themselves. For example, in the United States we have seen the emergence of strategic nuclear war doctrine, intended to destroy urban centers and military installations, through

1. second or preemptive nuclear strikes;
2. tactical nuclear war, which means the first or second use of nuclear weapons on the battlefield;
3. limited non-nuclear war, which means an engagement similar to that of Korea, Vietnam, or even the Second World War;
4. brushfire wars, which were meant to stop wars of national liberation, as in the end of Vietnam, Nicaragua, and Guatemala;
5. police actions, which were thought to be instruments of UN franchise or authority, as in the case of Korea;
6. low-intensity war, such as a continuing antiguerrilla war (Philippines);
7. low-intensity and high-intensity warfare to be waged against former allies, as in the case of fundamentalist Muslims and drug dealers in Afghanistan;
8. covert actions aimed at fomenting insurrection, inhibiting national self-determination, or overthrowing governments (Chile, Australia);
9. the diffident or gratuitous use of force to prove dominance, as in Panama, Granada, or Clinton's bombing of Iraq and the Sudan; and
10. homeland defense organized after September 11, which, as President George W. Bush stated, would mobilize the entire American Citizenry. They would become "soldiers" in the war against terrorism (or any war for that matter). Foreigners could be detained and tried before military tribunals. Through executive orders and the Patriot Act a president is authorized to set up internment camps. Who is to be placed in them is to be determined by the executive.

Added to these war categories are new modes of warfare involving biological viruses and viruses to destroy computer programs. Each of these methods begins from the principle of "violent rationality," by which I mean thinking and planning in and for the use of force. This idea gave rise to the attractive antiseptic notion that from the American perspective wars can be limited exercises because they do not include the use of nuclear weapons or American casualties.

What a limited war is to the outsider superpower is a catastrophe for a small nation. Even so, where the small nation perceives that it is fighting for its independence and self-determination (in other words, its ultimate values, irrespective of what outsiders may conceive of as facts), it may conclude that it has no choice but to accept the possibility of total destruction to maintain or achieve independence. The examples of the hapless Melians during the Peloponnesian Wars and the North Vietnamese come to mind. On the other hand, during the Korean War, when at least a million people died, American Cold War analysts thought the American engagement was a successful limited non-nuclear war.[15] The U.S.-led alliance in the Gulf War was deemed an even greater triumph, since there were few American and allied casualties, and the United States was allowed to bomb at will. This conception of success does not count the hundreds of thousands of Iraqis who were killed or starved without much proof of gain.[16] And there were costs to American soldiers. Substantial evidence made the existence of a Gulf War health syndrome undeniable. Over 125,000 soldiers suffered minor and debilitating illness from that "successful" war.

Perhaps as justification for participation in the expansion of twentieth century wars of ferocity, the rhetoric about war's political purposes also expanded. Wars were fought to end wars or to make the world safe for democracy. Wars were fought against evil, and smoldering religious wars emerged full force in the post-Cold War period. The populace was to be aroused through Christ or Mohammed. Perhaps Man (literally man) was struggling with violent aspects of his own nature to justify what he was doing with the sentiments and needs of another part of his nature that did not respond easily to murderous impulses. (Young Americans might say that governments psyched them up, as if before a football game, or getting "psyched" through religion because it offers God as the absolute. There is little that can "psyche a person up" that equals a sports contest or religion, both of which are dependent on zealotry.) All religions struggle with the absolutism of those who see the Other as the enemy in what is never a game. For the religious zealot nothing could more rapturous than killing or being killed in His, Allah's, God's name. There are only His laws, which know no boundaries. The zealot does not believe man exists. There is only God. No wonder Machiavelli feared religion, for there was no proportion in a political sense, only rationalization of blood lust for *beyond* that could not be appeased.

Modernism and progress claimed the linkage between rationality and peace. Kant's argument for perpetual peace found its way into the official documents of the twentieth century. The pacific self was accorded obeisance and public legitimacy through agreements prepared and used in the post-World War I period among the imperial nations. The 1928 Kellogg-Briand Pact was ineffective in outlawing war because it protected preexisting alliance systems against other nations and countenanced force over the colonies of signatory nations by their owners. However, the effort was important as an example of what the leadership of nations is prepared to do, under public pressure from social movements such as the outlawry of war movement, headed by Salmon Levinson and John Dewey.[17] For Dewey the outlawry of war was meant as a fundamental safeguard for the development of humanness among people, as well as the perfecting of democracy. It should be noted that the fundamental gravamen against the Nazis at Nuremberg was that the Nazi government had breached the Kellogg-Briand Pact. They had broken the peace.

More than others, the important English political scientist and Labour Party activist Harold Laski understood that after World War II the United States would have to choose between being the premier imperial military power or a democracy pressuring internal democratic social reconstruction and redistribution of political and economic power. The choice was made by 1947 to the detriment of democracy. Democratic ideas of citizenship clash with citizenship as a form of militarism. Democratic citizenship reaches beyond political boundaries. But its meaning is shaped by local cultures and control over productive processes and previously passive citizenry aroused by social movements. Vastly different meanings emerge.

Martin Luther King Jr.'s project had very little to do with simply scaling back war, as suggested by some members of the Democratic Party; nor did it have anything to do with the project of war as personified in General Curtis LeMay, who called for bombing the North Vietnamese back to the Stone Age. Lyndon Johnson's attempt to find a golden mean between these two opposing views foundered and cost him his presidency. There is no compromise between these two positions. Political attempts to mediate between them and find a "golden mean" subvert the human possibility of an expanding peace based on economic and social justice. The irony of the second Bush administration is that it is attempting to use the nonviolence movements as a cover story for continuous war; one of the great advertising tricks of American commerce is to package back marginality in a form that masks a different intention. Thus, the second Bush administration appears to accept universal values in his war with Iraq. Just as churchgoers visit God on Sunday morning and go on with their real business during the rest of the week, so American self-deception regarding its real policy purposes about freedom, justice, and even open markets is seldom believed by leaders and people of other nations. Yet, the second Bush administration claimed that he acted on the basis of universal values in his war with Iraq. The question is whether there are universal values, the second Bush administration's or anyone else's. For liberals, even the Left, the answer must be yes. But whose?

APPLICATION OF UNIVERSAL VALUES AND MINIMAL CITIZENSHIP

Universal values transform boundaries when they are applied in practice. They are third-stage liberal values, meant to strengthen the empathic sentiments for the known and the unknown Other. Boundary lines between the insider and the outsider are crossed, between the individual and the state within and between all aspects of society, from family to school to work. And each boundary crossing is cause for reconsideration of identity and definition for the participants in their relation to linked social activities among cooperation, empathy, and dignity. This is a frightening thought to those eager to hold onto the identity of self and the group against others. As I have suggested, such sentiments exist in all cultures. No idea of universalism can be successful if it does not take into account differences or the reasonable wishes of those who are not the zealots but who can act as brokers between both sides. In this context the "broker" is the emissary who seeks to accept people as they are and shift the language of good versus evil by ascertaining the nature of evil within institutions and developing rules of international law that change existing boundaries and subject matter. Thus, for example, the issue in the Middle East might not be Israeli presence but the disposition of water. It might be that nations and people read current events through historical moments that are traumatic and unforgettable. Thus, to continue with the Middle East problem, it is likely that Israelis are hard put to forget the role of the Grand Mufti during the Second World War, when he favored the Nazis. But surely Jews who had a rapprochement with the Germans can rethink their own position toward the Arab states and the Palestinian people. This is an astonishing psychological border crossing. Similarly, another border crossing could still occur in the Middle East, where nonviolent groups could organize themselves especially where they are least expected to occur, such as in armies or terrorist groups. Such organization is the "cutting edge" of international affairs.

There is one obvious boundary crossing that makes clear the need for universal standards requiring redefinitions of political rights in terms of fundamental empathic sentiments. Here I refer to migrations and refugees: the political or economic stateless, war refugees, and the wanderers who are the victims of power politics. The twentieth century was famous for creating the modern stateless refugee victim caused by the war system, broken empires, and at the end of the century, wolfish capitalism presenting itself as modernism and the quintessence of freedom. This form of capitalism used sophisticated technology and communications for the movement of capital whose mock investors had no interest in investing in any particular nation. The noted Pakistani political scientist Eqbal Ahmad distinguished between corrupt unproductive capitalism and corrupt capitalism, which sought to develop things and projects for use rather than making money through currency speculation. Corrupt but productive capitalism created its own misery. As tourists moved from North to South, migrant laborers moved in the opposite direction.

Unless the world is to descend into an international dystopia, it must find the means of confronting the changed technological condition from the standpoint of the marginal and the suffering. Dystopias for millions of people give rise to moral and legal solutions for the reformulation of citizenship that add to the protection of all people, including the dispossessed. Citizenship would cease to be a tool against the Other. Instead, citizenship would be recognized as an international human right guaranteed to all, irrespective of boundaries, stemming from recognition of the individual's personhood rather than the accident of birth, wealth, or geographic and cultural boundaries.

Thus, we may note two types of citizenship. The first is a "constructive" world citizenship, granted through the United Nations, to be upheld in international and domestic courts in which all people, but especially the most vulnerable, namely, the stateless and migrant labor, are accorded protections under international and domestic law. Protections must be enforceable in local courts, with transnational and international institutions and associations operating to protect the person. Municipal courts would begin applying international and world law standards within "sovereign" nations. International law, such as the Universal Declaration of Human Rights, would no longer be aspirational.

Such ideas do not require a wholesale attack on national sovereignty. However, they do require the recognition of the political, social, and economic human rights covenants informing in fundamental ways decisions of judges and legislature in the nations. Through this means the human rights covenants, treaties against torture, or treaties against the development of weapons of mass destruction would begin to seep into the consciousness of groups within nations.[18] These ideas would serve as the inherent dignity that all nations should work to ensure and accept as the basis of their national homelands. In this way a world civilization begins to organize itself around rights that are the basis of being human and acting in a humane manner.

Let us admit that such ideas smack of the utopian while crackpot rationality has a powerful hold on humanity. Let us admit that, destroying the environment and adding to global warming through unlimited fossil fuel productions is practical, or that the threatened use of weapons of mass destruction is the very meaning of human nature, or that zealots must be stamped out without analyzing what they say. Where does this leave political action on the part of various groups within civil societies or governments that are not enamored of the idea that humanity will be defeated by crackpots, be they rational or irrational, believers or disbelievers? To the disengaged, conventional politics seems to be the problem, because its dynamics have no counterweight. On the other hand, politics is the necessary instrument to organize just humane ends on the basis of our best knowledge. Such knowledge is developed in universities or is folk knowledge, believing in those human capacities that yield human dignity for one's self and the Other. The task of politics is to bring love and knowledge together, defeating absolutism and superpower arrogance.

Such ideas, which were thought to be mainstream at the end of the Second World War, dropped off of the radar screen because they did not fit with conservative, liberal, imperial notions of national security, sovereignty, and property. Congressional members who had worked together in groups such as Members of Congress for Peace through Law allowed their groups to wither and die. More important, the Democratic Party also abandoned the ideas of a universal consciousness of the kind reflected in

UN covenants. Both political parties replaced this possibility with the newest stage of imperialism, globalization and triumphant nationalism backed up and interlaced with military and covert power. A crack in the bipartisan foreign policy presented itself for a short period during the debates on the second President Bush's efforts to go to war. Democratic liberals, such as Edward Kennedy and Congressman Dennis Kucinich, sought to delay the decision on going to war, even arguing that the United States should abide by the charter and not arrogate to itself unilateral enforcement of the UN Security Council resolutions. Such sentiments are present in the American body politic and are even widely held. However, Democratic liberals are stymied when it comes to presenting their own comprehensive program of progressive change, one that could reflect the powerful cultural changes as a result of the struggles of the 1960s and early 1970s. These cultural shifts need to be complemented and sustained by changes in the purpose, direction, and manner of American foreign and national security policy. In turn, the changed culture has made changes possible in the actions of the state.

Third-stage liberalism articulates a program that seeks the internalization of intentional covenants in American law and also as an element in the consideration of domestic cases. Imagine the following situation: A nominee to the federal court is asked at his or her hearing about international law, the covenants, and how he or she would apply them. This line of questioning would expand the consciousness of federal judges. At least a struggle would occur about the role of international law in domestic decisions. Now virtually none exists.

The process of learning about and then developing a new world body of law that would integrate local decisions and vice versa would become one important element in securing dignity. The Declaration of Human Rights asserted a bold principle, that respect for the dignity and rights of all was a necessary prerequisite for human survival. It was not a recipe for the destruction of different cultures. It was, and remains, a statement about the possibilities and needs of a nascent world civilization. There are important practical legal aspects that should absorb a good portion of time in our law schools, both in the development of statutes and in comparing decisions on cases in one country as against another.

Such ideas do not have to be seen as outside the range of possibility given the development of international human rights law since the end of the Second World War. The question is how to build on the work of transnational groups such as Amnesty International and Human Rights Watch, which are in the business of uncovering abuses, shaming the abuser, and protecting the violated. As are the covenants, such protections are predicated on the universal rights of personhood.

In a number of ways these purposes were thought to be the very essence of progressive capitalism from 1944 to 1948 in America. It was not unheard of that some businessmen, such as Henry Wallace, supported, even championed, this understanding of international politics. The wars and famines of the twentieth century broadened international human rights for refugees seeking asylum, detainees, and displaced persons. From the United Nations Covenant on Political Rights and decisions of the UN Committee on Human Rights, as well as regional and national decisions, it is accepted international law that, on paper, both refugees and displaced persons must be accorded minimum human rights. The program of that UN committee is accepted as a legal principle, if not an everyday reality. It states that refugees and asylum seekers

> should not be penalized or exposed to any unfavorable treatment solely on the ground that their presence in the country is considered unlawful; they should not be subjected to restrictions on their movements other than those which are necessary in the interest of public health and public order. They should enjoy the fundamental civil rights internationally recognized; in particular those set out in the Universal Declaration of Human Rights; and they should receive all necessary assistance and be provided with the basic necessities of life including food, shelter, and basic sanitary and health facilities.[19]

It is true that a person does not have a right to be admitted to a particular nation under international law. But this right will mature as a result of labor migration across countries and the web of international rules that brings the plight of the migrant laborer, the refugee, and the displaced into focus as a fundamental issue. There are too many wailing in the bow of the whaling ship who insist that empathic notice be taken.

Through a heightened consciousness of human rights, people demand their own place, irrespective of their respective sovereign's will and irrespective of their political weakness. Submerged populations are seeking to be heard and counted, either through the recognition of their separate identities as a legitimate nation free from the oppression of the outsider or as part of a national entity saved from the badge of discrimination and oppression. If their claims are not recognized either as just, or the basis for negotiation, the problem will fester and expand. That is to say, the submerged want their grievances to be heard, and unless they are heard, and adjustments and resolutions are made, violent forms of communication will be attempted. The dispute may rise to the level of insurrection, civil war, or war. Violence becomes a substitute for law and brings with it its own law. As Richard McKeon, the leading architect of the philosophy of human rights and UNESCO, put it: "The question of power and sovereignty is less meaningful—both in the sense of corresponding to objective reality and in the sense of adapting to the situations and processes of change than the question of discovering and achieving realizable values and effective rights. In a period of social and cultural revolution violent change can be avoided only by institutionalized revolution and the only stable society is a self renewing society."[20]

Beyond unilateral domination by the United States there are four different types of grievance linked to the problems of the twenty-first century:

1. the struggle over resources, as in the case of water and fungible commodities;
2. the search for identity and recognition of that identity by submerged peoples, who seek political and economic development in the context of negotiated equity;
3. an end to reliance on weapons of mass destruction without causing the collapse of states or continued violence with less powerful weapons; and
4. morality, as in the case of Israel and Palestine, where both nations feel themselves victims, hooked on either historical or biblical claims.

Where one side refuses recognition of the other while the other does not define its boundaries, the role of the international community becomes critical. Its task is to politicize the struggle between competing parties by appealing over the heads of leaders to women, religious groups, and a citizenry that is invariably divided. For example, in the case of the Palestinians, submerged populations are seeking to be counted, through the recognition of their separate identities, as a legitimate nation-state free from the oppression of outsiders or sometimes their own leadership. At the least the submerged want their problems to be heard and will even adopt a mode of violent communication to that end. If their claims are not recognized either as just or as the basis for negotiation, the problem will fester, and without ongoing modes of resolution, the anger will fester and then flame in future generations. A surprising result occurs as future generations outside of government seek to universalize and politicize their own struggles, changing their deprivation into an international concern. If the camera sees it, many will hear and see. And some will act, seeing in the situation of others either their own predicament or their need to "stand with" the Other, on problems as seemingly disparate as the indigenous population of the Amazon and their concern for their livelihood, place, and the natural environment and the problems of the down winders in the American Southwest who suffer from uranium poisoning.

How such matters related to formidable international corporations that followed their own customs and self-regulated rules of behavior was only partially answered by UN international conferences, which at best operated as legitimation for those who sought environmental protections and human rights.[21] Human rights activists lived in a world of purgatory where they were recognized but not listened to.

Proponents of environmental protection and human rights were not central to the direction of the international system. Nevertheless, as criticism mounted, international corporations recognized the need to organize a public relations touch-up of their image. Depending on the corporation, this included some attempt at environmental, consumer, and worker protection—so long as these purposes did not interfere with the profitability of the firm. Some corporations accepted codes of conduct and international worker standards that occurred as a result of concerted effort and negotiation with workers and consumer advocates.[22]

Transnational movements began to see the value of making their voices heard beyond any one specific issue, using economic and political as the category to attain decency for those outside the circle of decency. This modern activity underscored the linkage among political freedom, responsible economic enterprise, and cultural diversity. Proponents of such activity used as their guide international law; nonviolent confrontation; and the twentieth-century attempts to mirror laws, UN covenants; and aspirational documents such as the Universal Declaration of Human Rights, through emphatic sentiments. In other words, they infused into the corporate culture elements of the democratic social character. The fragile empathic trope strengthened through social action and law fills the space of what has come to mean political freedom, common sense, and justice. Such sentiments had been in the air since the eighteenth-century revolutions. But each of these sentiments required confrontation with superpower arrogance and militarism. In other words, it became necessary to confront superpower arrogance while finding and organizing a world system beyond imperialism and war. The agencies for that purpose are weak so long as they are mediated solely through nation-states and classic views of power, violence, and coercion as the coin of relations between states.

THE SECURITY OF THE SECURE

The screams of the wounded, perhaps the dead as well, or novels about war and a humanistic sentiment emboldened those who hoped that an international organization committed to peace and security would replace an arms race and the international war system. These ideas were found not only on the Left. They could be found among conservative businessmen, especially those who believed that trade was the substitute for war. In self-interested terms they believed American business could dominate the trading process. Further, for a time conservatives were concerned that war increased the power of the state, centralizing more authority in the bureaucracy while upsetting stability. President George W. Bush is not part of that tradition. He believes in a strong and bellicose state encased in the language of freedom. (That is to say, weapons of mass destruction are what the Other has. Weapons and military superiority are to be maintained at all costs.) It is no surprise that according to his notions of superpower, bellicosity does not include peace agreements. Ideas about disarmament at one time thought to be critical to post-World War II statecraft are now thought of as quaint. Instead, phasing out "aging" weapons and replacing them with new ones that fit current military doctrine is defined as arms control.

In 1960 there was some discussion about general and complete disarmament; but such ideas were thought by "realists" to be propaganda. Instead, realists offered a palliative, arms control, which did not necessarily mean fewer weapons but in fact meant, in various cases, more weapons. Strategists and diplomats sold themselves the idea that they were able to manage and control arms races, local conflicts, and alliances, much in the manner of thinking that dominated the minds of general staffs and leaders before the First World War.

There was a difference. New experts (the counterpart to economic technicians) came to the fore to show how to "manage" conflict.[23] This new group comprised different ideological strands of scientists and strategies who believed that they were like Bead players keeping the earth on its axis. They advised on how and when to fight wars, and with what weapons, as well as what weapons could be bargained away if new technological replacements were constructed, such as more sophisticated weapons, missiles, or aircraft. As in a potlatch between two warring tribes that really did not want to go to war with the other, as part of bipartisan foreign policy, Cold War liberals and conservatives found one key to Soviet weakness. It was to spend on wasteful high-tech weapons, which the Soviets believed they had to answer in kind with greater defense expenditures. The American strategy caused much despair among Soviet leaders as their own economy fell into bankruptcy. In what was thought to be a brilliant stroke of realpolitik, the CIA trained, funded, and used radical Muslim fundamentalists to bring about the defeat of the Soviet Union's "invited" intervention in Afghanistan. One can only imagine the chagrin of national security managers when they found that radical fundamentalists turned on the United States and used American technology to war with the United States. As Machiavellians, crisis managers took on the task of managing their own blunders.

There was a further cost to the United States as well since its strategy meant spending on weapons systems that could not work, except as a bargaining tool in the fantasy world of the Cold War. Soviet scientists thought the Strategic Defense Initiative (SDI) was silly, but they could not be sure, so they sought ways of countering it. Congress was also fooled. Its members were told that tests for the SDI had proved successful when, in fact, they either were never performed or were failures.[24] So high expenditures continued and greater Soviet insecurity was ensured—until Gorbachev. He believed that the strength of socialism as a system and an ideal, linked to a re-evaluation of Western intentions, could lead to accommodations with the West that would end the Cold War and, therefore, the perceived need for unaffordable defense expenditures. By pursuing this course Mikhail Gorbachev believed that a frayed Soviet Union would have a chance to repair itself economically and finally close the book on Stalinism forever.

But reassessments can get out of hand. No one could control the pent-up fury that the Soviet republics and Russians felt against the Soviet system. The historian Crane Brinton's insight, that revolutionary changes occur both when conditions are improving and when greater attention is paid to people's feelings, proved to be correct for Gorbachev as he removed the cork from the political bottle. He could not regulate the complaints, animosity, and thrust for political freedom that had accumulated over almost three generations within what the subjects of the Soviet Union took to be a frightening, and then stifling, enclosed space. Gorbachev could neither balance himself like Nijinski nor act like Reagan. The Communist Party had become calcified, with none of the revolutionary fervor by which early members were unified—even those who were purged, like Nikolai Bukharin. For those concerned with cultural history, it should not be surprising that, in the twentieth century, the age of the image, Reagan provided a world stage for the collapse of the Soviet Union as a major player in the war system. Neither Alfred Hitchcock nor Bertholt Brecht could have improved on Reagan's fake props, such as SDI. A few years later, the moderate liberal governor who became the Democratic Party nominee for president, Michael Dukakis, sought his own military prop to prove his warrior mettle, posing in a tank when he ran against George H. W. Bush. Looking too small for the tank and his helmet, Dukakis merely proved his ineptitude in arranging military props and thereby his incapacity to be president.

Once the Cold War ended, another reality was noted. The American balance of payments deficits could be compensated only through arms sales abroad. The United States had 57 percent of the trade. It also, by its Cold War methods, had increased drug trafficking in Thailand, Afghanistan, Pakistan, and Latin America to epidemic proportions as a result of partnerships it struck with corrupt politicians, the military in other nations, drug dealers, and transporters. But such changes were thought to be the costs of being an engaged superpower, just as the American soldiers absorbed the enormous damage from the sale and use of drugs in Indochina, which resulted in a generation of soldiers who were felled by drug addiction long after they returned home. Indeed, by the beginning of the twenty-first century, one segment of the American elite had accepted, even championed, the proposition that war was the health of the American state and economy.[25] Thus, a war against Iraq came to be understood as integral to nurturing the nation's health and vitality, just as some believe that wars in Colombia are necessary to ensure the unchallenged status of the United States in Latin America.

OLD FEARS AND NEW INSECURITIES
By 1989 it had become clear that there were stunning changes in the big power politics game. For a few years, in the 1980s and immediately after the Berlin Wall came

down, it appeared that Germany and Japan were the economic victors in the Cold War. The major antagonists exhausted themselves in the shadow cold war, and in Germany and Japan a new nationalism was championed. Because of increasing burdens on the U.S. budget, American policymakers urged the Germans and Japanese to void that part of their respective constitutions that hampered a more robust role for their armed forces outside of their own territories.

Fifty years after the Second World War, the Germans and Japanese were ready to break out of the residual restraints placed on them by the victorious powers. The once-defeated nations could again become military powers, to come and go as they chose, unless the United States found a means of controlling their appetites once they sat at the table that emphasized the use of military power. On the one hand, the defeated World War II powers were cajoled by the United States into making their forces available for peacekeeping duty in different areas of the world. On the other hand, the question was how to ensure control over their activities and limit any aggrandizing sentiments that lingered from the past. American diplomats were split on methods to accomplish this task.

For some, this policy meant a covert entente with Russia and the People's Republic of China in a skewed replay of World War II power politics against Germany and Japan. For others, it meant holding Germany and Japan tightly to the American military and economic bosom, on the grounds that China and Russia were weak and would remain so for at least a generation.

Russia sought to keep what was left of its pride and nationhood so that it would not end up as a hollow empire destined to fight continuous wars on its periphery, as it did in Chechnya. With the breakup of the Soviet Union, the war system seemed to be uncontainable. The Cold War duopoly had seemed to give the world a certain amount of stability, wherein each superpower controlled its respective clients.

The United Nations counted 150 small wars and skirmishes between and within nations that were breaking apart and attempting to redefine themselves in a new nationalism. But these wars were of little importance to the United States during Clinton's presidency. Economic and cultural globalization had become the mantra of the American elite.[26]

New players and problems appeared on the horizon of international politics that seemed trivial compared to those that engulfed most of the twentieth century. The United States, as the undisputed world leader, was admired for its technological prowess, which seemed to redefine the universe and humankind's place in it. But admiration did not mask underlying conditions. Liberals, whether technocratically oriented or committed to reconstruction, were unable to find the political agency or leadership to deal with these underlying conditions. For example, liberals had not found a way to turn these conditions into problems that were understood and linked to economic issues that might galvanize the American middle and working classes to action against surface solutions that would merely deepen immiseration and waste.

American business and policymakers pursued a three-pronged strategy. The first was to press for open markets and the easy flow of capital to developing nations. This allowed for greater investment and intrusion in the economic affairs of other nations. (In the lexicon of economic public relations, imperial intrusion was replaced with the more sonorous sounding phrases "global interdependence" and "global governance.") A second strategy involved an effort to guarantee the flow of oil at such low cost that it would be economically foolish to investigate alternative sources of energy. The actual market cost for gas is undervalued as a result of the presence of American military power in the Middle East.[27] Further, the United States has access to Russian and Alaskan oil as backups. It would appear that the United States could continue its wasteful ways without harm to itself except that it is captive to oil at the expense of the environment and it protects the sheiks of the Middle East. And where necessary the United States would support coups (even in Saudi Arabia), as it did in Venezuela, organizing fig leaf democratic governments to its liking.

The third seemingly contradictory strategy relates to speculation by Western and American investors, who invested heavily in Asian and Latin American stock markets. However, the prosperity in these nations did not lead to wages for workers. Indeed, once Western investors pulled their funds out of Asian markets, stock valuation became depressed. Lending in Asian banks slowed, resulting in a continuing contraction of the economy. Banks called in their loans and, as is invariably the case, firings and lay-offs followed. Wage increases for Asian workers ended. In turn, greater pressures on American industry to reduce the wages of workers in the United States continued under the guise of the need for greater productivity to meet international competition and for an end to job security. Increasing numbers of middle class "consultants" in fact became part of a secondary labor market. The vulnerability of the American economy was understood in new ways, such as no long-term guarantees for workers, increasing costs for health, and heavy indebtedness. This everyday reality for Americans cannot be overemphasized, especially as it relates to problems of unemployment and a heavily indebted middle class, fearful of losing surface gains that it had made through the enjoyment of consumer goods that were financial liabilities. For this grouping, as is the case with the working class, cutting back social services and those activities thought to be part of the national heritage, such as parks, schools, museums, and public spaces, adds greatly to agitation within American society.

In this context one must judge the implications of George W. Bush's conception of a homeland defense. It will prove to be similar to the National Guard of the latter nineteenth century in American history, which was used to keep order against strikers, anarchists, and dissidents. In the case of the second Bush administration it will be used to keep order throughout society, accompanied as it is by acceptable incursions into civil liberties. And some will rationalize these actions on the ground that constitutional democracy does not fit with the needs of the time. Even the budgetary niceties for education, health, and environment may not be affordable as domestic needs are unmet and unproductive militarization of the society is reflected in federal war budgets. When a nation is engaged in a war without end, claiming that the Constitution is not a suicide pact, surface rationality would demand that the laws and organization of the government require radical change. Just as the national security state was necessary for the operations of an empire abroad, so it is that a war without end requires a war without end domestically, turning the citizenry into soldiers and informers.

The Department of Homeland Security, like the National Security Council, includes secret directives intended to govern and coordinate the various security agencies. Their governmental consequence is to add to the plethora of information and increase the system of pyramidal, centralized bureaucratic power. In this process a homeland security department will be protected from citizen inquiry by executive order and legislation. However, the establishment of new departments of government brings with it bureaucratic infighting, which can last as long as five years. But where the framework is established of a war without end, organizational structures will become permanent. This will mean that a suprainternal and national security council will coordinate virtually all nonsocial welfare aspects of governing. This has been a long-standing wish of those committed to reshaping the governmental structure of the United States who believed that the governmental machinery was inadequate to run an empire. Vice President Nelson Rockefeller had hoped for a prime minister role for the vice presidency, overseeing the major functions of government under an ornamental president and passive Congress. Just as the United States reorganized its state structure into a national security state at the end of the Second World War, so it appears that the thrust for a Homeland Security Council is "necessary" if the United States is to protect the homeland from within. Its task includes the justification for fighting continuous wars abroad and establishing through war "friendly" regimes that have the color of legitimacy, while ensuring secured levels of military supplies and unquestioning loyalty from a trusting citizenry that has chosen private gain over public and critical deliberation. The question of what and who to trust is to be driven beneath the surface of the national psyche, moved aside by the drumbeat of patriotic war. Love and knowledge, two staples of social existence, are to be surrendered.

ALLIANCE, INTERNATIONAL ORGANIZATION, AND THE SOVIET DEMISE

What had been a popular fantasy and the fear of nuclear strategists during the Cold War—that gangs would threaten and blackmail cities and nations with nuclear weapons—cannot in the twenty-first century be dismissed out of hand. In global free markets, everything is for sale, from sex slaves to nuclear weapons parts to biological viruses. Traditional enmities, suppressed by the Cold War and competing power blocs, came to the fore after 1990. Ethnic rivalries became more virulent, and pre-1914 nationalism took hold among competing factions, from Cambodia, Sri Lanka, and China to Tibet, Hungary, Romany, and the Balkans. In the latter case, the explosive situation seemed only to be held in check through international and U.S. engagement, which meant long-term military commitments of NATO forces.

While some argued that the NATO alliance system brought communism to its knees and that goal was quite sufficient, others argued that it was time for a new *cordon sanitaire* with the expansion of NATO to the borders of Russia. Supposedly this strategy would finally neutralize Russian power in Europe and restore that middle kingdom to nothing more than a buffer against a resurgent China. Others in the second Bush administration had no interest in the niceties of alliance. The United States intended to lead a condominium of nations in establishing a sphere of influence over Kazakhstan and Kyrgyzstan through military bases and domination over oil reserves and pipelines. The American policy was a fait accompli, and those who wanted to share in this largesse needed only accept American dominance. A question may be asked whether this way of conducting foreign and national security affairs was totally different or merely an extension, a teasing out, of what had been integral to American policy since the Second World War.

There were two competing views about the international system among those who did not favor the fortress America view Joseph Kennedy had put forward after the Second World War. One American position was an attempt to rebuild the League of Nations, but now as a United Nations, which over time would become a universal organization superseding all alliances and in which all foreign policies (except those concerned with U.S. relations to Latin America) would be mediated.[28] The other was a return to the alliance system.

The UN conception, predicated on limited sovereignty and the restriction of the traditional right of states to make war, soon found itself having to compete with more traditional notions of politics among nations, to use Hans Morgenthau's phrase. This meant the reinvigoration of the alliance system as understood by historians, such as Henry Steele Commager, to be nothing less than the defense of Western civilization against the new Sparta, the Soviet Union. The stated underlying claim American leaders made was that unless bullying leaders were stopped early and by force if necessary, wars would expand into larger wars. This was the ideological mantra of American policymakers who ran post-World War II foreign and national security affairs. (Note how this idea of international politics remains the rationalization for American military intervention in the twenty-first century.) Once Henry Wallace and left New Dealers found themselves marginalized by the new bipartisanship of the Cold War consensus, there was very little difference between liberals and moderate conservatives such as Dwight Eisenhower on foreign and national security policy. Cold War liberals were more bellicose and expansionist than conservatives, as was the case with Truman, who committed American troops to Korea using the United Nations Participation Act as the rationale, and then organized and committed American military forces to NATO. (The reason that the Korean War was referred to as a "police action" was that police actions were contemplated in the UN Participation Act, and it was not necessary therefore to obtain a declaration of war from Congress.) American policymakers had an unstated reason that went far beyond the scarecrow fear of Soviet invasion of West Europe.

That reason, which was crafted in evasive language for the American people (Americans had fought two wars in Europe during the twentieth century), was to control Germany, which had sought hegemony over Europe in the first half of the twentieth century. Thus, the Western alliance was an alliance against a nation that had been conquered in two wars and that was occupied by allied troops. NATO only *appeared* to be an alliance against the Soviets. Its military planning was an elaborate game, albeit with real consequences in spent material resources.[29] Similarly, the Warsaw Pact alliance of 1955 appeared to be an answer to NATO. However, Its fundamental political purpose was to keep Eastern Europe in line, controlled by the Soviet Union.

The Soviet rejection of the Marshall Plan meant that the Soviet bloc nations intended to take themselves out of the world capitalist system. Over time this turned out to be a mistaken calculation for the Soviet Union, because it had nowhere near the capacity to subsidize other nations and provide the level of military hardware, maintenance, and training its clients needed. Furthermore, the Soviets did not have a system of entrepreneurial innovation, which the United States was able to offer to its younger, technologically educated elites.

The Soviet Union was an economically underdeveloped nation, which throughout the Cold War was placed by the West in the position of heavyweight adversary when its capacities, in reality (except in the case of nuclear weapons), were fundamentally lightweight.[30] Yet, the Cold War became the global enterprise of the Americans and Soviets. It brought confrontations and responses around liberation movements; ideological pretensions; wars in the Third World; and a new form of jousting through propaganda, play acting at diplomatic meetings, and allowing both sides to increase military expenditures, which had a salutary effect on the employment situation, especially in the United States. Jousting kept a lid on domestic problems by ensuring internal loyalty for the higher good of national patriotism in both the United States and the Soviet Union.

In the United States state power expanded as the capacity and interest in solving internal problems outside of the market waned. War may be the health of the state, and certain sectors of government sponsored defense production. This has not led to the improvement of social services and the everyday well-being of American society. The Soviet government found that it could not financially keep up its side of the Cold War. Prior to the breakup of the Soviet Union, the last Soviet leadership looked for ways to scuttle the Warsaw Pact alliance because of its cost. The attempts of an older generation, which relied on military control to shore up allegiances in the Soviet Union and Eastern Europe, also failed for reasons that touch on the struggles of intellectual elites since the French Revolution for negative freedom.

The emphasis in Russia, from the tsars to the Communist Party, in its citizen socialization was the narrowing of negative freedom so that the public space, as defined by the state, preempted any concept of challenge to it or protection against it. Freedom of association, assembly, and press are part of negative freedom. The freedom of the press, of writing and publishing, was a power and right that the Soviets, beginning with Lenin, were not prepared to grant to noncommunists or independent publishing houses, as for example in the case of the anarchist Peter Kropotkin.

Human rights activists such as Andrei Sakharov understood the importance of negative freedom, although his fellow dissident, the religious reactionary Alexander Solzhenitsyn, had no interest in that part of eighteenth-century revolutions meant to be protective of the person in the context of a vibrant secular society. Solzhenitsyn had concluded that secularism was the enemy of man. His Pan-Slav nationalism could deliver God, but what could socialism deliver in the face of the evanescent and resentful? Socialism, which had done so much to catalyze the consciousness of people for economic security, could not find the means, either politically or economically, to champion human rights in the political sphere.

Movements and purposes had changed. State socialism was left behind, with its adherents still claiming that "bourgeois" rights such as free speech, or attempts (which invariably failed) to control all the social spaces of society, had to be top down, where unions did not represent workers' interests but those of the Party, which became increasingly calcified. On the other hand, liberation in the form of a radical liberalism was reflected initially in modern axial leaders such as Martin Luther King Jr., who inspirited the various solidarity and human rights movements of Eastern Europe almost a generation after his death.[31]

As a result of a new consciousness of human rights, people demanded their own place, irrespective of their sovereign's will or who the sovereign claimed it was or represented. Submerged populations throughout the world, including Eastern Europe (and Native Americans in the Southwest United States), sought to be heard and counted, either in terms of separate identities or at least in terms of their problems. Women, long thought to be war trophies, claimed new rights under international criminal law. By 1990 rape was commonly understood to be a war crime rather than a military benefit. These changes were profoundly important and necessitated what was to be included in a liberal foreign policy and the organization of Nuremberg-like tribunals. However, these efforts paled in the face of the modern conditions of war and war preparation, which had bedeviled the entire century. American foreign policy was of little help, for it did not accept an international criminal court. Progress was not a straight line, as believers in progress, modernists, and Marxists believed. The question was whether it could be the dominant spirit of a time.

Not if conservatives could help it. The United States delayed paying its assessments to the UN while stopping any kind of tax-deductible funding from American taxpayers for the UN. The second Bush administration added new targets to its rogue shooting gallery. Prior to September 11 it made clear that the United States would no longer be tethered by entangling alliances. It would now establish military bases in Central Asia never thought possible during the Cold War. The conservatives who supported Bush and his predecessors had claimed that liberals talked of moral equivalence between "them and us." But the issue was not one of moral equivalence. The issue was moral amnesia in which Americans cannot remember what the morally arrogant national security leaders do in the nation's name.[32] The commitment to political equality as a goal of liberalism is undercut by the cultivation of inequality through excess, as in the case of corporate managers who think nothing of having salaries and benefits hundreds of times greater than those of the average worker.

World capitalism presents itself as a hegemonic system, and since the defeat of state socialism in large part at its own hand, there is no organized, comprehensive challenge to it. In the twenty-first century the challenge must come from the weakness of this hegemony and its incapacity to solve problems of war, the environment, hunger, and disease. Its method, to ameliorate these conditions through the national security state (continuous small wars) and the control of local economies (the work of uncontrolled and unaccountable international corporations), merely adds to the human tragedy, the evisceration of other cultures that are now to become appendages of the aggresive international military and corporate system.

In the 1960s and 1970s Andre Gorz spoke of nonreformist reforms, that is, reforms that would lead to a transformed condition. Under the heading of liberal reconstruction I too was concerned that incrementalism could be easily co-opted. But this is only true when there is insufficient awareness of how each problem carries within itself the seeds and rules of other realities that necessitate opening the door even wider to democratic social change. For example, the Voting Rights Act of 1957, in itself a minor civil rights step, led to the further legitimacy of civil rights protest and more far-reaching laws.

Transnational movements that have human rights, peace, and economic justice at their core cannot be easily co-opted. Indeed, they become a world beacon once groups in different settings undertake projects and actions that are fought for and sustained by local and international actions. This, for example, was the strength of the human rights movement in the Soviet Union, in which Andrei Sakharov's project of human rights was supported by scientists of other nations. He took existential risks for the participants and reflected individual integrity. The project itself reformulated the meaning of world political justice. But because economic and social justice were not linked to peaceful endeavors, in practice Sakharov's purpose was a limited one predicated on conservative ideas of balance of power. He favored an American MIRV, putting multiple nuclear warheads on individual missiles in the 1980s. This direction was hardly the one to move the world beyond deterrence and first strike. In fact, Sakharov's views did nothing to change the possibilities of first strike and war.

Twenty-first-century human rights movements are more than the carrying of signs in demonstrations or individual witness. They are linked to finding the means for every person to develop and to do so where necessary in relation to others. In practice, this means pushing back social and psychological spaces that appear to be closed to the person and especially those who are directly oppressed. By acting to develop projects that show what could become the dominant features of society, by defending them and then linking with others who develop similar projects, whether a peace center, think tanks, a rape crisis center, an environmental study group, funds for reinvestment of union pensions into regions in need, a health policy clinic, a prison reform project, or an arts center, the vitality is present for opening social, political, and economic spaces. Such projects have to be fought for, and in the process participants must reach out to allies that undertake similar activities of thought and practice in other arenas. From these relationships movements are emerging that have a moral claim on what the contours of modern democracy and a world more just could be.

Notes

1. Marcus Raskin, *Visions and Revisions: Reflections on Culture and Democracy at the end of the Century* (New York: Olive Branch Press, 1996), 314. For a perceptive account of Machiavelli's hatred of the corrupt and the need to favor a universal humanity, see *Niccolo's Smile,* by Maurizio Vivilo (New York: Hill and Wang, 1998).
2. William Bennett, *Why We Fight* (New York: Doubleday, 2002).
3. Throughout the twentieth century liberation movements were opportunistic, turning for aid to any nation that would give it with the fewest strings attached.
4. Harry S. Truman, "Statement on Fundamentals of American Foreign Policy," *Department of State Bulletin* 13, October 27, 1945, 653.

5. Jean-Paul Sartre, preface to *The Wretched of the Earth*, by Frantz Fanon, trans. Constance Farrington (New York: Grove Press), 7–34; and Frantz Fanon in "Concerning Violence," in *The Wretched of the Earth*, 35–106.

6. Who could forget, for example, the signal contributions of Marcos in the Philippines, Diem of South Vietnam, Suharto of Indonesia, Mobuto of Zaire and many others.

7. Richard McKeon, ed., *Democracy in a World of Tensions: A Symposium Prepared by UNESCO* (Chicago: University of Chicago Press).

8. William James, "The Moral Equivalent of War," in *The Moral Equivalence of War and Other Essays and Selections from Some Problems on Philosophy*, ed. John K. Roth (New York: Harper Torchbooks, 1971), 3-16; Mary King, *Mahatma Gandhi and Martin Luther King* (Paris: UNESCO Publishing); Gene Sharp, *The Politics of Nonviolent Actton* (Boston: Porter Sargent, 1973).

9. Elias Canetti, *Crowds and Power,* trans. Carol Stewart (New York: Viking Press, 1962).

10. Raul Hilberg, *The Destruction of the European Jews,* 3 vols. (New York: Holmes & Meier, 1955).

11. Ernst Nolte, *Three Faces of Fascism* (New York: Henry Holt, 1966). The of the rather willing, albeit fraught with complexity, acceptance of the Nazi regime and its murderous ideology by the esteemed German philosophical community is told in Hans Slugcl, *Heidegger's Crisis: Philosophy and Politics in Nazi Germany* (Cambridge: Harvard University Press, 1993).

12. Churchill had very warm words to say about the Italian fascism of Mussolini as an antidote to Leninism when he visited Italy in 1926. He reaffirmed his adoration for Mussolini and his regime in 1935. See Robert R. James, *Churchill: A Study in Failure 1900–1939*. (New York: World Publishing Company, 1970), 285.

13. George Washington's farewell address after his second term as president. Marcus Raskin, "Presidential Disrespect," http://www.ips-dc.org/reports/presidential_disrespect (1996).

14. For a discussion of how World War II precipitated a large-scale capital transfer from public hands to big corporations, see Gabriel Kolko, *Century of War: Politics, Conflict and Society since 1914* (New York: New Press, 1994), 79–82.

15. See Robert E. Osgood, "The Korean War," in *Limited War: The Challenge to American Strategy* (Chicago: University of Chicago Press, 1957), 163–93.

16. Tens of thousands of American soldiers suffered a mysterious unidentified disease syndrome probably as a result of drugs taken as an antisepsis against chemical and biological warfare.

17. One may note that the nuclear freeze movement of the 1980s had great popular support, but once the nuclear freeze passed through the maw of the national security state apparatus and Congress, the popular movement became housebroken and irrelevant.

18. See the UN international Covenant on Economic, Social and Cultural Rights, appendix B.

19. "The Movement of Persons across Borders," in *Studies in International Legal Policy,*

eds. Louis Sohn and Thomas Buergenthal (Washington, D.C.: American Society of International Law, 1992), 121–22.

20. Richard McKeon, *Philosophy, Science and Culture*, vol. 1 (Berkeley: University of California Press, 2000), 456.

21. UN Conference on Environment and Development, Rio de Janeiro, June 3–14, 1992 (the "earth summit").

22. Note codes of conduct prepared and negotiated by the nongovernmental organization the International Labor Rights Fund for factories owned by American multinational corporations, including "suppliers." The corporations that negotiated this arrangement for doing business in China include Levi, Liz Claiborne, Phillip Van Huesen, Gear for Sports, Adidas, Reebok, and Nike.

23. Some few were members of the Pugwash group started at the height of the Cold War by pacific-minded scientists from the United States and the Soviet Union under the impetus of Cyrus Earon, Joseph Rotblat, and Bertrand Russell.

24. For an understanding of the young physicists involved in the SDI project, see William J. Broad, *Star Warriors* (New York: Simon & Schuster, 1985). As of 1999, Frances Fitzgerald completes the journalistic account of policy and scientific failure in *Way Out There in the Blue* (New York: Touchstone Books, 2001).

25. Such ideas are clothed in the rhetoric of triumphal democracy made popular by neo-conservatives such as the former Democratic advisor Richard Perle and columnist George Will, who joined with Vice President Dick Cheney. When Cheney was in Congress, he was the leader of the arch-conservative wing of the Republican Party.

26. Noam Chomsky, *World Orders. Old and New* (New York: Columbia University Press, 1994); Central Intelligence Agency, *Global Trends, 2015* (Langley, VA: CIA, 2000). With the election of Jimmy Carter to the presidency, his first Secretary of state, Cyrus Vance, enunciated the fundamental role of corporations in American foreign and economic policy. He resigned when the United Stares, under the tutelage of National Security Advisor Zbigniew Brzezinski, favored force as the primary instrument of foreign policy. Vance was an interesting man who believed in arms control, viewed war as irrational, and thought the American state's relationship to the Third World, responsiveness, would reflect or deny the nation's moral purpose. Vance resigned immediately after the failed military attempt to rescue the hostages at the U.S. embassy in Iran. Vance said the mission would fail. When he was overruled by Carter, Vance said that such an attempted military incursion would fail and continue to damage national interests of the United States in the Middle East. It is worth noting that the U.S. focus on oil during the Carter administration did not take seriously the Soviet concern about Islam fundamentalism, which the United States sought to use as an ideological instrument against the Soviet Union. Cyrus Vance, *Hard Choices* (New York: Simon & Schuster, 1983).

27. This can be seen when comparing oil and gas prices in other nations using Middle East oil to U.S. bills for oil.

28. There is an exception in which Nelson Rockefeller argued that the UN charter recognized Latin America as within the United States' sphere of influence.
29. Each nation, for example, was to have at least one detachment of troops on the front lines facing Eastern Europe, so that if a war did occur each nation's forces would he in harm's way and therefore committed to fight.
30. Struggles between the various national security and defense agencies continued throughout the Cold War.
31. But these movements carried an unwanted passenger in their bags, that of the unrestrained free market, which brought the picaro to the fore.
32. Not many know the recent history of Afghan-U.S. relations. Committed to anticommunism at all costs, the United Stares objected to rapprochement between social reformist King Daoad and the Soviet Union.

PART II
THE WARS AT HOME

6

America's Permanent War Economy

Seymour Melman

On September 10, 2001, Secretary of Defense Donald H. Rumsfeld made a stunning announcement: "We cannot track $2.3 trillion in transactions."[1]

In the realm of business, with its emphasis on profit maximizing, such looseness in accounting would be either evidence of monumental incompetence or deliberate falsification.

THE PENTAGON LOSES $2,300,000,000,000

But not in the Pentagon. For there, the dominant measure of success is gain in power, the ability to control the behavior of people, or the whole nation. On behalf of maximizing power, monetary efficiency is secondary. Thus it appears to be the characteristic among Pentagon managers to treat inability to match payments made with goods or services received as mere inconvenience that may be brushed off as so much "budget dust": Magnitudes such as 2.3 trillion, while ordinary in astronomy are unusual in economy. Note that $2.3 trillion exceeds the net value of the entire plant and equipment of U.S. manufacturing industries, measured as $1.8 trillion.

What sort of economic system is this that can accept uncertainty about how it has disposed of $2.3 trillion of goods and services?

The Pentagon managers' loss of $2.3 trillion has a far greater significance than as a mere exhibition of trashy administration.

In fact, the resources lost by the Pentagon are equal to the investments required to raise the quality of life of the whole American people. Finding this equality was unexpected. It emerged from examining the Report Card for America's Infrastructure by the American Society of Civil Engineers (ASCE), as well as the work of Professor John E. Ullmann on railroad electrification costs and the housing repair costs.

According to the ASCE, the current condition of U.S. infrastructure warrants a grade of D+. Achieving grade A infrastructure performance in the United States will

139

require reconstruction of many significant areas. These include: roads; bridges; transit facilities; aviation; schools; drinking water; wastewater disposal; dams; solid and hazardous waste disposal; navigable waterways; energy supply; provision for replacing several million "worst-case" housing units; and electrification of U.S. railroads.

This brief discussion defines a great choice. Where should we allocate the $2.3 trillion—to the permanent war economy, or to the reconstruction of American life?

Upon taking office the George W. Bush administration redirected billions of dollars to fund an ambitious effort to extend U.S. hegemony. This campaign for world hegemony for the United States as displayed in Iraq, Afghanistan, and preparations for potential wars, has consumer resources urgently needed in the U.S. civilian economy. Meanwhile, the U.S. has been accelerating industrial decay and major job losses for Americans as American managers—eager to garner the financial benefits of Chinese wages ranging from $60 to $95 a month—transfer production their U.S. bases to China. On the current path, what will be left for young men and women other than to enroll in one of the Pentagon's formations?

The central task of this book is to offer ways to reverse the decay. It will show how and orderly process of modernization in infrastructure and related industries—as outlined by the American Society of Civil Engineers—might well create between one and four million new productive jobs and give fresh life to the great manufacturing industries of the U.S. (See Appendices A and B below on, "National Employment and Income Effects From a Shift in Federal Priorities," by Dr. Greg Bischak and the 2003 Progress Report of the Report Card for America's Infrastructure.)

The experience that yielded Secretary Rumsfeld's loss of $2.3 trillion also included costs of the technological feats of WWII to 2001. These included production of large complex aircraft as though they were Model-T's, while researching and erecting the military industrial (atomic) establishment with vast physical assets, and a workforce that established it as by far the largest single enterprise in the United States. With those understandings, Americans could see losing or otherwise misplacing even $2.3 trillion without "batting an eyelash."

High level discussion among corporate and government chiefs regarding the continuing management of the U.S. war economy began as Hitler's armies were approaching military defeat in 1944. Leading business managers and senior government officials began to discuss a central problem of the post-war economy. The United States alone possessed an immense industrial system that was untouched by military destruction and therefore would be the final strategic location for producing and exporting the consumer and capital goods required for recovery in the rest of the world. Accordingly, the *Wall Street Journal* (January 6th, 1944) reported on the thinking of Vice Chairman Batt of the government's War Production Board. He urged the adoption of a plan for balancing the expected rush of machinery and other goods coming out of the United States.

The rest of the world, Batt suggested, could pay for American exports of goods and finance capital by making available to the United States large quantities of raw materials. These, in turn, could be "mothballed"—removed from the marketplace by placing them in buried stockpiles. Thereby, a strategic economic problem could be "solved" while affording the United States a stockpile of raw materials, to help cope with future national military emergencies.

In a January 1944 speech to·the Army Ordnance Association, Charles E. Wilson, president of the General Electric Corporation, proposed an alliance of business and the military in a permanent war economy. This was proposed as "a continuing program and not the creature of an emergency. . . The program must be insured and supported by the Congress in the beginning through resolution . . . later, by regularly scheduled and continuing appropriations. Industry's role in this program is to respond and cooperate . . . Let us make this 3-way [executive branch, congress and industry] partnership permanent and workable, not just an arrangement of momentary convenience."[2]

Recall that within the U.S. government the international political perspective at the close of World War II was dominated by the prospect of a worldwide competition between the United States and the Soviet Union. No long wait was required before the relentless competition that came to be called the Cold War was set in motion.

There is no question that the appearance of nuclear military capability in the Soviet Union, followed swiftly by Soviet invention of the hydrogen bomb, had a decisive effect in blurring a traditional "holding at arm's length" attitude among certain sectors of American business towards the federal government. The political and military aspects of the great contest between the U.S. government and Stalin's Russia bound the senior managers of the U.S. government with top corporate management of the United States.

A Permanent War Economy was no longer a speculation or merely a plan for smoothing U.S. economic relations with many countries in the world. The Permanent War Economy came to be the key strategy for waging the Cold War.

America's government and corporate managers joined in a favorable assessment of the post–World War II economy. From right to left the main verdict was that the U.S. economy could sustain both Guns and Butter. That was the verdict of both the government's National Security Council (1950) and the Marxist economist Paul Baran.[3]

PRODUCTIVE AND PARASITIC GROWTH: EISENHOWER'S ASSESSMENT

A different perspective on the subject of military spending was pronounced by President Dwight D. Eisenhower in a 1953 address to the American Society of Newspaper Editors. He stated that:

Every gun that is made, every warship launched, every rocket fired signifies, in the final sense, a theft from those who hunger and are not fed, those who are cold and are not clothed.

This world in arms is not spending money alone. It is spending the sweat of its laborers, the genius of its scientists, the hopes of its children.

The cost of one modern heavy bomber is this: a modern brick school in more than 30 cities. It is two electric power plants, each serving a town of 60,000 population. It is two fine, fully equipped hospitals. It is some 50 miles of concrete highway.

We pay for a single fighter with a half million bushels of wheat. We pay for a single destroyer with new homes that could have housed more than 8,000 people.

This, I repeat, is the best way of life to be found on the road the world has been taking.

This is not a way of life at all, in any true sense. Under the cloud of threatening war, it is humanity hanging from a cross of iron.

The economists deceived themselves (and most of the American people) by failing to take into account the difference between productive and parasitic growth. Productive growth is represented by goods and services used for consumption or further production. Parasitic growth refers to products that, (while money valued) are neither useful for consumption or for production. Though military industry is economically parasitic, the value of its production is included in the accounting of national wealth called Gross Domestic Product, (GDP). Thus, production of war materiel masked the decline in production of civilian items. In overlooking this point, the U.S. managers established a policy that would later devastate U.S. manufacturing, (particularly capital goods) infrastructure and population. [. . .]

THE AMERICAN CORPORATE-STATE REGIME

When a permanent war economy was established in the U.S., once separate government and corporate managements became merged. What exactly was the character of these separately identified groups of managers? How did they come to be "merged"? No provision for such a merger is found in the Constitution of the United States. What exactly caused this connection?

After World War II rapid growth in the size of America's leading industrial firms gave rise to new problems of managerial control. The chiefs of the larger firms discovered that it had become unwieldy to try to specify detailed rules, appointments of subordinates, decisions about products, production details etc.—all from one large management office. The component products and factories were too diverse and far-flung for such micro decision-making to be done in one place. The idea of a "Central Administrative Office" was developed to solve this problem.

A CAO was charged with formulating general policies to be followed by the managers of subordinate divisions (or firms) who reported on their key operations on a scheduled basis to the chiefs of the CAO. The CAO approved top appointments for the important subordinate units while charging them with executing broad policies as defined by the CAO. This style of operation lent itself to enlargement—without defined limit—of the number of "subordinate firms" that could be supervised by a CAO with an appropriate staff. A regionally dense array of contractor firms could be supervised subject to controls under a regional central administrative office. The regional CAOs, in turn, would then report to, and be subject to controls by the national CAO. All this combined elements of "decentralized" and nationally tight policy control.

President John F. Kennedy and his advisors drawn from schools of management sought ways for tighter control over the far-flung operations of the U.S. government, notably the important Department of Defense. For this task President Kennedy appointed, as Secretary of Defense, Robert McNamara who had been president of the Ford Motor Company and had won renown as an innovative organizer of that far-flung corporation. McNamara proceeded to install a Central Administrative Office type organization in the Pentagon to oversee the operations of the Department of Defense. This was deemed essential because the military establishment that emerged from World War II had never been reduced to its pre-WWII scale.

The creation of a state-management marked the transformation of President Dwight Eisenhower's "military-industrial complex." The "complex" referred to a loose collaboration of senior military officers, industrial managers, and legislators, operating mainly through market relations. McNamara's central-management office replaced the market with a management system that governed internal operations of the Pentagon serving firms as well as their relation to each other. In-place of the complex, there was now a structured central administrative control center that regulates tens of thousands of subordinate managers. Independently of the intention of the JFK White House, the central office managerial structure, by formalizing and tightening controls, strengthened the normal authoritarian, including anti-union features of Managerialism.

The Pentagon's managerial structure for controlling military-serving industry was made the more powerful owing to its access to the vast resources of America and the readiness of a population to allow its formally designated representatives, (as in the Congress) to draw upon those resources-even to the extent of allowing $2.3 trillion to be "lost" without complaint. The new state-management is by far the largest and single most important management in the United States, engaging about 290,000 men and women who arrange work assignments to subordinate managers (contract negotiation), and supervise compliance of submanagers of subdivisions with the top management's rules. This is the largest industrial central administrative office in the United States—perhaps in the world.

The state-management has also become the most powerful decision-making unit in the United States government. Thereby, the federal government does not "serve" business or "regulate" business. For the new management structure runs the largest business of them all. Government is business. It is state capitalism.

The normal operation, including expansion, of the new state-management has been based upon preemption of a lion's share of federal tax revenue and of the nation's finite supply of technical manpower. This use of capital and skill has produced parasitic economic growth—military products which are not part of the level of living and which cannot be used for further production.

Nevertheless the great social strength of American military institutions comes from what so many people see as its contributions: wages and salaries of military personnel; a graded system of pensions; veterans hospitals; wages and salaries of military industry workers of all grades; research grants to the universities; the GI Bill paying tuitions (from skills training to university degrees); the incomes of every sort of small business abutting military bases.

These and allied benefits help to cement popular support for the military institutions while obscuring the array of parasitic effects.

THE MONEY AND HUMAN COST OF DEFENSE

From 1990 to 2000, the United States government spent $2,956 billion on the Department of Defense. This sum of staggering size (try to visualize even one billion of anything) does not express the cost of the military establishment to the nation as a whole. The true cost is measured by the "opportunity cost", by what has been foregone, by the accumulated deterioration in many facets of life, by the inability to alleviate human wretchedness of long duration.

Here is part of the human inventory of depletion:

1. By 2001, huge numbers of US homes were decaying. 2 million homes have severe physical problems. 13 million have leaks from outside the structure. 1 million homes have holes in their floors. 1 million homes are infested with rats. 72,000 homes have no electricity.
2. In 2002, 9.3 million people in the U.S. were classified as "hungry" by the U.S. Department of Agriculture. Furthermore, almost 35 million people—12.5 percent of U.S. households—had no secure supply of food, due to lack of resources.
3. In 2002, 34.8 million people in the US lived in poverty. This is 12.4 percent of the population, and an increase of 1.4 million from 2001.

4. 2.3–3.5 million people (including 1.3 million children) in the U.S. experience homelessness each year.
5. 41.2 million people in the U.S. lacked health insurance during the entire year 2001. In 2002, 18,000 uninsured Americans died due to lack of treatment.
6. 14 million children go to class in deteriorating public schools. Two thirds of all public schools have troublesome environmental conditions.

The human cost of military priority is paralleled by the depletion of industrial technology caused by the concentration of manpower and capital on military technology and in military industry. For example:

1. In 1996, over 60% of the machine tools used in US industry were 11 + years old.
2. Congestion of roads causes 5.7 billion hours of delay in the US. each year. This is equivalent to 650,684 years of time wasted.
3. U.S. railways have become antiquated. Now the electrification of 60,000 miles of track is required before the US can use the modern, fast and efficient trains that exist in other countries.

As civilian industrial technology deteriorates or fails to advance, productive employment opportunity for Americans diminishes.

All of this only begins to reckon the true cost to America of operating the state military machine. (The estimated cost of the Vietnam War, for example, from 1965 to 1973 to the United States population is reckoned at $676 billions. This estimate includes not only the direct military outlays but also the military assistance to client governments, interest on the national debt and payments for veterans, which will endure for a long time. The cost to the Vietnamese people has no reckoning.)

No mere ideology or desire for individual power can account for the colossal costs of the U.S. military. Rather, the state-management represents an institutionalized power-lust. A normal thirst for more managerial power within the largest management in the United States gives the new state-management an unprecedented ability and opportunity for building a military-industry empire at home and for using this as an instrument for building an empire abroad.

Even individual operations of the DoD are of a monumental scale. Discussing Bush's supplemental funding requests for the occupation and reconstruction of Iraq, Senator Robert C. Byrd stated, "At $87 billion, the President's request is larger than the economies of 166 countries. It's larger than the individual economies of almost half the states of the Union." The scale of these operations shows that the state-management has in fact become a para-state, a state within a state.

The magnitude of the decision-power of the Pentagon management has reached that of a nation-state. Modeled after the central administrative offices of multi-division industrial firms—such as the Ford Motor Company, the General Motors Corporation, and the General Electric Company—the new top management in the Department of Defense was designed to control the activities of subsidiary managements of firms producing, in 2003, $115 billion of goods purchased by the Department of Defense.

By the measure of industrial activity governed from one central office, this new management in the Department of Defense is beyond compare the largest industrial management the United States, perhaps in the world. Never before in American experience has there been such a combination of economic and political decision-power in the same hands. Recall that the senior officers of the new state-management are also senior political officers of the government of the United States. Thus, one consequence of the establishment of the new state-management has been the installation, within American society, of an institutional feature of a totalitarian system.

The new industrial management has been created in the name of defending America from its external enemies and preserving a way of life of a free society. It has long been understood, however, that one of the safeguards of individual liberty is the separation of roles of a citizen and of an employee. When an individual relates to the same person both as a citizen and as an employee, then the effect is such— regardless of intention—that the employer-government official has an unprecedented combination of decision-making power over the individual citizen-employee.

In his final address to the nation as President, Eisenhower gave his countrymen a grave message. "In the councils of government we must guard against the acquisition of unwarranted influence, whether sought or unsought, by the military-industrial complex. The potential for the disastrous rise of misplaced power exists and will persist." Here and in subsequent speeches, Eisenhower did not offer a precise definition of what he meant by military-industrial complex. Military-industrial complex meant a loose, informally defined collection of firms producing military products, senior military officers, and members of the executive and legislative branches of the federal government—all of them having a common ideology as to the importance of maintaining or enlarging the armed forces of the United States and their role in American politics.

The new industrial management in the federal government is, by contrast, clearly structured and formally organized, with all the paraphernalia of a formal, centrally managed organization, whose budget draws upon 10 percent of the Gross National Product of the richest nation in the world.

Managers in both civilian and state-capitalist firms seek to expand their decision power, but they do so in different ways. Managers in civilian firms try to *reduce their costs of production,* so they will have greater profits (capital) that can then be used for other projects. Managers in state-capitalist firms are under no pressure to minimize their costs, because· new funds are made available each year with Congress's allocation to the DoD. Additions to the flow of capital funds from the Pentagon are welcomed. One example is the pulley puller for the F-16 fighter—essentially a steel bar two inches in length with three screws tapped in. In 1984, this small item was sold to the DoD by General Dynamics for $8,832 each. If the same equipment were custom ordered in a private shop it would cost only $25.

The Pentagon record—before, during, and after Robert McNamara—includes other obvious cost excesses. Before McNamara, average prices on major weapons systems were 3.2 times their initial cost estimates. Under McNamara, the famous multipurpose F-111 airplane was costing $12.7 million per plane by December, 1969, as compared to a first cost estimate of $3.9 million—or 3.25 times the initial estimate. (A 2003 example of the multiplication of weapons system costs exists in the F-22 Raptor, an ultra-sophisticated fighter. The price of the F-22 has increased from initial estimates of $159 to $250 million per plane, an increase of 57 percent.) Such performance under the well-advertised regime of the state-management's "cost effectiveness" programs has been characteristic. *The pattern of cost excesses during the rule of "cost effectiveness" is explicable, not as aberrant behavior, but as a pattern that is normal to the state-management. The state-management's control system includes monitoring for so-called cost overruns as a regular function. Payment for the cost overruns by the Pentagon has been the functional equivalent of a grant of capital from a central office to a division of its firm.*

The American people and the Congress have long accepted decision-making by the state-management in the belief that it possesses critical expertise, not only in military matters but also in the management of industry and the economy. In its 1966 Report, the Joint Economic Committee of the Congress declared:

> Let no one, at home or abroad, doubt the ability of the United States to support, if need be, simultaneous programs of military defense of freedom and economic and social progress for our people, or (2) our capacity and preference to live and grow economically without the stimulus of government spending on defense or a competitive arms race.

In a memorable address at the University of Connecticut, Senator Fulbright stated the contradiction:

> There is a kind of madness in the facile assumption that we can raise the many billions of dollars necessary to rebuild our schools and cities and public transport and eliminate the pollution of air and water while also spending tens of billions to finance an open-ended war in Asia.

Now in 2003, programs for civilian benefit have been denied necessary funds to make way for the gargantuan expense of a program of wars, such as the wars and occupation in Afghanistan and Iraq. Senator Robert C. Byrd commented on this point when discussing the funding needed for children's education:

> I wonder how the Senators who object to the cost of my amendment will view the President's request to add $60 billion or $65 billion or $70 billion to the deficit to fund military and reconstruction activities in Iraq. I wonder if they will be comfortable voting to support a massive spending program for Iraq if they cannot bring themselves to support a comparatively meager increase in education funding for American schoolchildren.

The very openness of operations of the state machine is one of its great sources of strength. During Kennedy's term, no conspiracy was required to get the American people to accept the myth of the missile gap (that helped place Jack Kennedy into the White House), and the subsequent nuclear war overkill program, which was produced at great expense. The American people were sold on the myth and thought they were buying defense. This was agreed to by a Congress and a public that was taught to believe that all this activity is useful for defense and that it also stimulates the economy, allowing a society to enjoy both guns and butter. In all of this, the controlling factor is not a political party or a single political theory, not a personality, not a conspiracy: it is the existence and normal operation of the Pentagon's management-institution.

CHARACTERISTICS OF THE MILITARY ECONOMY

In the classic private business capitalist economy, the chiefs of large industrial and financial firms had substantial political influence. Under state capitalism top political and economic decision power is joined in the hands of government managers. These state-managers dominate the entire economy even though private business may still operate within it. Examples of civilian state capitalism can be found in various economies of Western Europe and in Japan. In the United States with its permanent war economy, military power is a chief component of the state management. Thus to a large degree, the U.S. can be understood as a *militarized* state capitalism.

In state capitalism, the top managers' control extends throughout the entire economy, even affecting privately owned and privately controlled enterprises. For example, this power can be used to guarantee a firm's access to capital, or to guarantee the market for a firm's products. In military state capitalism, the exercise of these powers becomes more prominent and is used in direct conflict with the civilian economy (see below).

State capitalist economy is largely regulated by a system of subsidies, which replace the self-correcting market mechanism of private business capitalism. This is true of the United States as well, despite the odes to "the free market" and "the invisible hand" sung by the president and his economic advisors.

Subsidy payments from government do appear under private capitalism—when government moves in to regulate parts of the economy. Subsidy systems flourish to their fullest under state capitalism, where the chiefs of the economy use their political decision power to enforce their economic priorities. In the case of military state capitalism the subsidy is rendered on behalf of economically parasitic activity, and yields no return to society.

A military economy has unique characteristics that affect its relationship with the surrounding economy and society. A set of key characteristics is summarized here, without pretending completeness, in order to portray the range of consequences from the system as a whole. These are in three parts: first, the parasitic quality of military economy; second, the expansionist propensity of the managers of military economy; and finally, major impact or *opportunity cost* on the civilian economy.

THE PARASITIC NATURE OF MILITARY ECONOMY

To appreciate the nature and effects of a permanent war economy, a functional differentiation is essential. Productive growth means goods and services that either are part of the level of living or can be used for further production of whatever kind. Hence, they are by these tests economically useful.[4] Parasitic growth includes goods and services that are not economically useful either for the level of living or for further production.

For most Americans, effects attributable to parasitic economic growth are not apparent. The generations of Americans who have been instructed by standard economics texts and courses are not equipped to see a part of the economy as parasitic. Instead, their appreciation of economy is dominated by theories about competitive market relations, the allocation of incomes, taxes, interest rates, and the role of government as a regulator of economy.

Ordinarily a civilian economy can look forward to making advances in its total productivity because of the gains that can be made in the efficiency of machinery, hence in productivity of *capital,* and thereby in the efficiency of labor. However; if new machinery, however efficient, is installed for producing military materiel, then what emerges is military materiel, which no factory can use for any further production. The result is that the normally available addition to production capability that stems from making and installing new production equipment is forgone for the whole society. That is also the reason why investment in military industry, while adding to the flow of money, does not successfully offset declining investment in new productive machinery.

In a permanent war economy whole industries and regions that specialize in military economy are placed in a parasitic economic relationship to the civilian economy, from which they take their sustenance and to which they contribute (economically) little or nothing. This results in the operation of a system of "internal imperialism" among the states of the Union.

The economic significance of parasitic economic growth is often rendered obscure by the apparently small magnitude of some of the spending involved. Money spent on military research and development (R&D) reflects economically parasitic activity, but R&D costs are rarely a major item of expense in manufacturing industry. U.S. manufacturing firms spend about 3.3 percent of their net sales dollars for R&D. But the significance of this activity cannot be measured by its proportionately small cost. Thus, when R&D is not properly done, results like poor product design or poor production methods can have disastrous effects on the economic position of an industry.

There is little or no ambiguity in understanding how large, continuing military budgets can generate military abundance at the side of civilian scarcities. These contrasts show up sharply in the accompanying display on Military Abundance and Civilian Scarcity. Like it or not, the reality of our physical universe does not permit energy or materials to occupy two places at once.

THE PROPENSITY TO EXPAND
A second basic feature of state capitalism is the relentless thrust for enlargement of decision power that is normal to managers. Under state capitalism this conventional managerial imperative is given unprecedented capability in terms of the resources that can be applied to these goals. By 1965 the state managers of the Pentagon actually advertised for advice on how to "maintain world hegemony."

The Army Research Office announced a public request for bids for a wide-ranging study on methods of achieving a Pax Americana. Here is the exact announcement as it appeared in the U.S. Department of Commerce Daily Bulletin asking for bids for government work:

Service and materials to perform a RESEARCH STUDY ENTITLED "PAX AMERICANA" consisting of a phased study of the following: (a) elements of National Power; (b) ability of selected nations to apply the elements of National Power; (c) a variety of world power configurations to be used as a basis for the U.S. to maintain world hegemony in the future. Quotations and applicable specifications will be available upon request at the Army Research Office, 3845 Columbia Pike, Arlington, Va., until 1 May 1965.

Table 6-1

How the Pentagon Robs the People

Cost of building housing for the 600,000 homeless families in the U.S.	= $59 billion =	Army Comanche Helicopter Program 48.1 BN and Navy Point Standoff Weapon Program $11.2 BN (SAR)
Investment needed to provide 20% of U.S. electricity supply from renewable and clean resources	= $80 billion =	Navy SSN 774 Virginia Class Submarine $71 BN and Navy Advanced Amphibious Assault Vehicle Program $8.7 BN (SAR)
Annual shortfall to meet federal safe drinking water standards and replace aging facilities	= $11 billion =	Total cost of the Navy's Future Surface Combatant Program (SAR)
Additional annual investment needed to improve the condition of U.S. roads and bridges	= $42 billion =	Navy Trident sub program $35 BN and Army Interim Assault Vehicle program $7 BN
Rehabilitation of all unsafe U.S. dams	= $2 billion =	Tactical Tomohawk Cruise Missile (SAR)
Electrification of 50 miles of mainline railroad	= $210 million =	One Global Hawk Unmanned Drone (PAC)
Annual cost to provide sanitary water to the 2.4 billion people worldwide	= $10 billion =	2 Navy CVN6-B Aircraft Carriers (SAR)
3,500 miles of Maglev (magnetic levitation) Train Lines, running at 266 miles per hour	= $99 billion =	F-22 Raptor Advanced Fighting Program ($228 million/plane) (SAR)
100 New Natural Gas school buses to replace high polluting diesel buses	= $12.7 million =	One Longbow Apache helicopter (PAC)
Annual cost to enroll 1100 children in Head Start pre school programs	= $7.9 million =	One "upgraded" Abrams Tank (SAR)
Five years of funding for a global tuberculosis control program	= $9.1 billion =	E-8C Joint Surveillance Target Attack radar system program (SAR)
Fix deteriorating U.S. school buildings	= $268 billion =	One third of the estimated cost of the Joint Strike Fighter program
Cost of salaries for an additional 561,000 nurses, an increase that will be necessary by 2010	= $20 billion =	DDG-51 Guided Missile Destroyer program (SAR)

SAR = DoD Selected Acquisition Report, PAC = DoD Program Acquisition Costs.

With a stated goal of such dimensions—"to maintain world hegemony"—we can understand why there has been a sustained growth of the budgets of the Department of Defense.

Franklin C. Spinney, a former staff analyst of the Department of Defense, has presented a number of important portraits of the military budgets of the United States presented before congressional committees. The fiscal year 2003 budget of the DoD, said Spinney, "would be higher than that averaged during the Cold War, when America faced the threat of a nuclear-tipped Soviet superpower instead of a criminal network of terrorists funded by a fanatical anti-American Saudi millionaire." He shows how patterns of mismatch between plans and reality have the effect of misrepresenting the future consequences of current decisions owing to a bias to underestimate future costs. This creates a constant pressure to implement new increases in budgets—even while the ink on current increases is still wet.

Addressing "Defense Power Games", Spinney indicated that, "a repetitive bias to grossly understate future costs is typical of programs in the early stages of their acquisition lifecycles." Thus, "the early plans predicted that the 400th F-18A [a navy fighter] would cost about $20 million, but it actually cost about $41 million." He called attention to a number of biases that reflect what he terms a "ubiquitous two step bureaucratic gaming strategy, known as Front Loading and Political Engineering." Spinney notes that, "these strategies are explained in detail in a report that can be downloaded from the internet." There is a regular pattern of behavior here, he points out. Part A is a mismatch between plans and reality. Part B really gets down to business—"Brutally stated, the aim of this gaming strategy is to turn on the money spigot and lock it open."

You don't have to be a specialist to go along with Spinney as he asks, "how much spending is enough?—accounting for the external threat." Any ambiguity that these questions might ordinarily pose is totally dispelled when you turn to Spinney's bar graph ("The 20 Power Standard"). It takes the 20 next largest national defense budgets put together to match the U.S. level of spending.

What is all this about? According to Spinney, the Congressional Budget Office has concluded that "policy changes to Social Security and Medicare (read changes to reduce expenditures per capita) would be needed, because under current policies . . . 'federal deficits are likely to reappear and eventually drive federal debt to unsustainable levels,' once the baby boomers start collecting social security and Medicare. If those programs are not changed, CBO concluded in January 2002, decision makers will face the prospect of approving steep tax increases, big cuts in other government spending, or large budget deficits."

Table 6-2

Military Spending by the United States Compared to Other Nations
(In Millions of Dollars)

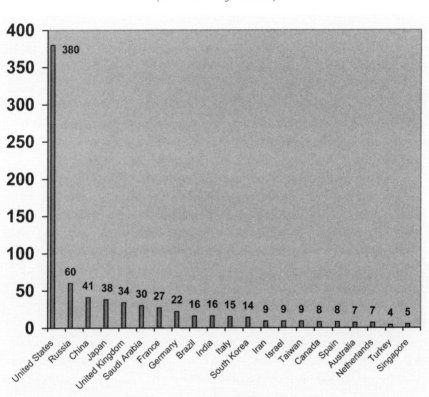

Countries

International Institute for Strategic Studies of Department of Defense, *The Military Economy and the Decline of the United States*, or *War Ltd.*, Seymour Melman. (2006)

The Pentagon has undercut funding for Social Security and other programs in a second manner. According to a G.A.O. report, "More than 27,000 military contractors, (1 in 9) are evading taxes and still continuing to win new business [from the Pentagon]. . . ." "The tax cheats owed an estimated $3 billion at the end of the 2002 fiscal year, mainly in Social Security and other payroll taxes that were diverted for business or personal use instead of being forwarded to the government, actions that could bring criminal prosecution." Senator Norm Coleman—the chairman of the Senate Permanent Subcommittee on Investigations—stated that, "The Pentagon needs to start targeting more firepower on the management side on fraud and abuse in the system, and go after the thousands of defense contractors that routinely renege on paying their taxes." The G.A.O. found that the DoD could have collected $100 million in 2002 from these tax evading firms, under the Taxpayer Relief Act of 1997. However, "in the six years since passage of the legislation to do such levying, the Defense Department has collected only about $687,000. . . ." The Pentagon managers—assured of unlimited funding for their own projects—have seen no reason to prevent military contractors from cheating both the nonmilitary branches of the federal government and U.S. taxpayers.

The non-partisan citizen's lobbying group *Common Cause* has provided us with a good sample of how Pentagon influence has superseded Congressional powers and obligations to regulate defense spending to restrain fraud by Pentagon contractors.

> "Congress in its final Iraq spending bill did not even include language offered by Senator Patrick Leahy (D-VT) to penalize war profiteers for defrauding American taxpayers. The Senate Appropriations Committee unanimously approved a provision to ensure that contractors who cheated the American taxpayer would face fines of up to $1 million and jail time of up to 20 years. Senators of both parties supported the provision, but Republican House negotiators refused to include the language in the final bill."

THE "OPPORTUNITY COST" OF MILITARISM

Franklin Spinney predicted, without ambiguity, the consequences of proposals to greatly increase the defense budget. Spinney said such moves are, "tantamount to a declaration of total war on Social Security and Medicare in the following decade." He has also reminded us that in all but a handful of states Department of Defense dollars account for by far the majority of Federal dollars spent in each state. If money talks then the Pentagon clearly has the loudest voice by far.

The operation of a permanent war economy entails large continuing costs for American society, measured in terms of what has been forgone in order to build and operate an immense military system. From 1946 to 2001 combined budgets of the Department of Defense were $17.9 trillion (in 2001 constant dollars). $17.9 trillion equals the value of every private building existing in the United States in 2001. In other words, the resources devoted to the DoD from the end of World War II until 2001 were large enough to duplicate all commercial and residential structures, (every skyscraper, factory and house) that was present in the U.S. in 2001. The decay in areas such as roads, bridges, schools, housing, energy production & transmission, public transportation, drinking water, and toxic waste cleanup represents items crucial for life that were passed up because the funds were spent on the military system instead.

When the investment in fresh educational competence, at whatever level, is subsequently applied to nonproductive economic activity, then once again the community loses the potential economic gain from human competence that ordinarily accrues to it when that capability is applied to productive work.

A second major form of impact of the military on the civilian economy is a process of industrial deterioration that generates uninvestable capital and unemployable labor. An unprecedented phenomenon has appeared in the United States: the formation of a large network of depleted industries and a flight of capital from the country. (Chapter Three will give details on "depleted" industries: those that have lost capability for serving all or part of their domestic markets and have been replaced by foreign producers because of a combination of technical, managerial and economic deterioration.)

Many theorists of capitalist economy, especially those in the Marxist tradition, have sought to explain recurring problems of capitalism as a result of the tendency of a business-based economy to generate surpluses of capital and surpluses of labor. Uninvestable capital and unemployable labor were certainly fundamental features of what happened in the United States during the Great Depression, 1929-39. The World War II economy soaked up surpluses of capital and of labor. But surplus capital in the U.S. is now long gone and surplus labor is now the product of deindustrialization.

THE NUCLEAR ARSENAL

By far the single most complicated and costly U.S. military program of the 20th century has been the drive for production and use of nuclear weapons. Everyone knows that modern weapons have capability for vast destruction. Nuclear weapons that are now in place could conceivably destroy all of mankind. In discussions of military affairs so much emphasis has been given to the destructiveness of nuclear weapons that the idea that military power can have limits has been characteristically bypassed. An understanding of what can be done with military power requires a parallel assessment of what cannot be done. This latter approach has not been encouraged by American military institutions or by the committees of Congress that formally oversee them.

For the purpose of appreciating America's War Economy, two central features of military power require identification here: first, the nature of guerilla warfare and second the scale, cost and consequences of nuclear weapons.

"During a long span of the cold war, from 1940 to 1996, U.S. military outlays totaled about $17 trillion, measured in dollars of 1996 purchasing power. Of this amount, $5.8 trillion was spent on nuclear weapons. This includes research, testing, production, delivery systems, command, control and early-warning networks, defense against nuclear attack, and the management and disposition of nuclear waste.

Over the course of fifty years, the government produced more than 70,000 nuclear explosives.

"There is surely this real limit to military power: a person or community can be destroyed only once. We need reminding that Hiroshima was ravaged on August 6, 1945, by a single nuclear explosive with a power of 15,000 tons of TNT. About 140,000 were killed by that single blast.

"Consider, as purely hypothetical nuclear targets, the combined present populations of Russia and China: 1,351,000,000 or the equivalent of 9,650 Hiroshimas of 1945. Using the Hiroshima yardstick, warheads with the combined power of 144.7 million tons of TNT (9,650 X 15,000 tons) would be required to destroy these two countries. (As the nuclear planners would remind us, selection of warhead sizes and dispersion would have to take into account that blast effect does not increase proportionately with size.) If we allow for an additional 30 percent to account for possible launch and warhead failures, 188.2 million tons of TNT would be needed.

"What is the size of the current nuclear arsenal? The United States now deploys warheads with the power of some 2.3 billion tons of TNT. Thus, the 188.2 million tons required to destroy both Russia and China is merely 8 percent of the power of the active U.S. nuclear arsenal. The remaining 92 percent represents a vast reservoir of excess killing power and military spending, or in the language of nuclear strategy, overkill."

Prior to the invention of nuclear explosives and their delivery systems, armed forces stockpiled bullets, shells and various forms of explosives which, on a one-to-one basis, could even exceed in number the military personnel and the populations of possible enemy countries. Nevertheless, there were no efficient means by which these bullets, shells, etc., could be brought to bear on an opposing force or an enemy population with sufficient concentration to destroy all or virtually all of them. It is this critical element of concentration in time and place that was contributed by nuclear weapons. The destruction of Dresden at the close of World War II military operations in Europe was performed by hundreds of planes dropping thousands of explosives over many hours. The destruction of Hiroshima and Nagasaki was done in each instance by one explosive carried by one plane, and was accomplished in a few seconds. This concentration of energy release now possible with nuclear explosives is well in excess of the amount required to destroy entire communities. This excess of destructive capability, new in human experience, required the invention of a new word, "overkill." That invention implied that strategic military technology had become absurd. Weapons have been developed in kind and quantity to exceed any plausible estimate of requirement for destruction of armed forces and populations. Nevertheless, for the top managers and officers of the U.S. military establishment, the

American nuclear weapons stockpile is not at all absurd. For the getting and practicing the use of these weapons has been the justification of their working lives.

Two nuclear explosives, by destroying Hiroshima and Nagasaki in August 1945, played a decisive role in compelling the surrender of Japan and ending the Second World War. Thereafter, until this writing in 2004, there was no further military use of nuclear weapons. Nevertheless, the U.S. government now retains about 10,650 nuclear warheads, and a great variety of associated technologies in the form of control and delivery systems.[5] These have ranged from nuclear warheads designed to be hand carried or Jeep delivered, onto warheads to be delivered by multi-billion dollar vehicles like aircraft carriers and submarines, and earth circling aircraft.

The cost of nuclear weapons invites a many-sided calculation: the budgets of the federal agencies that sponsor research, design and production of nuclear warheads; the development and fabrication of diverse delivery systems; the costs of educating, training and maintaining the labor force required for federal agencies that sponsor research, design and production of nuclear warheads; the development and fabrication of diverse delivery systems; and the costs of educating, training and maintaining the labor force required for competent performance of these diverse functions.

Despite the apparent extensiveness of this enumeration, it falls short of measuring the costs to the wider community that are owing to wide-ranging military-nuclear operations. These wider costs are made visible as "opportunity cost"—money valued assessments of what has been foregone for the wider community owing to using up vast resources for researching, designing, fabricating and operating the main parts of the nuclear military technologies and their manpower forces.[6]

The Bush Administration intends to further increase the nuclear overkill, as seen by the FY 2004 National Nuclear Security Administration nuclear weapons budget request of $6.38 *billion*. Now, the Bush Administration is claiming that we have a *penetration gap*. They say the U.S. ability to destroy subterranean facilities which we know or imagine contain or control Weapons of Mass Destruction is severely lacking. Supposedly new, usable Earth Penetrating Weapons are needed. These weapons penetrate the ground above the target before exploding. Current Earth Penetrating technology (the 80 kiloton *B61-11*) penetrates 10 ft into hard rock and the explosion will produce damage down to a maximum of 400 ft. The administration has expressed an interest in low-yield Earth Penetration Weapons because of their presumed ability to destroy deeply buried targets while reducing the damage done to the surrounding population from blast and fallout.

There is a contradiction however, between the two requirements of damaging hardened targets and minimal "collateral damage." "EPWs, sufficient to damage hardened buried targets at even moderate depths, cannot penetrate nearly deep enough to achieve substantial containment of the radioactive debris created by their detonation. This 'fallout' actually increases with the increasing depth, due to the greater volume of earth lifted by the blast."

HOW THE MILITARY ECONOMY WORKS: THE FIRM

A young engineer was employed by an aerospace firm and assigned the task of preparing cost and price estimates for new products on which the firm would submit bids to the Department of Defense. For this work he was expressly prohibited from having any access to or communication with the accounting department. Neither was he permitted to read any of the firm's own internal accounting reports. Hence, he had no information available on the details of previous costs of similar work. On the face of it this is preposterous. How do you go about preparing cost and price estimates without access to cost data? The management wanted no critical assessment of the components of total cost. A restriction of this kind would be unthinkable in any rational, cost-minimizing, business firm.

Our young engineer in this aerospace firm proceeded to prepare price estimates, using prices (not costs) of former products of his own firm, prices of aircraft products of other firms, and occasional information obtained informally from inside competing firms. This sort of job requirement proved to be unnerving to the engineer in question. He had been trained to apply techniques for engineering costing that required a critical assessment of every factor used in production. He resigned.

The industrial engineer develops the cost of each element by considering not only the actual experience of the enterprise in making a similar product, as recorded by the accounting department, but *possible alternative methods for each element of cost.* Ordinarily, then, the task of engineering costing is to tell the management what something *should cost,* using the best available methods. Obviously, in the performance of this function the actual costs previously incurred (historical costs) are only a starting point. For the industrial engineer is charged with seeking out the minimum possible cost, not with simply repeating previous practices.

From about 1961, under Robert McNamara, President Kennedy's Secretary of Defense, military-industry firms we're required to use historical price information as a basis for future price estimates without necessarily diagnosing and evaluating the separate costs that build up to the price. Engineering costing is essential if one is trying to minimize costs. Historical costing, based upon past prices for price bidding, contains a built-in escalator for increasing costs and prices.

When Robert McNamara was installed as Secretary of Defense in 1961, (he held the office until 1968) bilking of the public treasury by the military-industrial complex was supposed to change. Cadres of men trained in the techniques of statistical analysis and managerial control were recruited for top positions at the Pentagon for the purpose of designing and operating the largest industrial central office in the world. The new Pentagon chiefs formalized control methods that were appropriate to the task of regulating more than twenty thousand subfirms. They emphasized the introduction of analytical methods and standardized computer routines. In combination, these control techniques were supposed to yield "cost effectiveness" in the military-industrial system.

From a statistical point of view, behavior is "under control" when it varies within predictable and acceptable magnitudes. In the world of military economy, "under control" has meant control around a rising average trend where the rising costs are incorporated as an inherent part of the price process. By accepting the historical record as a given condition, the Pentagon management perpetuated rising costs without determining whether the rising cost "history" was necessary—or why there is rising cost at all, especially since many technological-improvement options have tended to reduce costs. Following a lengthy and heated dispute between the advocates of "engineering costing" and "historical costing", the latter method was formally designated as preferred procedure.

In October 1965 the Air Force Systems Command formalized these methods by publishing a manual entitled *Cost Estimating Procedures*. In the section headed "Estimating Methodology," the following instruction is given for cost estimating on new products: "The estimating methods are based on projections from historical data. Historical data are used to project future costs." The manual stipulated that the industrial-engineering approach to cost estimating was prohibited.

McNamara's preferred methods allowed the managements to incorporate whatever methods, including inefficiencies, had been part of making product A, B and C into the historical trend of costs and prices used for justifying yet further cost and price increases for product D.

For the military-industry enterprise, higher costs mean more activity, more facilities, more employees, more cash flow, and a larger cost based for calculating profits. For the military-industry top managers in the Pentagon, cost increases in the subfirms denote more activity under their control and are the basis for enlarged budget requests to the Congress. There is no built in limitation on the cost-maximization process. The limits are external: the political acceptability of Pentagon budgets to the Congress and to the population as a whole.

In response to the sort of political pressures brought to bear by Senator Proxmire and others, the Air Force, by February 13–15, 1973, sponsored meetings for its supplier firms on the idea of designing something with "Cost as a Design Parameter." An Air Force Systems Command Classified Symposium in Los Angeles described a session on this subject as follows:

"The near-geometric growth in costs of weapons systems over the past decade and more has prompted the Defense Department to initiate major steps to bring this problem under control.

The session will present speakers who will discuss the evolution of the design-to-price philosophy, its implementation, and its expected impact. Selected examples of design-to-price hardware developments for both the commercial and military marketplaces will be described to highlight the effect which constrained price has on the design approach. The problem of limiting total system cost (operation as well as acquisition) will also be discussed. The session will conclude with a panel discussion directed toward encouraging audience participation."

Until a major turnabout is visible in weapons prices, it is prudent to appreciate such sessions as serving to show Congressional critics an Air Force effort to restrain costs.[7]

Also, from a national economic vantage point, the McNamara-type methods and their results were entirely justified by the standards of the ideological consensus as contributing to the disbursement of government funds, thereby creating job opportunities. In these ways the cost- and subsidy-maximizing aims of industrial firms and the goals of the Pentagon managers for enlarging their decision power became mutually complementary and mutually supporting.

Indeed, Pentagon chiefs applied punitive measures against men whose offense was to try to introduce and practice well-known methods of cost-minimization in the military economy and who, as a last resort, spoke out publicly against the outrageous avarice of leading military-industry firms.

Principal names that come to mind are Ernest Fitzgerald (Air Force) and Gordon Rule (Navy). As senior civilian officials responsible for cost management, both were subjected to professional victimization for no other reason than their effort to restrain the cost maximization process in military industry. In Fitzgerald's case President Nixon announced that he had himself passed on the decision to fire him. Ernest Fitzgerald's professional autobiography, *The High Priests of Waste* (Norton, 1972) is a unique account of the experience of trying to apply ordinary industrial criteria of efficiency in military industry.

Administrative costs are part of the necessary expense for operating any enterprise. In order to have production there must be decision-making. Someone must do the acceptable problem solving, record-keeping and allied routines. In U.S. manufacturing industry as a whole by 1992; for every hundred production workers there were about fifty-seven administrative, technical and clerical employees. In many military serving manufacturing industries, the 1992 numbers of administrative and allied workers per 100 production workers (A/100 P) have been significantly higher.

Table 6-3

Administration to Production Ratios in Select Military Industries

INDUSTRY, 1992	A/100 P
Guided Missile and Spacecraft	218
Military Aircraft	162
Ordinance and Accessories (howitzers, mortars)	144
Ammunition (except for small arms)	73
Tanks and Tank Components	72
A/100 P ratio in all U.S. mfg.	57

Obviously, administrative overhead ratios that are as much as 3.8 times the average for manufacturing as a whole translate into heavy fixed costs in these enterprises. This is the result of more intensive managerial controls. Military-industry firms, for example, prepare more accounting reports in greater detail and with greater frequency than is usually acceptable in civilian firms. The records of American industry since the beginning of the twentieth century show steady growth in the cost of administration. However, the top managers of the military-industry empire speeded and intensified the ordinary processes by extending the scope and intensity of internal controls.

Giant-size administrative overheads in military industry seem to be an American specialty. The French designed and built the Mirage III with a total engineering staff of fifty design draftsmen. The Air Force's F-15 Program Office alone has had a staff of over 240, just to monitor the people doing the work.

"Who cares about the cost?" is one of the common themes among product developers inside military firms. If the product is more complex, it costs more and justifies a higher price; all this is called "gold-plating" in the trade. In one major enterprise the product-development staffs engaged in contests for designing the most complex, "Rube Goldberg" types of devices. Why bother putting brakes on such professional games as long as they can be labeled "research," charged to "cost growth" and billed to the Pentagon? Obviously, the military is penalized by receiving unreliable equipment—devices that are too complex, requiring hard-to-find skilled maintenance talent and prone to malfunction. But that is in the realm of unintended consequences.

Capital, both fixed and working capital, is made available to military-industry firms in ways that are unthinkable for the civilian industry enterprise. The Pentagon is empowered by law and its own regulations to supply not only buildings and equipment but also advance grants of funds, progress payments on work in process (but before delivery), and guarantees on loans that might be obtained by the military-industry firm from a private bank or similar institution. By these means the military-industry firm has access to quantities of capital under conditions that cannot be matched by a civilian-industry firm.

After 2000 the ambitions of the Pentagon rose to new heights. For example: a new aircraft design program was launched–the Joint Strike Fighter with a prospective outlay of $750 billion. The new plane would be used by all branches of the U.S. military and also by many other nations. By the start of the 21st century there had already been a half-century of experience with new Pentagon programs in the multi-billion class. These had become characteristic of U.S. military programs that have been launched without regard to what is foregone.

The quality of production management in military industry and the quality of its products are for the most part inaccessible to outsiders. However, the performance of the Lockheed Company, the largest military-industry firm, was partially opened to public view, especially with respect to its work on the important C-5 airplane. These aircraft, originally designed to carry heavy equipment or large numbers of soldiers over intercontinental ranges, were supposed to cost about $29 million per plane and have wound up at prices of $62 million per plane and more. We are informed that the C-5 had suffered a major technical breakdown once an hour during every hour of flight time. The unenviable pilot of the giant jet should anticipate, according to the General Accounting Office, that his landing gear alone will fail once every four hours. One of the planes already accepted by the Air Force and picked at random by the GAO auditors for inspection had 47 major and 149 minor deficiencies. Fourteen of the defects, the GAO reported to Congress, "impair the aircraft's capability to perform all or a portion of six missions" assigned to it.

The Lockheed saga includes the experience of Henry Durham, a former production manager at Marietta, Georgia, who tried to bring to the attention of Lockheed top management what he had discovered after being assigned as general manager for all production-control activities on the flight line. Durham has reported:

"When planes arrive at the flight line of the assembly line they're supposed to be virtually complete except for a few engineering changes and normal radar and electronic equipment installation, but I noticed these serious deficiencies. These weren't just minor deficiencies; these aircraft were missing thousands and thousands of parts when the Lockheed records showed the aircraft to be virtually complete.

"At first I thought it was an error in the papers. Then I initiated an audit. I found it was true. I was amazed. But I still thought there was some kind of mistake going on. Later I figured out what was happening was the company was consciously indicating through the inspection records that they had done the work so that they could receive credit payment from the Air Force when actually they weren't on schedule and hadn't done the work."

The recent fortunes of the Boeing Company illustrate core characteristics of how the military economy firm actually works. During 2002, Boeing had received $19.6

billion in government contracts. In support of such results the Boeing management spent $3.8 million for lobbying of various sorts and made campaign contributions to members of Congress amounting to $1.7 million.

The Boeing Company had been in internal transition toward ever-greater dependence on U.S. government contracts for its revenue. During recent years the Airbus Corporation of Western Europe had proven itself able to out-compete in designing and finally shipping commercial aircraft. Another part of Boeing's corporate redesign was its plan for greater dependence on design engineers located abroad. By 1993 the *Wall Street Journal* of March 17th reported that

> "As Boeing thins the ranks of its U.S. engineers, the aerospace giant is shifting professional design and engineering work abroad. A few years ago, Boeing hired, through a subcontractor, 300 Japanese engineers for its biggest airplane project, the 777. Then last year, Boeing said it planned to hire hundreds of engineers in Taiwan and Russia."

Evidently, the Boeing management's lobbying, campaign contributions and desperate efforts to obtain proprietary information from competitors—was insufficient to offset the Airbus firm's competing design and production capability. Therefore, at this writing, there is doubt whether Boeing's strategic plan for selling and leasing $100 billion worth of refueling tankers to the Air Force would actually go through. Senator John McCain, an Arizona Republican, pulled no punches in his assessment of Boeing management, saying, "this has already been revealed to be a corrupt if not terribly flawed program. . . ." Neither was Boeing Management's position improved by the report that "among those who promoted the tanker deal were Richard N. Perle, a top Pentagon advisor who is a member of the Defense Policy Board. Mr. Perle also runs an investment firm in which Boeing invested $20 million last year, and on August 14th he co-wrote an op-ed article titled "Gas Stations in the Sky" in the *Wall Street Journal* in which the Air Force would have leased all 100 tanker aircraft from Boeing."

Evidently, the Boeing Corporation has focused on aggressive methods for financial accumulation rather than solving the problems of running a stable production system.

At Columbia University from 1961 to 1990 there was a yearly seminar on problems of conversion of industry from military to civilian economy. We sought out managers, engineers and others from military industry to tell us about various efforts by their firms to enter civilian fields. The typical story was failure, traceable to one or another style of operating that was just fine in the military economy but economically lethal in the civilian arena.

The military-industrial firm is controlled by the central administrative office in the Pentagon. Considerable detail on this institution is available in *Pentagon Capitalism*. Anyone interested in industrial organization will find the details on *The Armed Services Procurement Regulations* fascinating reading. These are not, as the name seems to imply, a set of purchasing regulations. Rather, they are rules formulated by Pentagon management for the guidance of the central-office staff itself and the guidance of Pentagon-serving firms.

The extent of the Pentagon's control apparatus is indicated by the fact that in one important military-industry firm a staff of 210 Pentagon employees is in permanent residence, in addition to a group of ten military officers representing the armed-service branch primarily served by the firm in question.

The concept of the subsidy-maximizing policy of the state management was set forth early on in a dramatic exchange between Senator William A. Proxmire and Secretary of the Treasury John B. Connally on June 8, 1971, as the Senate Banking Committee was considering the special legislation to guarantee a $250-million loan to the Lockheed Corporation.

> Senator Proxmire: . . . I would remind you in a subsidy program it is different, there is a quid pro quo. You make a payment to a railroad and in return they build trackage; you make a payment to an airline and they provide a certain amount of service for it. In welfare, of course, you make a payment and there is no return. In this case we have a guarantee and there is no requirement on the part of Lockheed to perform under that guarantee. A guarantee of $250 million and no benefit, no quid pro quo.
>
> Secretary Connally: What do you mean, no benefit?
>
> Senator Proxmire: Well, they don't have to perform.
>
> Secretary Connally: What do we care whether they perform? We are guaranteeing them basically a $250 million loan. What for? Basically so they can hopefully minimize their losses, so they can provide employment for 31,000 people throughout the country at a time when we desperately need that type of employment. That is basically the rationale and justification.

Without formal announcement, including American experience during a half-century of cold war and hot wars in Korea and Vietnam, the government of the United States was revised into a form not anticipated by any act of Congress or textbook on American government. Corporate managers were mobilized to operate a continuing war economy while accumulating resources without equal in other parts of the government. The drive for profit was matched by a drive for power over whole populations. Thereby, much of the American economy was transformed, without debate or formal announcement, into a species of state-capitalism, with the establishment of a war economy as its primary component.

Notes

1. Veterans of Pentagon administration confirm major points made by Secretary Rumsfeld in his Sept. 10, 2001 address on Pentagon accounting, including understanding that money paid out by the Pentagon is good for the economy.

2. US Department of Commerce, *Survey of Current Business*, September 2002.

3. NSC-68, "A Report to the National Security Council by the Executive Secretary on the United States Objectives and Programs for National Security, April 14, 1950," *Naval War College Review*, May-June 1975; Paul A. Baran, "The Political Economy of Growth," *Monthly Review Press*, 1957, 41.

4. There are, of course, other kinds of usefulness: political, esthetic, military, religious. Here we are interested primarily in economic usefulness. Thus the absence of economic usefulness does not preclude other effects.

5. Natural Resources Defense Council.

6. In my book, *After Capitalism*, I offered an estimate of the many-sided opportunity cost of U.S. nuclear weaponry. See Chapter 5.

7. Readers with an interest in the general theory of the coast- and subsidy-maximizing firm should examine N. Finger, *The impact of Subsidy system on Industrial Management* (Praeger, 1971), chapter 5. For evidence of the pervasiveness of the cost-maximizing process, see U.S. General Accounting Office, *Cost Growth in Major Weapons Systems, Report to the House Committee on Armed Services*, March 26, 1973.

7

Schenck v. United States

Justice Oliver Wendell Holmes Jr. (Opinion)

Schenck v. United States, (1919) 249 U.S. 47

Nos. 437, 438

Argued January 9, 10, 1919

Decided March 3, 1919

ERROR TO THE DISTRICT COURT OF THE UNITED STATES
FOR THE EASTERN DISTRICT OF PENNSYLVANIA

SYLLABUS

Evidence *held* sufficient to connect the defendants with the mailing of printed circulars in pursuance of a conspiracy to obstruct the recruiting and enlistment service, contrary to the Espionage Act of June 15, 1917.

Incriminating document seized under a search warrant directed against a Socialist headquarters, *held* admissible in evidence, consistently with the Fourth and Fifth Amendment, in a criminal prosecution against the general secretary of a Socialist party, who had charge of the office.

Words which, ordinarily and in many places, would be within the freedom of speech protected by the First Amendment may become subject to prohibition when of such a nature and used in such circumstances a to create a clear and present danger that they will bring about the substantive evils which Congress has a right to prevent. The character of every act depends upon the circumstances in which it is done.

A conspiracy to circulate among men called and accepted for military service under the Selective Service Act of May 18, 1917, a circular tending to influence them to obstruct the draft, with the intent to effect that result, and followed by the sending of such circulars, is within the power of Congress to punish, and is punishable under the Espionage Act, § 4, although unsuccessful.

The word "recruiting," as used in the Espionage Act, § 3, means the gaining of fresh supplies of men for the military forces, as well by draft a otherwise.

The amendment of the Espionage Act by the Act of May 16, 1918, c. 75, 40 Stat. 553, did not affect the prosecution of offenses under the former.

AFFIRMED

The case is stated in the opinion.

MR. JUSTICE HOLMES delivered the opinion of the court.

This is an indictment in three counts. The first charges a conspiracy to violate the Espionage Act of June 15, 1917, c. 30, § 3, 40 Stat. 217, 219, by causing and attempting to cause insubordination, &c., in the military and naval forces of the United States, and to obstruct the recruiting and enlistment service of the United States, when the United States was at war with the German Empire, to-wit, that the defendants willfully conspired to have printed and circulated to men who had been called and accepted for military service under the Act of May 18, 1917, a document set forth and alleged to be calculated to cause such insubordination and obstruction. The count alleges overt acts in pursuance of the conspiracy, ending in the distribution of the document set forth. The second count alleges a conspiracy to commit an offence against the United States, to-wit, to use the mails for the transmission of matter declared to be nonmailable by Title XII, § 2 of the Act of June 15, 1917, to-wit, the above mentioned document, with an averment of the same overt acts. The third count charges an unlawful use of the mails for the transmission of the same matter and otherwise as above. The defendants were found guilty on all the counts. They set up the First Amendment to the Constitution forbidding Congress to make any law abridging the freedom of speech, or of the press, and bringing the case here on that ground have argued some other points also of which we must dispose.

It is argued that the evidence, if admissible, was not sufficient to prove that the defendant Schenck was concerned in sending the documents. According to the testimony, Schenck said he was general secretary of the Socialist party, and had charge of the Socialist headquarters from which the documents were sent. He identified a book found there as the minutes of the Executive Committee of the party. The book showed a resolution of August 13, 1917, that 15,000 leaflets should be printed on the other side of one of them in use, to be mailed to men who had passed exemption boards, and for distribution. Schenck personally attended to the printing. On August 20, the general secretary's report said "Obtained new leaflets from printer and started work addressing envelopes" &c., and there was a resolve that Comrade Schenck be allowed $125 for sending leaflets through the mail. He said that he had about fifteen or sixteen thousand printed. There were files of the circular in question in the inner office which he said were printed on the other side of the one sided circular, and were there for distribution. Other copies were proved to have been sent through the mails to drafted men. Without going into confirmatory details that were proved, no reasonable man could doubt that the defendant Schenck was largely instrumental in sending the circulars about. As to the defendant Baer, there was evidence that she was a member of the Executive Board, and that the minutes of its transactions were hers. The argument as to the sufficiency of the evidence that the defendants conspired to send the documents only impairs the seriousness of the real defence.

It is objected that the documentary evidence was not admissible because obtained upon a search warrant, valid so far as appears. The contrary is established. *Adams v. New York,* 192 U.S. 585; *Weeks v. United States,* 232 U.S. 383, 232 U.S. 395, 232 U.S. 396. The search warrant did not issue against the defendant, but against the Socialist headquarters at 1326 Arch Street, and it would seem that the documents technically were not even in the defendants' possession. *See Johnson v. United States,* 228 U.S. 457. Notwithstanding some protest in argument, the notion that evidence even directly proceeding from the defendant in a criminal proceeding is excluded in all cases by the Fifth Amendment is plainly unsound. *Holt v. United States,* 218 U.S. 245, 218 U.S. 252, 218 U.S. 253.

The document in question, upon its first printed side, recited the first section of the Thirteenth Amendment, said that the idea embodied in it was violated by the Conscription Act, and that a conscript is little better than a convict. In impassioned language, it intimated that conscription was despotism in its worst form, and a monstrous wrong against humanity in the interest of Wall Street's chosen few. It said, "Do not submit to intimidation," but in form, at least, confined itself to peaceful measures such as a petition for the repeal of the act. The other and later printed side of the sheet was headed "Assert Your Rights." It stated reasons for alleging that anyone violated the Constitution when he refused to recognize "your right to assert your opposition to the draft," and went on, "If you do not assert and support your rights, you are helping to deny or disparage rights which it is the solemn duty of all citizens and residents of the United States to retain." It described the arguments on the other side as coming from cunning politicians and a mercenary capitalist press, and even silent consent to the conscription law as helping to support an infamous conspiracy. It denied the power to send our citizens away to foreign shores to shoot up the people of other lands, and added that words could not express the condemnation such cold-blooded ruthlessness deserves, etc., etc., winding up, "You must do your share to maintain, support and uphold the rights of the people of this country." Of course, the document would not have been sent unless it had been intended to have some effect, and we do not see what effect it could be expected to have upon persons subject to the draft except to influence them to obstruct the carrying of it out. The defendants do not deny that the jury might find against them on this point.

But it is said, suppose that that was the tendency of this circular, it is protected by the First Amendment to the Constitution. Two of the strongest expressions are said to be quoted respectively from well-known public men. It well may be that the prohibition of laws abridging the freedom of speech is not confined to previous restraints, although to prevent them may have been the main purpose, as intimated in *Patterson v. Colorado,* 205 U.S. 454, 205 U.S. 462. We admit that, in many places and in ordinary times, the defendants, in saying all that was said in the circular, would have been within their constitutional rights. But the character of every act depends upon the circumstances in which it is done. *Aikens v. Wisconsin,* 195 U.S. 194, 195 U.S. 205, 195 U.S. 206. The most stringent protection of free speech would not protect a man in falsely shouting fire in a theatre and causing a panic. It does not even protect a man from an injunction against uttering words that may have all the effect of force. *Gompers v. Bucks Stove & Range Co.,* 221 U.S. 418, 221 U.S. 439. The question in every case is whether the words used are used in such circumstances and are of such a nature as to create a clear and present danger that they will bring about the substantive evils that Congress has a right to prevent. It is a question of proximity and degree. When a nation is at war, many things that might be said in time of peace are such a hindrance to its effort that their utterance will not be endured so long as men fight, and that no Court could regard them as protected by any constitutional right. It seems to be admitted that, if an actual obstruction of the recruiting service were proved, liability for words that produced that effect might be enforced. The statute of 1917, in § 4, punishes conspiracies to obstruct, as well as actual obstruction. If the act (speaking, or circulating a paper), its tendency, and the intent with which it is done are the same, we perceive no ground for saying that success alone warrants making the act a crime. *Goldman v. United States,* 245 U.S. 474, 245 U.S. 477. Indeed, that case might be said to dispose of the present contention if the precedent covers all *media concludendi.* But, as the right to free speech was not referred to specially, we have thought fit to add a few words.

It was not argued that a conspiracy to obstruct the draft was not within the words of the Act of 1917. The words are "obstruct the recruiting or enlistment service," and it might be suggested that they refer only to making it hard to get volunteers. Recruiting heretofore usually having been accomplished by getting volunteers, the word is apt to call up that method only in our minds. But recruiting is gaining fresh supplies for the forces, as well by draft as otherwise. It is put as an alternative to enlistment or voluntary enrollment in this act. The fact that the Act of 1917 was enlarged by the amending Act of May 16, 1918, c. 75, 40 Stat. 553, of course, does not affect the present indictment, and would not even if the former act had been repealed. Rev. Stats., § 13.

8

Detention, Treatment, and Trial of Certain Non-Citizens in the War Against Terrorism

Executive Order of the President of the United States

MILITARY ORDER OF NOVEMBER 13, 2001

By the authority vested in me as President and as Commander in Chief of the Armed Forces of the United States by the Constitution and the laws of the United States of America, including the Authorization for Use of Military Force Joint Resolution (Public Law 107-40, 115 Stat. 224) and sections 821 and 836 of title 10, United States Code, it is hereby ordered as follows:

Section 1. Findings.

(a) International terrorists, including members of al Qaida, have carried out attacks on United States diplomatic and military personnel and facilities abroad and on citizens and property within the United States on a scale that has created a state of armed conflict that requires the use of the United States Armed Forces.

(b) In light of grave acts of terrorism and threats of terrorism, including the terrorist attacks on September 11, 2001, on the headquarters of the United States Department of Defense in the national capital region, on the World Trade Center in New York, and on civilian aircraft such as in Pennsylvania, I proclaimed a national emergency on September 14, 2001 (Proc. 7463, Declaration of National Emergency by Reason of Certain Terrorist Attacks).

(c) Individuals acting alone and in concert involved in international terrorism possess both the capability and the intention to undertake further terrorist attacks against the United States that, if not detected and prevented, will cause mass deaths, mass injuries, and massive destruction of property, and may place at risk the continuity of the operations of the United States Government.

(d) The ability of the United States to protect the United States and its citizens, and to help its allies and other cooperating nations protect their nations and their

citizens, from such further terrorist attacks depends in significant part upon using the United States Armed Forces to identify terrorists and those who support
them, to disrupt their activities, and to eliminate their ability to conduct or support such attacks.

(e) To protect the United States and its citizens, and for the effective conduct of military operations and prevention of terrorist attacks, it is necessary for individuals
subject to this order pursuant to section 2 hereof to be detained, and, when tried,
to be tried for violations of the laws of war and other applicable laws by military
tribunals.

(f) Given the danger to the safety of the United States and the nature of international
terrorism, and to the extent provided by and under this order, I find consistent
with section 836 of title 10, United States Code, that it is not practicable to apply
in military commissions under this order the principles of law and the rules of
evidence generally recognized in the trial of criminal cases in the United States
district courts.

(g) Having fully considered the magnitude of the potential deaths, injuries, and
property destruction that would result from potential acts of terrorism against the
United States, and the probability that such acts will occur, I have determined
that an extraordinary emergency exists for national defense purposes, that this
emergency constitutes an urgent and compelling government interest, and that
issuance of this order is necessary to meet the emergency.

Sec. 2. Definition and Policy.

(a) The term "individual subject to this order" shall mean any individual who is not
a United States citizen with respect to whom I determine from time to time in
writing that:

(1) there is reason to believe that such individual, at the relevant times,

(i) is or was a member of the organization known as al Qaida;

(ii) has engaged in, aided or abetted, or conspired to commit, acts of international terrorism, or acts in preparation therefor, that have caused,
threaten to cause, or have as their aim to cause, injury to or adverse effects on the United States, its citizens, national security, foreign policy,
or economy; or

(iii) has knowingly harbored one or more individuals described in subpara-
graphs (i) or (ii) of subsection 2(a)(1) of this order; and

(2) it is in the interest of the United States that such individual be subject to
this order.

(b) It is the policy of the United States that the Secretary of Defense shall take all
necessary measures to ensure that any individual subject to this order is detained

in accordance with section 3, and, if the individual is to be tried, that such individual is tried only in accordance with section 4.

(c) It is further the policy of the United States that any individual subject to this order who is not already under the control of the Secretary of Defense but who is under the control of any other officer or agent of the United States or any State shall, upon delivery of a copy of such written determination to such officer or agent, forthwith be placed under the control of the Secretary of Defense.

Sec. 3. Detention Authority of the Secretary of Defense.

Any individual subject to this order shall be—

(a) detained at an appropriate location designated by the Secretary of Defense outside or within the United States;

(b) treated humanely, without any adverse distinction based on race, color, religion, gender, birth, wealth, or any similar criteria;

(c) afforded adequate food, drinking water, shelter, clothing, and medical treatment;

(d) allowed the free exercise of religion consistent with the requirements of such detention; and

(e) detained in accordance with such other conditions as the Secretary of Defense may prescribe.

Sec. 4. Authority of the Secretary of Defense Regarding Trials of Individuals Subject to This Order.

(a) Any individual subject to this order shall, when tried, be tried by military commission for any and all offenses triable by military commission that such individual is alleged to have committed, and may be punished in accordance with the penalties provided under applicable law, including life imprisonment or death.

(b) As a military function and in light of the findings in section 1, including subsection (f) thereof, the Secretary of Defense shall issue such orders and regulations, including orders for the appointment of one or more military commissions, as may be necessary to carry out subsection (a) of this section.

(c) Orders and regulations issued under subsection (b) of this section shall include, but not be limited to, rules for the conduct of the proceedings of military commissions, including pretrial, trial, and post-trial procedures, modes of proof, issuance of process, and qualifications of attorneys, which shall at a minimum provide for—

(1) military commissions to sit at any time and any place, consistent with such guidance regarding time and place as the Secretary of Defense may provide;

(2) a full and fair trial, with the military commission sitting as the triers of both fact and law;

(3) admission of such evidence as would, in the opinion of the presiding officer of the military commission (or instead, if any other member of the commission so requests at the time the presiding officer renders that opinion, the opinion of the commission rendered at that time by a majority of the commission), have probative value to a reasonable person;

(4) in a manner consistent with the protection of information classified or classifiable under Executive Order 12958 of April 17, 1995, as amended, or any successor Executive Order, protected by statute or rule from unauthorized disclosure, or otherwise protected by law, (A) the handling of, admission into evidence of, and access to materials and information, and (B) the conduct, closure of, and access to proceedings;

(5) conduct of the prosecution by one or more attorneys designated by the Secretary of Defense and conduct of the defense by attorneys for the individual subject to this order;

(6) conviction only upon the concurrence of two-thirds of the members of the commission present at the time of the vote, a majority being present;

(7) sentencing only upon the concurrence of two-thirds of the members of the commission present at the time of the vote, a majority being present; and

(8) submission of the record of the trial, including any conviction or sentence, for review and final decision by me or by the Secretary of Defense if so designated by me for that purpose.

Sec. 5. Obligation of Other Agencies to Assist the Secretary of Defense.

Departments, agencies, entities, and officers of the United States shall, to the maximum extent permitted by law, provide to the Secretary of Defense such assistance as he may request to implement this order.

Sec. 6. Additional Authorities of the Secretary of Defense.

(a) As a military function and in light of the findings in section 1, the Secretary of Defense shall issue such orders and regulations as may be necessary to carry out any of the provisions of this order.

(b) The Secretary of Defense may perform any of his functions or duties, and may exercise any of the powers provided to him under this order (other than under section 4(c)(8) hereof) in accordance with section 113(d) of title 10, United States Code.

Sec. 7. Relationship to Other Law and Forums.

(a) Nothing in this order shall be construed to—

(1) authorize the disclosure of state secrets to any person not otherwise authorized to have access to them;

(2) limit the authority of the President as Commander in Chief of the Armed Forces or the power of the President to grant reprieves and pardons; or

(3) limit the lawful authority of the Secretary of Defense, any military commander, or any other officer or agent of the United States or of any State to detain or try any person who is not an individual subject to this order.

(b) With respect to any individual subject to this order—

(1) military tribunals shall have exclusive jurisdiction with respect to offenses by the individual; and

(2) the individual shall not be privileged to seek any remedy or maintain any proceeding, directly or indirectly, or to have any such remedy or proceeding sought on the individual's behalf, in (i) any court of the United States, or any State thereof, (ii) any court of any foreign nation, or (iii) any international tribunal.

(c) This order is not intended to and does not create any right, benefit, or privilege, substantive or procedural, enforceable at law or equity by any party, against the United States, its departments, agencies, or other entities, its officers or employees, or any other person.

(d) For purposes of this order, the term "State" includes any State, district, territory, or possession of the United States.

(e) I reserve the authority to direct the Secretary of Defense, at any time hereafter, to transfer to a governmental authority control of any individual subject to this order. Nothing in this order shall be construed to limit the authority of any such governmental authority to prosecute any individual for whom control is transferred.

Sec. 8. Publication.

This order shall be published in the Federal Register.

GEORGE W. BUSH
THE WHITE HOUSE,
November 13, 2001

9

The Propaganda of History

W. E. B. Du Bois

How the facts of American history have in the last half century been falsified because the nation was ashamed. The South was ashamed because it fought to perpetuate human slavery. The North was ashamed because it had to call in the black men to save the Union, abolish slavery and establish democracy.

What are American children taught today about Reconstruction? Helen Boardman has made a study of current textbooks and notes these three dominant theses:

1. All Negroes were ignorant.
"All were ignorant of public business." (Woodburn and Moran, "Elementary American History and Government," p. 397.)

"Although the Negroes were now free, they were also ignorant and unfit to govern themselves." (Everett Barnes, "American History for Grammar Grades," p. 334.)

"The Negroes got control of these states. They had been slaves all their lives, and were so ignorant they did not even know the letters of the alphabet. Yet they now sat in the state legislatures and made the laws." (D. H. Montgomery, "The Leading Facts of American History," p. 332.)

"In the South, the Negroes who had so suddenly gained their freedom did not know what to do with it." (Hubert Cornish and Thomas Hughes, "History of the United States for Schools," p. 345.)

"In the legislatures, the Negroes were so ignorant that they could only watch their white leaders—carpetbaggers, and vote aye or no as they were told. (S. E. Forman, "Advanced American History," Revised Edition, p. 452.)

"Some legislatures were made up of a few dishonest white men and several Negroes, many too ignorant to know anything about law-making." (Hubert Cornish and Thomas Hughes, "History of the United States for Schools," p.349.)

175

2. All Negroes were lazy, dishonest and extravagant.

"These men knew not only nothing about the government, but also cared for nothing except what they could gain for themselves." (Helen F. Giles, "How the United States Became a World Power," p. 7.)

"Legislatures were often at the mercy of Negroes, childishly ignorant, who sold their votes openly, and whose 'loyalty' was gained by allowing them to eat, drink and clothe themselves at the state's expense." (William J Long, "America—A History of Our Country," p. 392.)

"Some Negroes spent their money foolishly, and were worse off than they had been before." (Carl Russell Fish, "History of America," p. 385.)

"This assistance led many freed men to believe that they need no longer work. They also ignorantly believed that the lands of their former masters were to be turned over by Congress to them, and that every Negro was to have as his allotment 'forty acres and a mule." (W. F. Gordy, "History of the United States," Part II, p. 336.)

"Thinking that slavery meant toil and that freedom meant only idleness the slave after he was set free was disposed to try out his freedom by refusing to work." (S. E. Forman, "Advanced American History," Revised Edition.)

"They began to wander about, stealing and plundering. In one week, in a Georgia town, 150 Negroes were arrested for thieving." (Helen F. Giles, How the United States Became a World Power," p. 6.)

3. Negroes were responsible for bad government during Reconstruction.

"Foolish laws were passed by the black law-makers, the public money was wasted terribly and thousands of dollars were stolen straight. Self-respecting Southerners chafed under the horrible regime." (Emerson David Fite, "These United States," p. 37.)

"In the exhausted states already amply 'punished' by the desolation of war the rule of the Negro and his unscrupulous carpetbagger and scalawag patrons, was an orgy of extravagance, fraud and disgusting incompetency." (David Saville Muzzey, "History of the American People," p. 408.)

"The picture of Reconstruction which the average pupil in these sixteen States receives is limited to the South. The South found it necessary to pass Black-Codes for the control of the shiftless and sometimes vicious freedmen. The Freedmen's Bureau caused the Negroes to look to the North rather than to the South for support and by giving them a false sense of equality did more harm than good. With the scalawags, the ignorant and non-propertyholding Negroes under the leadership of the carpetbaggers, engaged in a wild orgy of spending in the legislatures. The humiliation and distress of the Southern whites was in part relieved by the Ku Klux Klan, a secret organization which frightened the superstitious blacks."[1]

Grounded in such elementary and high school teaching, an American youth attending college today would learn from current textbooks of history that the Constitution recognized slavery; that the chance of getting rid of slavery by peaceful methods was ruined by the Abolitionists; that after the period of Andrew Jackson, the two sections of the United States "had become fully conscious of their conflicting interests. Two irreconcilable forms of civilization . . . in the North, the democratic . . . in the South, a more stationary and aristocratic civilization." He would read that Harriet Beecher Stowe brought on the Civil War; that the assault on Charles Sumner was due to his "coarse invective" against a South Carolina Senator; and that Negroes were the only people to achieve emancipation with no effort on their part. That Reconstruction was a disgraceful attempt to subject white people to ignorant Negro rule; and that, according to a Harvard professor of history (the italics are ours), "Legislative expenses were grotesquely extravagant; the *colored members in some states engaging* in *a saturnalia of corrupt expenditure.*" (*Encyclopaedia Britannica*, 14th Edition, Volume 22, p. 815, by Frederick Jackson Turner.)

In other words, he would in all probability complete his education without any idea of the part which the black race has played in America; of the tremendous moral problem of abolition; of the cause and meaning of the Civil War and the relation which Reconstruction had to democratic government and the labor movement today.

Herein lies more than mere omission and difference of emphasis. The treatment of the period of Reconstruction reflects small credit upon American historians as scientists. We have too often a deliberate attempt so to change the facts of history that the story will make pleasant reading for Americans. The editors of the fourteenth edition of the *Encyclopaedia Britannica* asked me for an article on the history of the American Negro. From my manuscript they cut out all my references to Reconstruction. I insisted on including the following statement:

"White historians have ascribed the faults and failures of Reconstruction to Negro ignorance and corruption. But the Negro insists that it was Negro loyalty and the Negro vote alone that restored the South to the Union; established the new democracy, both for white and black, and instituted the public schools."

This the editor refused to print, although he said that the article otherwise was "in my judgment, and in the judgment of others in the office, an excellent one, and one with which it seems to me we may all be well satisfied." I was not satisfied and refused to allow the article to appear.

War and especially civil strife leave terrible wounds. It is the duty of humanity to heal them. It was therefore soon conceived as neither wise not patriotic to speak of all the causes of strife and the terrible results to which sectional differences in the United States had led. And so, first of all, we minimized the slavery controversy which convulsed the nation from the Missouri Compromise down to the Civil War. On top of that, we passed by Reconstruction with a phrase of regret or disgust.

But are these reasons of courtesy and philanthropy sufficient for denying Truth? If history is going to be scientific, if the record of human action is going to be set down with that accuracy and faithfulness of detail which will allow its use as a measuring rod and guidepost for the future of nations, there must be set some standards of ethics research and interpretation.

If, on the other hand, we are going to use history for our pleasure and amusement, for inflating our national ego, and giving us a false but pleasurable sense of accomplishment, then we must give lip the idea of history either as a science or as an art using the results of science, and admit frankly that we are using a version of historic fact in order to influence and educate the new generation along the way we wish.

It is propaganda like this that has led men in the past to insist that history is "lies agreed upon"; and to point out the danger in such misinformation. It is indeed extremely doubtful if any permanent benefit comes to the world through such action. Nations reel and stagger on their way; they make hideous mistakes; they commit frightful wrongs; they do great and beautiful things. And shall we not best guide humanity by telling the truth about all this so far as the truth is ascertainable?

Here in the United States we have a clear example. It was morally wrong and economically retrogressive to build human slavery in the United States in the eighteenth century. We know that now, perfectly well; and there were many Americans, North and South, who knew this and said it in the eighteenth century. Today, in the face of new slavery established elsewhere in the world under other names and guises, we ought to emphasize this lesson of the past. Moreover, it is not well to be reticent in describing that past. Our histories tend to discuss American slavery so impartially, that in the end nobody seems to have done wrong and everybody was right. Slavery appears to have been thrust upon unwilling helpless America, while the South was blameless in becoming its center. The difference of development, North and South, is explained as a sort of working out of cosmic social and economic law. . . .

Yet in this sweeping mechanistic interpretation, there is no room for the real plot of the story, for the clear mistake and guilt of rebuilding a new slavery of the working class in the midst of a fateful experiment in democracy; for the triumph of sheer moral courage and sacrifice in the abolition crusade; and for the hurt and struggle of degraded black millions in their fight for freedom and their attempt to enter democracy. Can all this be omitted or half suppressed in a treatise that calls itself scientific?

Or, to come nearer the center and climax of this fascinating history: What was slavery in the United States? Just what did it mean to the owner and the owned? Shall we accept the conventional story of the old slave plantation and its owner's fine, aristocratic life of cultured leisure? Or shall we note slave biographies, like those of Charles Ball, Sojourner Truth, Harriet Tubman and Frederick Douglass; the careful observations of Olmsted and the indictment of Hinton Helper?

No one can read that first thin autobiography of Frederick Douglass and have left many illusions about slavery. And if truth is our object, no amount of flowery romance and the personal reminiscences of its protected beneficiaries can keep the world from knowing that slavery was a cruel, dirty, costly and inexcusable anachronism, which nearly ruined the world's greatest experiment in democracy. No serious and unbiased student can be deceived by the fairy tale of a beautiful Southern slave civilization. If those who really had opportunity to know the South before the war wrote the truth, it was a center of widespread ignorance, undeveloped resources, suppressed humanity and unrestrained passions, with whatever veneer of manners and culture that could lie above these depths.

Coming now to the Civil War, how for a moment can anyone who reads the *Congressional Globe* from 1850 to 1860, the lives of contemporary statesmen and public characters, North and South, the discourses in the newspapers and accounts of meetings and speeches, doubt that Negro slavery was the cause of the Civil War? What do we gain by evading this clear fact, and talking in vague ways about "Union" and "State Rights" and differences in civilization as the cause of that catastrophe?

Of all historic facts there can be none clearer than that for four long and fearful years the South fought to perpetuate human slavery; and that the nation which "rose so bright and fair and died so pure of stain" was one that had a perfect right to be ashamed of its birth and glad of its death. Yet one monument in North Carolina achieves the impossible by recording of Confederate soldiers: "They died fighting for liberty!"

On the other hand, consider the North and the Civil War. Why should we be deliberately false, like Woodward, in "Meet General Grant," and represent the North as magnanimously freeing the slave without any effort on his part?

"The American Negroes are the only people in the history of the world, so far as I know, that ever became free without any effort of their own. . . .

"They had not started the war nor ended it. They twanged banjos around the railroad stations, sang melodious spirituals, and believed that some Yankee would soon come along and give each of them forty acres of land and a mule."[2]

The North went to war without the slightest idea of freeing the slave. The great majority of Northerners from Lincoln down pledged themselves to protect slavery, and they hated and harried Abolitionists. But on the other hand, the thesis which Beale tends to support that the whole North during and after the war was chiefly interested in making money, is only half true; it was abolition and belief in democracy that gained for a time the upper hand after the war and led the North in Reconstruction; business followed abolition in order to maintain the tariff, pay the bonds and defend the banks. To call this business program "the program of the North" and ignore abolition is unhistorical. In growing ascendancy for a calculable time was a great moral movement which turned the North from its economic defense of slavery and led it to Emancipation. Abolitionists attacked slavery because it was wrong and their moral battle cannot be truthfully minimized or forgotten. Nor does this fact deny that the majority of Northerners before the war were not abolitionists, that they attacked slavery only in order to win the war and enfranchised the Negro to secure this result.

One has but to read the debates in Congress and state papers from Abraham Lincoln down to know that the decisive action which ended the Civil War was the emancipation and arming of the black slave; that, as Lincoln said: "Without the military help of black freedmen, the war against the South could not have been won." The freedmen, far from being the inert recipients of freedom at the hands of philanthropists, furnished 200,000 soldiers in the Civil War who took part in nearly 200 battles and skirmishes, and in addition perhaps 300,000 others as effective laborers and helpers. In proportion to population, more Negroes than whites fought in the Civil War. These people, withdrawn from the support of the Confederacy, with threat of the withdrawal of millions more, made the opposition of the slaveholder useless, unless they themselves freed and armed their own slaves. This was exactly what they started to do; they were only restrained by realizing that such action removed the very cause for which they began fighting. Yet one would search current American histories almost in vain to find a clear statement or even faint recognition of these perfectly well-authenticated facts.

All this is but preliminary to the kernel of the historic problem with which this book deals, and that is Reconstruction. The chorus of agreement concerning the attempt to reconstruct and organize the South after the Civil War and Emancipation is overwhelming. There is scarce a child in the street that cannot tell you that the whole effort was a hideous mistake and an unfortunate incident, based on ignorance, revenge and the perverse determination to attempt the impossible; that the history of the United States from 1866 to 1876 is something of which the nation ought to be ashamed and which did more to retard and set back the American Negro than anything that has happened to him; while at the same time it grievously all wantonly wounded again a part of the nation already hurt to death.

True it is that the Northern historians writing just after the war had scant sympathy for the South, and wrote ruthlessly of "rebels" and "slave-drivers." They had at least the excuse of a war psychosis. . . .

First of all, we have James Ford Rhodes' history of the United States. Rhodes was trained not as an historian but as an Ohio business man. He had no broad formal education. When he had accumulated a fortune, he surrounded himself with a retinue of clerks and proceeded to manufacture a history of the United States by mass production. His method was simple. He gathered a vast number of authorities; he selected from these authorities those whose testimony supported his thesis, and he discarded the others. . . .

Above all, he begins his inquiry convinced, without admitting any necessity of investigation, that Negroes are an inferior race:

"No large policy in our country has ever been so conspicuous a failure as that of forcing universal Negro suffrage upon the South. The Negroes who simply acted out their nature, were not to blame. How indeed could they acquire political honesty? What idea could barbarism thrust into slavery obtain of the rights of property? . . .

"From the Republican policy came no real good to the Negroes. Most of them developed no political capacity, and the few who raised themselves above the mass, did not reach a high order of intelligence."[3]

Rhodes was primarily the historian of property; of economic history and the labor movement, he knew nothing; of democratic government, he was contemptuous. He was trained to make profits. He used his profits to write history. He speaks again and again of the rulership of "intelligence and property" and he makes a plea that intelligent use of the ballot for the benefit of property is the only real foundation of democracy.

The real frontal attack on Reconstruction, as interpreted by the leaders of national thought in 1870 and for some time thereafter, came from the universities and particularly from Columbia and Johns Hopkins.

The movement began with Columbia University and with the advent of John W. Burgess of Tennessee and William A. Dunning of New Jersey as professors of political science and history.

Burgess was an ex-Confederate soldier who started a little Southern college with a box of books, a box of tallow candles and a Negro boy; and his attitude toward the Negro race in after years was subtly colored by this early conception of Negroes as essentially property like books and candles. Dunning was a kindly and impressive professor who was deeply influenced by a growing group of young Southern students and began with them to re-write the history of the nation from 1860 to 1880, in more or less conscious opposition to the classic interpretations of New England.

Burgess was frank and determined in his anti-Negro thought. He expounded his theory of Nordic supremacy which colored all his political theories:

"The claim that there is nothing in the color of the skin from the point of view of political ethics is a great sophism. A black skin means membership in a race of men which has never of itself succeeded in subjecting passion to reason, has never, therefore, created any civilization of any kind. To put such a race of men in possession of a 'state' government in a system of federal government is to trust them with the development of political and legal civilization upon the most important subjects of human life, and to do this in communities with a large white population is simply to establish barbarism in power over civilization."

Burgess is a Tory and open apostle of reaction. He tells us that the nation now believes "that it is the white man's mission, his duty and his right, to hold the reins of political power in his own hands for the civilization of the world and the welfare of mankind."[4]

For this reason America is following "the European idea of the duty of civilized races to impose their political sovereignty upon civilized, or half civilized, or not fully civilized, races anywhere and everywhere in the world."[5]

He complacently believes that "There is something natural in the subordination of an inferior race to a superior race, even to the point of the enslavement of the inferior race, but there is nothing natural in the opposite."[6] He therefore denominates Reconstruction as the rule "of the uncivilized Negroes over the whites of the South."[7] This has been the teaching of one of our greatest universities for nearly fifty years.

Dunning was less dogmatic as a writer, and his own statements are often judicious. But even Dunning can declare that "all the forces [in the South] that made for civilization were dominated by a mass of barbarous freedmen"; and that "the antithesis and antipathy of race and color were crucial and ineradicable. . . ."[8]

The Columbia school of historians and social investigators have issued between 1895 and the present time sixteen studies of Reconstruction in the Southern States, all based on the same thesis and all done according to the same method: first, endless sympathy with the white South; second, ridicule, contempt or silence for the Negro; third, a judicial attitude towards the North, which concludes that the North under great misapprehension did a grievous wrong, but eventually saw its mistake and retreated.

These studies vary, of course, in their methods. Dunning's own work is usually silent so far as the Negro is concerned. Burgess is more than fair in law but reactionary in matters of race and property, regarding the treatment of a Negro as a man as nothing less than a crime, and admitting that "the mainstay of property is the courts."

In the books on Reconstruction written by graduates of these universities and others, the studies of Texas, North Carolina, Florida, Virginia, and Louisiana are thoroughly bad, giving no complete picture of what happened during Reconstruction, written for the most part by men and women without broad historical or social background, and all designed not to seek the truth but to prove a thesis. Hamilton reaches the climax of this school when he characterizes the black codes, which even Burgess condemned, as "not only . . . on the whole reasonable, temperate and kindly, but, in the main, necessary."[9]

Thompson's "Georgia" is another case in point. It seeks to be fair, but silly stories about Negroes indicating utter lack of even common sense are included, and every noble sentiment from white people. When two Negro workers, William and Jim, put a straightforward advertisement in a local paper, the author says that it was "evidently written by a white friend." There is not the slightest historical evidence to prove this, and there were plenty of educated Negroes in Augusta at the time who might have written this. Lonn's "Louisiana" puts Sheridan's words in Sherman's mouth to prove a petty point.

There are certain of these studies which, though influenced by the same general attitude, nevertheless have more of scientific poise and cultural background. Garner's "Reconstruction in Mississippi" conceives the Negro as an integral part of the scene and treats him as a human being. With this should be bracketed the recent study of "Reconstruction in South Carolina" by Simkins and Woody. This is not as fair as Garner's, but in the midst of conventional judgment and conclusion, and reproductions of all available caricatures of Negroes, it does not hesitate to give a fair account of the Negroes and of some of their work. It gives the impression of combining in one book two antagonistic points of view, but in the clash much truth emerges.

Ficklen's "Louisiana" and the works of Fleming are anti-Negro in spirit, but, nevertheless, they have a certain fairness and sense of historic honesty. Fleming's "Documentary History of Reconstruction" is done by a man who has a thesis to support, and his selection of documents supports the thesis. His study of Alabama is pure propaganda.

Next come a number of books which are openly and blatantly propaganda, like Herbert's "Solid South," and the books by Pike and Reynolds on South Carolina, the works by Pollard and Carpenter, and especially those by Ulrich Phillips. One of the latest and most popular of this series is "The Tragic Era" by Claude Bowers, which is an excellent and readable piece of current newspaper reporting, absolutely devoid of historical judgment or sociological knowledge. It is a classic example of historical propaganda of the cheaper sort.

We have books like Milton's "Age of Hate" and Winston's "Andrew Johnson" which attempt to re-write the character of Andrew Johnson. They certainly add to our knowledge of the man and our sympathy for his weakness. But they cannot, for students, change the calm testimony of unshaken historical facts . Fuess' "Carl Schurz" paints the picture of this fine liberal, and yet goes out of its way to show that he was quite wrong in what he said he saw in the South.

The chief witness in Reconstruction, the emancipated slave himself, has been almost barred from court. His written Reconstruction record has been largely destroyed and nearly always neglected. Only three or four states have preserved the debates in the Reconstruction conventions; there are few biographies of black leaders. The Negro is refused a hearing because he was poor and ignorant. It is therefore assumed that all Negroes in Reconstruction were ignorant and silly and that therefore a history of Reconstruction in any state can quite ignore him. The result is that most unfair caricatures of Negroes have been carefully preserved; but serious speeches, successful administration and upright character are almost universally ignored and forgotten. Wherever a black head rises to historic view, it is promptly slain by an adjective— "shrewd," "notorious," "cunning"—or pilloried by a sneer; or put out of view by some quite unproven charge of bad moral character. In other words, every effort has been made to treat the Negro's part in Reconstruction with silence and contempt.

When recently a student tried to write on education in Florida, he found that the official records of the excellent administration of the colored Superintendent of Education, Gibbs, who virtually established the Florida public school, had been destroyed. Alabama has tried to obliterate all printed records of Reconstruction.

Especially noticeable is the fact that little attempt has been made to trace carefully the rise and economic development of the poor whites and their relation to the planters and to Negro labor after the war. . . .

The whole development of Reconstruction was primarily an economic development, but no economic history or proper material for it has been written. It has been regarded as a purely political matter, and of politics most naturally divorced from industry.[10]

All this is reflected in the textbooks of the day and in the encyclopedias, until we have got to the place where we cannot use our experiences during and after the Civil War for the uplift and enlightenment of mankind. We have spoiled and misconceived the position of the historian. If we are going, in the future, not simply with regard to this one question, but with regard to all social problems, to be able to use human experience for the guidance of mankind, we have got clearly to distinguish between fact and desire.

In the first place, somebody in each era must make clear the facts with utter disregard to his own wish and desire and belief. What we have got to know, so far as possible, are the things that actually happened in the world. Then with that much clear and open to every reader, the philosopher and prophet has a chance to interpret these facts; but the historian has no right, posing as scientist, to conceal or distort facts; and until we distinguish between these two functions of the chronicler of human action, we are going to render it easy for a muddled world out of sheer ignorance to make the same mistake ten times over.

One is astonished in the study of history at the recurrence of the idea that evil must be forgotten, distorted, skimmed over. . . . The difficulty, of course, with this philosophy is that history loses its value as an incentive and example; it paints perfect men and noble nations, but it does not tell the truth. . . .

Not a single great leader of the nation during the Civil War and Reconstruction has escaped attack and libel. The magnificent figures of Charles Sumner and Thaddeus Stevens have been besmirched almost beyond recognition. We have been cajoling and flattering the South and slurring the North, because the South is determined to re-write the history of slavery and the North is not interested in history but in wealth.

This, then, is the book basis upon which today we judge Reconstruction. In order to paint the South as a martyr to inescapable fate, to make the North the magnanimous emancipator, and to ridicule the Negro as the impossible joke in the whole development, we have in fifty years, by libel, innuendo, and silence, so completely misstated and obliterated the history of the Negro in America and his relation to its work and government that today it is almost unknown. This may be fine romance, but it is not science. It may be inspiring, but it is certainly not the truth. And beyond this it is dangerous. It is not only part foundation of our present lawlessness and loss of democratic ideals; it has, more than that, led the world to embrace and worship the color bar as social salvation and it is helping to range mankind in ranks of mutual hatred and contempt, at the summons of a cheap and false myth.

Nearly all recent books on Reconstruction agree with each other in discarding the government reports and substituting selected diaries, letters, and gossip. Yet it happens that the government records are an historic source of wide and unrivaled authenticity. . . .

Certain monographs deserve all praise, like those of Kendrick and Pierce. The work of Flack is prejudiced but built on study. The defense of the carpetbag regime by Tourgee and Allen, Powell Clayton, Holden, and Warmoth are worthy antidotes to the certain writers. . . .

It will be noted that for my authority in this work I have depended very largely upon secondary material; upon state histories of Reconstruction, written in the main by those who were convinced before they began to write that the Negro was incapable of government, or of becoming a constituent part of a civilized state. The fairest of these histories have not tried to conceal facts; in other cases, the black man has been largely ignored; while in still others, he has been traduced and ridiculed. If I had had time and money and opportunity to go back to the original sources in all cases, there can be no doubt that the weight of this work would have been vastly strengthened, and as I firmly believe, the case of the Negro more convincingly set forth.

Various volumes of papers in the great libraries like the Johnson papers in the Library of Congress, the Sumner manuscripts at Harvard, the Schurz correspondence, the Wells papers, the Chase papers, the Fessenden and Greeley collections, the

McCulloch, McPherson, Shennan, Stevens, and Trumbull papers, all must have much of great interest to the historians of the American Negro. I have not had time nor opportunity to examine these, and most of those who have examined them had little interest in black folk.

Negroes have done some excellent work on their own history and defense. It suffers of course from natural partisanship and a desire to prove a case in the face of a chorus of unfair attacks. Its best work also suffers from the fact that Negroes with difficulty reach an audience. But this is also true of such white writers as Skaggs and Bancroft who could not get first-class publishers because they were saying something that the nation did not like.

The Negro historians began with autobiographies and reminiscences. The older historians were George W. Williams and Joseph T. Wilson; the new school of historians is led by Carter G. Woodson; and I have been greatly helped by the unpublished theses of four of the youngest Negro students. It is most unfortunate that while many young white Southerners can get funds to attack and ridicule the Negro and his friends, it is almost impossible for firstclass Negro students to get a chance for research or to get finished work in print.

I write then in a field devastated by passion and belief. Naturally, as a Negro, I cannot do this writing without believing in the essential humanity of Negroes, in their ability to be educated, to do the work of the modern world, to take their place as equal citizens with others. I cannot for a moment subscribe to that bizarre doctrine of race that makes most men inferior to the few. But, too, as a student of science, I want to be fair, objective, and judicial; to let no searing of the memory by intolerable insult and cruelty make me fail to sympathize with human frailties and contradiction, in the eternal paradox of good and evil. But armed and warned by all this, and fortified by long study of the facts, I stand at the end of this writing, literally aghast at what American historians have done to this field.

What is the object of writing the history of Reconstruction? Is it to wipe out the disgrace of a people which fought to make slaves of Negroes? Is it to show that the North had higher motives than freeing black men? Is it to prove that Negroes were black angels? No, it is simply to establish the Truth, on which Right in the future may be built. We shall never have a science of history until we have in our colleges men who regard the truth as more important than the defense of the white race, and who will not deliberately encourage students to gather thesis material in order to support a prejudice or buttress a lie.

Three-fourths of the testimony against the Negro in Reconstruction is on the unsupported evidence of men who hated and despised Negroes and regarded it as loyalty to blood, patriotism to country, and filial tribute to the fathers to lie, steal, or kill in order to discredit these black folk. This may be a natural result when a people have been humbled and impoverished and degraded in their own life; but what is inconceivable is that another generation and another group should regard this testimony as scientific truth, when it is contradicted by logic and by fact. This chapter, therefore, which in logic should be a survey of books and sources, becomes of sheer necessity an arraignment of American historians and an indictment of their ideals. With a determination unparalleled in science, the mass of American writers have started out so to distort the facts of the greatest critical period of American history as to prove right wrong and wrong right. I am not familiar enough with the vast field of human history to pronounce on the relative guilt of these and historians of other times and fields; but I do say that if the history of the past has been written in the same fashion, it is useless as science and misleading as ethics. It simply shows that with sufficient general agreement and determination among the dominant classes, the truth of history may be utterly distorted and contradicted and changed to any convenient fairy tale that the masters of men wish.

I cannot believe that any unbiased mind, with an ideal of truth and of scientific judgment, can read the plain, authentic facts of our history, during 1860–1880, and come to conclusions essentially different from mine; and yet I stand virtually alone in this interpretation. So much so that the very cogency of my facts would make me hesitate, did I not seem to see plain reasons. Subtract from Burgess his belief that only white people can rule, and he is in essential agreement with me. Remember that Rhodes was an uneducated money-maker who hired clerks to find the facts which he needed to support his thesis, and one is convinced that the same labor and expense could easily produce quite opposite results.

One fact and one alone explains the attitude of most recent writers toward Reconstruction; they cannot conceive Negroes as men; in their minds the word "Negro" connotes "inferiority" and "stupidity" lightened only by unreasoning gayety and humor. . . .

Assuming, therefore, as axiomatic the endless inferiority of the Negro race, these newer historians, mostly Southerners, some Northerners who deeply sympathized with the South, misinterpreted, distorted, even deliberately ignored any fact that challenged or contradicted this assumption. If the Negro was admittedly sub-human, what need to waste time delving into his Reconstruction history? Consequently historians of Reconstruction with a few exceptions ignore the Negro as completely as possible, leaving the reader wondering why an element apparently so insignificant filled the whole Southern picture at the time. The only real excuse for this attitude is loyalty to a lost cause, reverence for brave fathers and suffering mothers and sisters, and fidelity to the ideals of a clan and class. But in propaganda against the Negro since emancipation in this land, we face one of the most stupendous efforts the world ever saw to discredit human beings, an effort involving universities, history, science, social life, and religion. . . .

Notes

1. "Racial Attitudes in American History Textbooks," *Journal of Negro History*, XIX, 257.
2. W. E. Woodward, *Meet General Grant*, 372.
3. Rhodes, *History of the United States*, VII, 232–33.
4. Burgess, *Reconstruction and the Constitution*, viii, ix.
5. Ibid., 218.
6. Ibid., 244–45.
7. Ibid., 218.
8. Dunning, *Reconstruction, Political and Economic*, 212–13.
9. Hamilton, "Southern Legislation in Respect to Freedmen," in *Studies in Southern History and Politics*, 156.
10. *The Economic History of the South* by E. Q. Hawk is merely a compilation of census reports and conventionalities.

10

Some Economics of Class

Michael Perelman

How much more will be required before the U.S. public awakes from its political slumber? Tepid action in the workplace, the voting booth, and the streets have allowed the right wing to steamroll revolutionary changes that have remade the entire sociopolitical structure of the United States. Since the election of Franklin Roosevelt in 1932, every Democratic administration with the exception of Lyndon Johnson's has been more conservative—often far more conservative—than the previous Democratic administration. Similarly, every elected Republican administration, with the single exception of George Herbert Walker Bush's, has been more conservative than the previous Republican administration. The deterioration in the distribution of income is a symptom of a far larger problem. Perhaps formulating the situation in the United States might help people understand their class interests as well as reveal who has benefited from the right-wing revolution.

Critics of Marx have long taken pleasure in claiming that the rise of the middle class in the United States and other advanced capitalist economies disproves Marx's "predictions" of the course of capitalism. In recent decades, however, the distribution of income in the United States is coming to resemble that of many poor Latin American economies, with a shrinking middle class and an obscene share of wealth going to the richest members of society.

While proponents of the U.S. model pretend that recent economic trends represent a success, in truth, they are signs of capitalism's failure. Once capitalism began to falter in the late 1960s, the ruling class in the United States was unable to gain ground by ordinary business practices. So, the ruling class pursued a two-fold strategy: attacking workers rights while pursuing tax cuts, deregulation, and government subsidies. In effect, when forces integral to the normal functioning of capitalism began to depress the rate of profit, the ruling class adopted measures to change the balance of power in a way that would shift wealth and income in its direction.

189

Between 1970 and 2003, the Gross Domestic Product (GDP) adjusted for inflation almost tripled, from $3.7 trillion to $10.8 trillion.[1] Because the population also increased by about 35 percent during that same period, per capita income more than doubled. However, not everyone's income rose. Hourly wage earners certainly did not benefit from the economic growth. According to government statistics, hourly wages corrected for inflation peaked in 1972 at $8.99 measured in 1982 dollars. By 2003 hourly wages had fallen to $8.29, although they rose modestly using a different measure of inflation.[2]

Economists Thomas Piketty from the French research institute, CEPREMAP, and Emmanuel Saez of the University of California at Berkeley assembled detailed information about the distribution of income using data from the Internal Revenue Service. They defined income in current 2000 dollars as annual gross income reported on tax returns, excluding capital gains and all government transfers (such as Social Security, unemployment benefits, welfare payments, etc.) and before individual income taxes and employees' payroll taxes. For the bottom 90 percent of the population, the average income stood at $27,041 in 1970, then peaked in 1973—at the same time as hourly wages—at $28,540. This figure bottomed out in 1993 at $23,892. By 2002, average income for this group stood at $25,862, about 4.5 percent below where it stood in 1970.[3]

This estimate does not mean that everybody in the bottom 90 percent fell behind but that the losses among the vast majority of these people were sufficient to counterbalance the gains of the more fortunate members of the bottom 90 percent. So probably 80 percent of the population was worse off in 2002 than in 1970.

At the top, matters were quite different. Piketty and Saez found that in 1970 the top ten corporate CEOs earned about forty-nine times as much as the average wage earner. By 2000, the ratio had reached the astronomical level of 2,173 to 1. The rate of growth of executive pay has also outstripped the rate of growth of profits. For example, between the periods 1993–1995 and 2001–2003, the ratio of total compensation to the top-five executives of public companies to those companies' total earnings increased from 4.8 percent to 10.3 percent.[4]

Despite the decline in the average well-being of people in the bottom 90 percent of the population, because the population grew by approximately 30 percent, this group probably still received about 30 percent of the increase in the GDP. In addition, the GDP does not exactly equal the income figures of the Internal Revenue Service, but the figures are close enough to conclude that the top 10 percent of the population received the lion's share of all economic growth between 1970 and 2000.

You can quibble with the Piketty and Saez estimates about the distribution of income. Including transfers, such as Social Security, and by using a different estimate of inflation, the incomes of the bottom 90 percent of the population appear to have grown by about 20 percent between 1970 and 2002—approximately a mere 0.6 percent per year. However, looking at the situation from another perspective, this data may be far too conservative in estimating how much the poor have fallen behind and the rich have prospered. First of all, the data exclude capital gains, which represent a major share of the income going to the very rich. In addition, as Richard Titmuss observed in 1962, efforts by the rich to avoid taxes makes the distribution of income appear far more equal than it actually is.[5]

Academic economics has done little to investigate the extent of this distortion, although David Cay Johnston's outstanding book, *Perfectly Legal*, which describes the contribution of the tax system to inequality, forcefully demonstrates how the law permits the rich to use ingenious means to hide their wealth and income in order to avoid paying taxes.[6] Many of the tax avoidance schemes are perfectly legal, even though they may violate the spirit of the law; others, what economist Max Sawicky calls do-it-yourself tax cuts, are not.[7]

For example, in a globalized economy, hiding money offshore is not particularly difficult. One recent study estimated that the world's richest individuals have placed about $11.5 trillion worth of assets in offshore tax havens, mainly to avoid taxes. This amount is roughly equal to the GDP of the United States. Of course, citizens of the United States are not responsible for the entire $11.5 trillion, but then the report does not take account of the assets that corporations stash in tax havens.[8] Although the Internal Revenue Service (IRS) occasionally convicts an unsophisticated offender, this practice is relatively safe.

In addition, taxpayers underestimate their tax liabilities by inflating the cost basis of assets on which they take capital gains. One estimate puts the extent of this inflation at about one-quarter trillion dollars.[9] This practice obviously serves to benefit the richest taxpayers, although it does not affect the Saez and Piketty results, which exclude capital gains.

Of the estimated 16 percent of the legal tax obligation that goes unpaid, according to the latest data from the IRS, we can rest assured that the vast majority comes from the wealthiest members of society. The clever tactics of tax avoidance prevent the IRS data from capturing a good deal of the wealth and income of the top 10 percent of the population. In short, as hotel magnate Leona Helmsley famously said, "Only the little people pay taxes." The government facilitates shenanigans, such as those used by Helmsley, by steadily increasing the complexity of the tax code while reducing the resources for enforcement. Helmsley served eighteen months in jail for her financial transgressions, but not because of diligence on the part of the government. She refused to pay money due to contractors. The resulting civil suit incidentally exposed her tax fraud.

The IRS also reinforces inequities between rich and poor by devoting a dispro-portionate share of its scrutiny to those without substantial resources, especially poor people who declare an Earned Income Tax Credit.[10]

Over and above tax-related distortions of the distribution of income, the wealthy have access to resources that do not count as income. Consider Johnston's description of the personal use of corporate jets:

> When William Agee was running the engineering firm Morrison-Knudsen into bankruptcy, he replaced its one corporate jet, already paid off, with two new ones and boasted about how the way he financed them polished up the financial reports. His wife, Mary Cunningham Agee, used the extra as her personal air taxi to hop around the United States and Europe. When Ross Johnson ran the cigarette-and-food company RJR Nabisco, which had a fleet of at least a dozen corporate jets, he once had his dog flown home, listed on the manifest as "G. Shepherd." And Kenneth Lay let his daughter take one of Enron's jets to fly across the Atlantic with her bed, which was too large to go as baggage on a commercial flight.[11]

Here again, Johnston understates the situation. Consider this fuller description of the RJR-Nabisco case:

> After the arrival of two new Gulfstreams, Johnson ordered a pair of top-of-the-line G4s, at a cool $21 million apiece. For the hangar, Johnson gave aviation head Linda Galvin an unlimited budget and implicit instructions to exceed it. When it was finished, RJR Nabisco had the Taj Mahal of corporate hangars, dwarfing that of Coca-Cola's next door. The cost hadn't gone into the hangar itself, but into an adjacent three-story building of tinted glass, surrounded by $250,000 in landscaping, complete with a Japanese garden. Inside, a visitor walked into a stunning three-story atrium. The floors were Italian marble, the walls and floors lined in inlaid mahogany. More than $600,000 in new furniture was spread throughout, topped off by $100,000 in *objets d'art*, including an antique Chinese ceremonial robe spread in a glass case and a magnificent Chinese platter and urn. In one corner of the ornate bathroom stood a stuffed chair, as if one might grow fatigued walking from one end to the other. Among the building's features: a walk-in wine cooler; a "visiting pilots' room," with television and stereo; and a "flight-planning room," packed with state-of-the-art computers to track executives' where-abouts and their future transportation wishes. All this was necessary to keep

track of RJR's thirty-six corporate pilots and ten planes, widely known as the RJR Air Force.[12]

David Yermack of New York University's Stern School of Business produced a paper with the delightful title "Flights of Fancy: Corporate Jets, CEO Perquisites, and Inferior Shareholder Returns," in which he investigated the relationship between this particular luxury and corporate efficiency. He found that the cost for CEOs who belong to golf clubs far from their company's headquarters is two-thirds higher, on average, than for CEOs who have disclosed air travel but are not long-distance golf-club members.[13]

Based on Yermack's paper, a *Wall Street Journal* article entitled "JetGreen" described corporate jets "as airborne limousines to fly CEOs and other executives to golf dates or to vacation homes where they have golf-club memberships."[14] To add insult to injury, the government subsidizes corporate jets. For example, the government waves the hefty landing fees that commercial aircraft must pay in order to support the air traffic control system. The value of these subsidies amounts to billions of dollars.[15] A significant amount of these subsidies benefits the private lives of corporate executives.

High-level corporate executives enjoy many other perquisites besides free travel, including the provision of luxury boxes at sports stadia, chefs, lawn care, and a multitude of other benefits that ordinary people would have to pay for on their own, if only they could afford them. *New York Times* business columnist, Gretchen Morgenson, described the excesses of Donald J. Tyson, former chairman of Tyson Foods, ranging from the personal use of corporate jets to housekeeping and lawn care. Echoing Leona Helmsley, she appropriately titled her article "Only the Little People Pay for Lawn Care."[16]

The Piketty and Saez data also overestimate the welfare of the poor, especially if one considers the fact that ordinary people must increasingly work more hours to get what they earn. For example, between 1970 and 2002, annual hours worked per capita rose 20 percent in the United States, while falling in most other advanced economies.[17] Besides, for ordinary people, benefits, such as pensions and health care, are in rapid decline. Finally, the reported income of the poorer segments of society does not take account of many expenses that poor people pay. For example, the data ignores the late fees that banks and other corporations charge, along with usurious interest rates, and various other costs that fall mostly on the least fortunate. Even though the government disregards these factors in assembling its statistics about wealth and income, they can be significant. For example, in 2004, banks, thrifts, and credit unions collected a record $37.8 in service charges on accounts, more than double what they got in 1994, according to the Federal Deposit Insurance Corporation and the National Credit Union Administration. Banks are also raising fees for late payments, low balances, and over-the-limit charges to as much as $39 per violation. Some banks even charge for speaking with a service representative. These fees predominately fall on the poor.[18]

Even among the richest 10 percent of the population, the unseemly distribution of income is increasingly skewing toward the richest of the rich. In 1970, the top 0.01 percent of taxpayers had less than 0.53 percent of total income. By the year 2000, their share had soared to 3.06 percent. In other words, the income of these 13,400 taxpayers from being fifty-three times the national average to an almost unbelievable 306 times, slightly less than it was in the peak year of 1928, before the Great Depression. These 13,400 richest families in the States had about the same income as the poorest 25 percent of households in the country.[19] Of course, membership in this elite group was not unchanging, but it was probably relatively stable. Certainly, few of these fortunate people ever fell into the bottom 25 percent.

Ownership of wealth is even more concentrated than income. With the bursting of the dot-com bubble, wealth inequality had temporarily fallen a bit, as it usually does during an economic decline. Even so, by 2001, the top 1 percent of households owned 40 percent of the financial wealth in the United States.[20] Had the calculation of the wealth holdings of the richest 1 percent been made while the stock market had still been expanding, the number would have been even more extreme than the reported 40 percent. I have no doubt that inequality will continue its upward climb in the absence of a new recession or a rapid change in the political climate.

At the same time, ordinary people are rapidly losing their pensions and medical benefits, while government programs upon which they depend, such as Medicare and Medicaid, are becoming less generous. Robert K. Merton, the sociologist and father of a Nobel Prize winning economist, writing in the context of the accumulation of scientific prestige by the elite, called attention to the "Matthew effect," alluding to the biblical passage: "For to everyone who has will more be given, and he will have abundance but from him who has not even what he has will be taken away.[21] Today, we are witnessing an economic Matthew effect beyond what anybody could have imagined only a few decades earlier.

Whether the Piketty and Saez estimates are overstated or too conservative, I will leave for others to decide. No matter which estimate you prefer, nobody can deny that the business offensive has certainly paid off handsomely. Since the election of George W. Bush in 2000, the transfer of wealth and income has accelerated at an alarming rate.

Even that arch free-marketeer, former Federal Reserve chairman, Alan Greenspan, was moved to express concern about the extent of inequality in the United States today, admitting to Senator Jack Reed, "I think that the effective increase in the concentration of incomes here, which is implicit in this, is not desirable in a democratic society.[22] Admittedly, one might question the chairman's sincerity considering his preferred remedies. For example, in response to a question about Social Security from Senator Schumer at a hearing before the same Senate committee a few months later, Greenspan responded, "I've been concerned about the concentration of income and wealth in this nation . . . and this [meaning the privatization of Social Security], in my judgment, is one way in which you can address this particular question.[23] Here is a more genuine expression of concern from Warren Buffett, perennially the second richest person in the world regarding the excessive tax cuts:

> Corporate income taxes in fiscal 2003 accounted for 7.4 percent of all federal tax receipts, down from a post-war peak of 32 percent in 1952. With one exception (1983), last year's percentage is the lowest recorded since data was first published in 1934. . . . Tax breaks for corporations (and their investors, particularly large ones) were a major part of the Administration's 2002 and 2003 initiatives. If class warfare is being waged in America, my class is clearly winning.[24]

Buffett's figures actually overstate the corporate tax contribution. In fact, the Federal Reserve System— the purpose of which is supposed to be the public welfare, not profits—paid 16 percent of all corporate income taxes in 2002. Of those real corporations, many of the largest pay no taxes whatsoever. A fair number of these large corporations even pay negative taxes.

One study of 275 profitable Fortune 500 corporations with total U.S profits of $1.1 trillion over the three-year period, 2001 through 2003 found that 82 of these corporations:

> . . . paid zero or less in federal income taxes in at least one year from 2001 to 2003. Many of them enjoyed multiple no-tax years. In the years they paid no income tax, these companies reported $102 billion in pretax U.S. profits. But instead of paying $35.6 billion in income taxes as the statutory 35 percent corporate tax rate seems to require, these companies generated so many excess tax breaks that they received outright tax rebate checks from the U.S. Treasury, totaling $12.6 billion. These companies' "negative tax rates" meant that they made more after taxes than before taxes in those no-tax years.[25]

Twenty-eight of these companies had a negative tax rate over the entire three-year period. The report continues, suggesting that the inequities are getting worse year by year:

In 2003 alone, 46 companies paid zero or less in federal income taxes. These 46 companies, almost one out of six of the companies in the study, reported U.S. pretax profits in 2003 of $42.6 billion, yet received tax rebates totaling $5.4 billion. In 2002, almost as many companies, 42, paid no tax, reporting $43.5 billion in pretax profits, but $4.9 billion in tax rebates. From 2001 to 2003, the number of no-tax companies jumped from 33 to 46, an increase of 40 percent.[26]

Putting this erosion of corporate taxes into perspective, the authors conclude:

Corporate taxes paid for more than a quarter of federal outlays in the 1950s and a fifth in the 1960s. They began to decline during the Nixon administration, yet even by the second half of the 1990s, corporate taxes still covered 11 percent of the cost of federal programs. But in fiscal 2002 and 2003, corporate taxes paid for a mere 6 percent of our government's expenses.[27]

A follow-up study showed that the erosion of taxes on the state level was even more extreme.[28]

Gaining a perspective on the extent of the effect of cuts in personal income taxes may be easier. In 2005, President Bush was campaigning to make his tax cuts permanent. If he succeeds the benefits for the top 1 percent of the population over the following seventy-five years will amount to an estimated $2.9 trillion.[29] In other words, the tax cuts for this smaller segment of the population over this period would equal about one quarter of the current annual GDP of the United States.

The lethal combination of tax cuts for the rich and the growing burdens on the poor threaten to annihilate what is left of social mobility. In the words of Thomas Piketty, mentioned earlier for his startling work on income inequality:

These new high-income tax cuts, together with all the previous tax cuts (including the repeal of the estate tax), will eventually contribute to rebuild a class of rentiers in the U.S., whereby a small group of wealthy but untalented children controls vast segments of the U.S. economy and penniless, talented children simply can't compete. . . . If such a tax policy is maintained, there is a decent probability that the U.S. will look like Old Europe prior to 1914 in a couple of generations.[30]

I do not mean to imply that the right wing is totally indifferent about people not carrying their share of the tax burden. Without betraying a trace of irony, a famous *Wall Street Journal* editorial wailed about "the non-taxpaying class," complaining about the "lucky duckies."[31]

The lucky duckies in question were those people who were too poor to make enough to pay taxes, not the affluent beneficiaries of the rightwing revolution. And what a revolution it was! Even if we correct for population growth and transfer payments, while ignoring all the reasons why the gains of the wealthy may be an understatement, we can safely say that the right-wing revolution still represents the largest transfer of wealth and income in the history of the world—far larger than what occurred during either the Russian or Chinese revolutions. After all, neither China nor China nor Russia had an economy that came anywhere near $7 trillion, the amount by which the annual U.S. GDP grew between 1970 and 2002.

In terms of wealth, the differences are far more extreme because creating an annual income flow requires a much greater level of wealth, comparable to the difference between the annual rent of a house and its purchase price. Government policies continue to promote an even more extreme redistribution of wealth and income to the rich. Most economists manage to turn a blind eye or to make an effort to explain those policies as necessary to create jobs or to make the economy more productive. The short-term victory in capturing virtually all of the growth of wealth and income shedding tax obligations may seem like cause for jubilation—at least within some circles—but this victory may turn out to be hollow, even at the top of the pyramid. The right-wing revolution is ruthlessly pursuing policies that are undermining education, health care, and virtually every other public institution that supports the economy in an effort to extract more surplus value from ordinary people. In the process, the right wing is undermining the very foundation of the economy.

Notes

1. President of the United States, *Economic Report of the President* (Washington, D.C.: GPO, 2005), table B-2, 286.

2. President of the United States, *Economic Report of the President* (Washington, D.C.: GPO, 2004), table B-47, 340.

3. Thomas Piketty and Emmanuel Saez, "Income Inequality in the United States, 1913–1998," in Anthony B. Atkinson & T. Piketty, eds., *Top Incomes Over the Twentieth Century: A Contrast Between the European and English Speaking Countries* (Oxford: Oxford University Press, forthcoming), http://emlab.Berkeley.edu/users/saez/piketty-saez OUP04US.pdf; see also David Cay Johnston, *Perfectly Legal* (New York: Portfolio, 2003), 38–39; and Paul Krugman, "For Richer," *New York Times Magazine* (October 20, 2002).

4. Lucian Bebchuk & Yaniv Grinstein, "The Growth of Executive Pay," *Oxford Review of Economic Policy* 21, no. 2 (2005), http://law.harvard.edu/faculty/bebchuk/pdfs/ Bebchuk-Grinstein.Growth-of.Pay.pdf.

5. Richard M. Titmuss, *Income Distribution and Social Change* (London: Allen & Unwin, 1962), 22.

6. Johnston, *Perfectly Legal.*

7. Max B. Sawicky, "Do-It-Yourself Tax Cuts: The Crisis in U.S. Tax Enforcement," Economic Policy Institute Briefing Paper No. 160 (April 12, 2005), http://www.epinet .org/content.cfm/bp160.

8. Nick Mathiason, "Super-Rich Hide Trillions Offshore," *The Observer* (March 27, 2005).

9. Joseph M. Dodge & Jay A. Soled, "Inflated Tax Basis and the Quarter-Trillion-Dollar Revenue Question" *Tax Notes* 106, no. 4 (January 24, 2005).

10. Johnston, *Perfectly Legal,* 129ff.

11. Johnston, *Perfectly Legal,* 62.

12. Nell Minow, "The Use of Company Aircraft," http://www.thecorporatelibrary.com /special/misc/aircraft.html; Bryan Burrough and John Helyar, *Barbarians at the Gate* (New York: Harper and Row, 1990), 94; Gary Strauss, "Pricey Perk Lets Executives Fly High," *USA Today* (August 5, 2003).

13. David Yermack, "Flights of Fancy" (September 2004), http://public.kenan-flagler .unc.edu/faculty/shivdasani/uncduke%20corporate%20finance/David_Yermack_ Aircraft0904.pdf.

14. Mark Maremont, "Frequent Fliers: Amid Crackdown, the Jet Perk Suddenly Looks a Lot Pricier For CEOs," *Wall Street Journal* (May 25, 2005).

15. Joseph E. Stiglitz, *The Roaring Nineties* (New York: W. W. Norton, 2004).

16. Gretchen Morgenson, "Only the Little People Pay for Lawn Care," *New York Times* (May 1, 2005).

17. Organisation for Economic Co-operation and Development, *Clocking In and Clocking Out* (October 2004), http://www.oecd.org/dataoecd/42/49/33821328.pdf.

18. Kathy Chu, "Rising Bank Fees Hit Consumers," *USA Today* (October 4, 2005); Dean Foust, "Protection" Racket?: As Overdraft and Other Fees Become Huge Profit Sources For Banks, Critics See Abuses," *Business Week* (May 2, 2005).

19. Piketty and Saez, "Income Inequality in the United States"; see also Krugman, "For Richer."

20. Edward N. Wolff, "Changes in Household Wealth in the 1980s and 1990s in the U.S." Levy Economics Institute Working Paper No. 407 (May 2004).

21. Robert K. Merton, "The Matthew Effect in Science," *Science* 159, no. 3810 (January 5, 1968): 56–63.

22. Senate Banking, Housing and Urban Affairs Committee, *Federal Reserve's Second Monetary Policy Report for 2004,* 108th Congress, 2nd sess., July 20, 2004.

23. Senate Banking, Housing and Urban Affairs Committee, *Federal Reserve's First Monetary Policy report for 2005,* 109th Congress, 1st sess., February 16, 2005.

24. Warren Buffett, "Annual Letter to the Shareholders of Berkshire Hathaway Inc." (February 27, 2004), http://www.berkshirehathaway.com/letters/2003ltr.pdf.

25. United States Department of Commerce, Bureau of Economic Analysis, National Income and Product Accounts, "Table 3.2. Federal Government Current Receipts and Expenditures" (2004), http://www.bea.gov/bea/dn/nipaweb/TableView.asp#Mid.

26. Robert S. McIntyre and T. D. Coo Nguyen, *Corporate Income Taxes in the Bush Years* (Washington, D.C.: Citizens for Tax Justice, Institute on Taxation and Economic Policy, 2004), http://www.ctj.org/corpfed04pr.pdf.

27. McIntyre and Nguyen, *Corporate Income Taxes in the Bush Years*.

28. Robert S. McIntyre and T. D. Coo Nguyen, *Corporate Tax Avoidance in the States Even Worse Than Federal* (Washington, D.C.: Citizens for Tax Justice, Institute on Taxation and Economic Policy, 2005), http://www.ctj.org/pdf/corp0205an.pdf.

29. Richard Kogan and Robert Greenstein, "President Portrays Social Security Shortfall as Enormous, but His Tax Cuts and Drug Benefit Will Cost at Least Five Times as Much," Center on Budget and Policy Priorities (February 11, 2005), http://cbpp.org/1-4-05socsec.htm.

30. Daniel Altman, "Efficiency and Equity (In the Same Breath)," *New York Times* (April 20, 2003).

31. "The Non-Taxpaying Class," *Wall Street Journal* (November 20, 2002).

11

The Social Construction of Disaster

New Orleans as the Paradigmatic American City

Chester Hartman and Gregory D. Squires

The water- and wind-driven devastation that wracked New Orleans and the entire Gulf Coast region during and after the 2005 hurricane season is virtually without parallel in recent U.S. history. A staggering 2 million people were displaced (Hsu 2006). In the wake of Katrina and Rita came a series of striking events, most of which were also without parallel. Illustrations include:

- Credible accusations of dereliction, even financial improprieties, on the part of national sacred cows such as the Red Cross and the Humane Society, leading to firings, resignation of the Red Cross president, criticisms by international Red Cross organizations, and official state and federal investigations (Strom 2005, 2006a, 2006b; Salmon 2006a, 2006b; Nossiter 2006a). Workers for the Federal Emergency Management Agency (FEMA) also have been accused of bribery (Lipton 2006c).
- Foreign aid coming to us, not from us—and then mishandled. The United Arab Emirates was the leader, contributing $100 million (Lipton 2006b). (Cuba, on the other hand, proposed to send medical personnel and equipment—as it does with many countries—which the State Department ignored.)
- Pets taking center stage: Many flood-endangered folks, the elderly in particular, refused evacuation when they learned from government workers that they could not take their pets—in effect, their family—with them. In response, full-page ads, with maudlin photos, later appear in the *New York Times* and the *Washington Post*. The Humane Society of the United States cleverly entitled them "No Pet Left Behind" in their attempt to generate support for the Pets Evacuation and Transportation Standards (PETS) Act, signed into law in late 2006.

- A mandating of moratoriums (albeit ephemeral) on mortgage foreclosures and evictions—an intervention in the housing market virtually unheard of since Depression days.
- Absentee voting problems (only partially resolved) on an unprecedented scale for the April 22 New Orleans primary and May 20, 2006, runoff elections.
- The limitations of insurance coverage, as insurance companies flee coastal areas and the federal flood insurance program goes into the red to the tune of $23 billion as a result of post-Katrina claims (Treaster 2006a; Treaster and Dean 2006).
- The Iraq war comes home, as a strapped U.S. military, bogged down in the Middle East, was unable to send National Guard, reservists, or active personnel and equipment to help out in the many ways the federal government has supplemented state and local resources in the past.

But of course the most salient and ongoing story in New Orleans and cities throughout the United States is one of poverty and racism—all those dramatic, pathetic shots, on television and in the papers, showing who the prime victims were, and their helplessness, suffering, and abandonment—reflecting the current realities of race and poverty in America. Correspondent Wolf Blitzer, on Sept. 1, 2005, lamented on CNN: "You simply get chills every time you see these poor individuals . . . so many of these people . . . are so poor and are so black, and this is going to raise lots of questions for people who are watching this story unfold" (CNN 2005).

While such images were no surprise to the community organizers, journalists, academics, and others who deal with these issues every day, for all too large segments of America this was regarded as a "wake-up call" (Turner and Zedlewski 2006; Brookings Institution 2005; Pastor et al. 2006; Dyson 2006). Speaking from New Orleans just a few weeks after the storms, President Bush asserted: "Poverty has its roots in racial discrimination, which cut off generations from the opportunity of America. . . . We have a duty to confront this poverty with bold action. . . . Let us rise above the legacy of inequality." Conservative *New York Times* columnist David Brooks, while mislabeling the events as merely a "natural disaster," recognized that they "interrupted a social disaster" (Brooks 2005).

And so the real questions are these: What created the pre-Katrina world? What should the post-Katrina world be? How might we get from here to there? And since Katrina is really a shorthand for a set of economic, social, and political conditions that characterize most of metropolitan America, what lessons and models does this provide for the nation as a whole? Ironically, we might say that in some sense we are fortunate that iconic New Orleans is the focus: One can hardly imagine equivalent national attention had the locus been Spokane, Toledo, or Utica.

PRE-KATRINA NEW ORLEANS

Pre-Katrina New Orleans, like most major U.S. cities, was characterized by extreme levels of poverty and racial segregation. The local poverty rate has long been high, and poor residents have been heavily concentrated. New Orleans' poverty rate in 2000 was 28 percent, compared to 12 percent for the nation. The number of high-poverty census tracts (tracts where 40 percent or more of the residents are poor) grew from thirty in 1980 to forty-nine in 2000. The number of people living in these tracts increased from 96,417 to 108,419. Consequently, among U.S. cities, New Orleans had the second highest share of its poor citizens (38 percent) living in such neighborhoods in 2000. In addition, the black poverty rate of 35 percent was more than 3 times the white rate of 11 percent, and 43 percent of poor blacks lived in poor neighborhoods (Jargowsky 1996, 2003; Brookings Institution 2005; Wagner and Edwards 2006). And New Orleans has long been highly segregated. According to two common indicators of racial segregation—the Index of Dissimilarity and the Isolation Index—New Orleans is one of the ten or fifteen most racially segregated among the nation's fifty largest metropolitan areas. As a Brookings Institution report summed up the situation: "By 2000, the city of New Orleans had become highly segregated by race and had developed high concentrations of poverty.... [B]lacks and whites were living in quite literally different worlds before the storm hit."

But where New Orleans stands relative to other metropolitan areas is almost beside the point. Big cities throughout the U.S. all contain large numbers of poor people, many neighborhoods of concentrated poverty, and highly segregated housing patterns. Why is this? What are the consequences? Oddly enough—and even though nothing from his personal history or his followup actions reflects such understanding and analysis (in his January 2007 State of the Union address, there was not a single mention of Katrina)—George W. Bush got it right: We need to understand the history and the legacy of inequality, and why generations of Americans have been and continue to be cut off from opportunity (Massey and Denton 1993; Briggs 2005).

Structural Racism

Racial disparities and poverty are not the result primarily of individual actions or character traits, as the culture-of-poverty theory asserts. They are the cumulative result of a long history of institutional arrangements and structures that have produced current realities. We can start with the 250 years of African-American slavery and the longer-term effects that status had on wealth creation, family life, and white attitudes toward—as well as treatment of—blacks. Eleven Southern states (including Louisiana) seceded; a bloody civil war followed: and the defeated states (selectively) asserted a claim of "states' rights" as a means of limiting national intervention. Afterwards, a century of legal segregation throughout the South—overturned by the Civil Rights Movement and several court rulings—ensued, with less formal barriers at work in other parts of the country. Even progressive federal policies—in particular, those introduced in the New Deal period—were racially discriminatory.

The Social Security system, when introduced, categorically excluded two occupations, courtesy of Southern members of Congress: farmworkers and domestics. Not coincidentally, these were occupations dominated by racial minorities, particularly African Americans. Federal housing programs provided minimal home ownership assistance to minority households and reinforced patterns of residential segregation. The GI Bill following World War II similarly provided relatively little education and housing assistance to minorities, compared to the massive benefits whites secured from this program. Even when African Americans received these federal benefits, all too often they were still effectively denied by educational institutions, housing providers, and employers.

But, of course, this is not "just history"—and in any case history has clear and powerful continuing impacts. "Redlining" by lending institutions and insurance companies is still all too common. School conditions for black and white students are very different, and, *Brown* notwithstanding, K-12 schools are resegregating all over the country, providing minorities with inferior education, which in turn perpetuates intergeneraional disadvntage. Housing and employment discrimination, often hard to pinpoint and prove, is rife, as demonstrated by reams of scholarly literature. Exclusionary zoning regulations, racial steering by real estate agents, federally-subsidized highways, and tax breaks for homeowners as well as suburban business development prop up the system. Racial health disparities abound. The criminal justice system—incarceration rates, sentencing patterns, the laws themselves—reflects extreme racial disparities. Need we go on? Concentrated poverty and racial segregation severely reduce opportunity of all types. As sociologist Douglas Massey, co-author of the classic *American Apartheid*, observes: "Any process that concentrates poverty within racially isolated neighborhoods will simultaneously increase the odds of socioeconomic failure".

The racial segregation and concentration of poverty resulting from these forces have shaped development in New Orleans and metropolitan areas around the country. One consequence is that in New Orleans those with means left when they knew the storm was coming: They had access to personal transportation or plane and train fare, money for temporary housing, in some cases second homes. Guests trapped in one luxury New Orleans hotel were saved when that chain hired a fleet of buses to get them out. Patients in one hospital were saved when a doctor who knew Al Gore contacted the former Vice President, who was able to cut through government red tape and charter two planes that took them to safety. This is what is meant by the catch phrase "social capital"—a resource most unevenly distributed by class and race. Various processes of racial segregation have resulted in middle- and upper-income whites being concentrated in the outlying (and in New Orleans, literally higher) suburban communities, while blacks have been concentrated in the low-lying central city, where the flooding was most severe. And they had difficulty escaping: most notoriously, on August 31, 2005, police in the West Bank city of Gretna blocked a bridge from New Orleans, preventing large numbers of African-American evacuees from leaving the deluged city.

Infrastructure and Uneven Development

A related key issue is the failure to maintain critical public services, including the infrastructure (e.g., levees in flood-prone areas). In the Katrina case, officials long knew the protective levees surrounding the city were inadequate, leaving it vulnerable to precisely the type of disaster that occurred on August 29. But whether it is the levees in New Orleans, the bridges in the San Francisco Bay Area and the Twin Cities, or the public schools in almost every city, such public services are generally viewed as expenses that need to be minimized rather than essential investments to be maximized for the purpose of enhancing the quality of life in the nation's cities. In its *2005 Report Card for America's Infrastructure,* the American Society of Civil Engineers concluded: "Congested highways, overflowing sewers and corroding bridges are constant reminders of the looming crisis that jeopardizes our nation's prosperity and quality of life." Assessing twelve infrastructure categories, the Society gave the nation a "D" for its maintenance efforts, noting there had been little improvement in recent years and asserting an as yet unfunded $1.6 trillion investment need over the next five years. The consequences have not been and will not be race- or class-neutral. Low-income people and people of color are disproportionately dependent on public transportation to get to work and to shop; on local police to keep their neighborhoods safe; and on emergency services of all types. They have fewer private resources to serve as cushions in times of stress caused not only outside forces like hurricanes but by personal disasters such as sudden unemployment, unexpected illness or injury, or other vagaries of modern life. As James Carr observed, if the city of New Orleans had been a more diverse community, it may well have had the political clout to secure the levees long ago.

The clear "bottom line" is that, while there still is plenty of racist behavior by individuals, incompetence by FEMA and other public and private bureaucracies, corruption on the part of government contractors and their partners in the public sector, and other forms of malfeasance and misfeasance, by far the most potent force in creating these extreme disparities is institutional racism—"color-blind racism," as it is often termed —something that most black people understand and experience, but most white people do not. Consequently, it should have been no surprise when Katrina hit New Orleans that the areas damaged were 45.8 percent black, compared to 26.4 percent in undamaged areas, and that 20.9 pecent of the households in damaged areas were poor, compared to 15.3 percent in undamaged areas. And if nobody is allowed to return to damaged areas, New Orleans will lose 80 percent of its black population, compared to just 50 percent of its white population.

New Orleans and the Gulf Coast region generally, like virtually all metropolitan areas in the U.S., experience many costs of racism, concentrated poverty, and uneven development. These forces may well shape, and hinder, redevelopment efforts in and around New Orleans as well as other communities seeking paths to prosperity for their citizens. Inequities associated with race, class, gender, and other socially constructed markers are not inevitable. They reflect the conscious choices made by political and economic decision-makers and implemented by public and private institutions. Different choices are available in a post-Katrina world.

SPECIFIC COSTS AND SPECIFIC LESSONS OF KATRINA

Not all past U.S. disasters were so poorly handled by government. While there were mistakes as well as positive lessons to be learned, a look at the Chicago Fire of 1871, the 1906 San Francisco Earthquake, the 1927 Mississippi flood, the 1930s Dustbowl, and Hurricane Andrew in 1992 is highly instructive, showing the importance of a comprehensive revitalization approach to recovery, rather than simple rebuilding; involvement of the affected persons in their own recovery; the importance of oversight and accountability; the need for ecological balance; and the appropriate division between private- and public-sector responsibilities. Recovery in some instances focused on restoring the status quo, in others on true reform—depending on who was in the decision-making role (Powers 2006). Recovery in New Orleans, no doubt, has been and will be a contested process. A brief examination of key areas illustrates these dynamics.

Housing

Housing and rehousing (temporary and permanent) are of course critical issues: for family life, access to jobs, schools and other community facilities, and household finances. The extent of destruction (of both privately-owned as well as public and assisted housing) was unprecedented— a National Low Income Housing Coalition September 2005 analysis showed 302,405 housing units seriously damaged or destroyed by Hurricane Katrina, 73 percent of all units in the jurisdictions studied. Slightly under half (47 percent) were rental units, 71 percent affordable to low-income households (Crowley 2006). Subsequent HUD data showed that 932,944 homes were damaged in Alabama, Louisiana, Mississippi, Texas and Florida, 30 percent of which sustained severe or major damage (U.S. Department of Housing and Urban Development 2006). Of the 103,019 occupied public or assisted units (including privately-owned units rented by Section 8 voucher-holders) in the Katrina-affected areas of Louisiana, Mississippi and Alabama, 41,161 were damaged, 15,199 so severely damaged as to render them uninhabitable (Jackson 2006).

And the government—national, state, and local—largely botched efforts at relocation and replacement housing (Fischer and Sard 2006; Frank and Waters 2005; Hsu and Connolly 2005; Lipton 2006a; Steinhauer and Lipton 2006; Torpy 2005; Weisman 2005). In the scramble to find shelter for displaced people as they were dispersed to cities across the county, HUD encouraged local public housing authorities to give admission priority to evacuees over people on the waiting lists—thereby pitting one needy group against another, a predictable situation at a time when there are 4.5 million more extremely low-income households in the United States than there are affordable rental units (Pelletiere 2006).

FEMA's initial response after the disaster was its standard disaster response: it ordered trailers, providing them rent-free for up to eighteen months. Other FEMA housing relief programs provide funding for emergency shelters and cash grants to individuals for rental assistance, home repairs and other personal costs. FEMA ordered 300,000 travel trailers and mobile homes, but placed them mostly in trailer camps ("FEMAvilles") they set up, removed from transportation, jobs, schools, health care and shopping (Cohn 2005). The agency was able to install only 500 a day, with a waiting list of 40,000 in Louisiana alone (Collins and Lieberman 2006). News images of thousands of trailers awaiting delivery and installation sinking into the mud in a field near Hope, Arkansas became a symbol of FEMA's incompetence (Brand 2005; Neuman 2006). Siting of trailers has been met with "Not in my backyard!" resistance by some parish governments in Louisiana and by neighbors in New Orleans (Hustmyre 2005; Jensen 2005; Tizon 2005; Reuters 2006).

Perhaps the most bizarre problem with trailers is that they are structurally unsuitable for hurricane-prone areas (Barbour 2006). Added to that are the serious health perils to occupants from high-formaldehyde-emitting particle board and composite wood, causing serious eye, lung and nose irritation; the Gulf's hot, humid climate increases the rate at which these toxic, carcinogenic vapors are released. The vast majority of the trailers FEMA ordered were built very quickly, likely with poor quality control (Spake 2007). More than 500 hurricane survivors living in these trailers and mobile homes have sued 14 manufacturers in federal court, accusing them of using inferior materials in a profit-driven rush to build the temporary homes ("Storm

Victims Sue Over Trailers," Associated Press, Aug. 9, 2007). Most disturbingly, since early 2006 FEMA knew and suppressed warnings from its own heath workers about these trailer hazards—the agency stopped testing occupied trailers after discovering formaldehyde levels 75 times the U.S.-recommended safety threshold for workplaces, and more stringent standards likely are appropriate for tight living spaces where occupants (many of whom are children) spend more time than at their workplace (Hsu 2007b, 2007c; Palank 2007).

As of late April 2007, some 86,000 families were still living in government trailers, under unstable conditions (Eaton 2007a). A typical account of one such FEMA trailer park, in Hammond, Louisiana—a rural area an hour north of New Orleans—was headed, quoting one resident, "We called it Hurricane FEMA" (Whoriskey 2007a). Five trailer parks in Baton Rouge, on airport land, are closing as the airport has declined to renew the lease. "What trauma victims need most, stability, is just what has proved most elusive," noted one *New York Times* story (Dewan 2006e). Nor is the agency's profound dereliction limited to the housing area or the 2005 events: as one account noted, "As many as six million prepared meals stockpiled near potential victims of the 2006 hurricane season spoiled in the Gulf Coast heat last summer when the Federal Emergency Management Agency ran short of warehouse and refrigeration space" (Hsu 2007a). In July 2007, FEMA announced it was throwing away the last of 42,000 tons of ice purchased at a price of $24 million for the total 112,000 ton buy when Katrina struck—after paying $12.5 million in storage fees, plus $3.4 million to melt what's left (*Washington Post* 2007b).

Yet another expensive and contentious form of temporary housing was hotel/motel rooms, furnished first by the Red Cross, then taken over by FEMA. At the peak of hotel usage, FEMA reported paying for 85,000 rooms a night (U.S. Department of Homeland Security 2006). FEMA's repeated attempts to end the hotel program and compel the evacuees to move elsewhere., when there were no alternative quarters available, resulted in widespread public outcry and a lawsuit (*McWaters v. FEMA* 2005; Blumenthal and Lipton 2005; Driver 2005; "FEMA's Latest Fumble" 2005; Newsom Slams 2005; What Next 2005; With Holidays Coming 2005). A Louisiana-based Federal Judge issued a temporary restraining order enjoining FEMA from proceeding with its December 15, 2005 hotel assistance deadline, calling FEMA's actions "numbingly insensitive" and "unduly callous" (*McWaters v. FEMA* 2005). And in late November 2006, a federal judge ordered FEMA to restore housing assistance and pay back rent to at least 11,000 families, calling the agency's cut-off unconstitutional and "Kafkaesque" (Dewan 2006d; "Kafka and Katrina" 2006)—a decision FEMA has appealed. In other lawsuits against FEMA, other federal judges used such terms as "incomprehensible" and "a legal disaster" (Apuzzo 2006). The details of other, mostly inadequate government rehousing efforts are catalogued in Crowley 2006 and Quigley 2007.

Insurance has been a further and quite serious problem. Insurance companies have been insisting that their policies do not cover water damage caused by flooding—and proving that there was wind damage (which is covered) rather than water damage has been highly contentious (Treaster 2006c). Some 6,600 insurance-related lawsuits have landed in Federal District Court in New Orleans alone, and as a recent summary of popular sentiment put it: "Every neighborhood [in New Orleans] is full of horror stories about companies that reneged on their promises, offered only pennies on the dollar in settlements, dribbled out payments, deliberately underestimated the costs of repairs, dropped longtime customers and sharply increased the price of coverage" (Eaton and Treaster 2007). And yet, as an October 2006 *New York Times* headline reported, "Earnings for Insurers Are Soaring"—with the jump page headlined, "Record Profits Expected for Insurers in '06" (Treaster 2006b). The Mississippi Attorney General has sued one of the major carriers, State Farm and Casualty, and a Mississippi Grand Jury heard testimony on possible criminal charges against State Farm (*New York Times* 2007).

A further dimension of the housing problem has been salvaging, rebuilding, and reoccupying New Orleans' damaged homes—deciding what houses or parts of houses are salvageable, how to carry out the salvage and rebuilding work expeditiously and at modest cost; who will do the work; and of course how to do it in way that does not endanger the health and safety of those carrying out these tasks. "Deconstructing" homes, rather than bulldozing them—careful dismantling in order to re-use the building materials, provide skilled employment, reduce landfill dumping—has been suggested (Zdenek et al. 2006).

A related problem has been the overwhelming focus on homeowners, with wholly inadequate attention paid to the rental housing supply, both private and public—which of course is disproportionately where the region's poor families live (Carr 2005). Despite the huge hit the region's rental stock took, few replacement units have been built or restored for renters; consequently, rents have risen markedly: HUD's Fair Market Rent (a measure used for the agency's Section 8 rent subsidy program) for a two-bedroom apartment in the New Orleans metropolitan area was $987 in mid-2007, up from $676 in pre-Katrina 2005 (Brookings Institution 2007).

But neither is Louisiana's Road Home program—to assist homeowners in repairing or replacing their damaged homes—anywhere near successful: as of June 2007, it was estimated that the federally funded program may be as much as $5 billion short, and as of May 2007, only 16,000 of 130,000 applicants had received money (*Washington Post* 2007a; Whoriskey 2007b).

New Orleans's public housing program and projects—a major source for low-rent housing for the cities poor—were in poor shape before the storms. HUD went so far as to place the city's Housing Authority in receivership in 2002. There is considerable pressure not to replace or renovate damaged and destroyed units, instead to redevelop those projects located in potentially upscale neighborhoods—the city's public housing population was nearly 100% black—for entirely different uses and users (Nelson and Varney 2005; Filosa 2006b; Wilgoren 2005). Louisiana Congressman Richard Baker was heard to say, a few days after the storm, "We finally cleaned up public housing in New Orleans. We couldn't do it, but God did it" (Babington 2005).

In December 2006, HUD vastly added to the city's housing problems with its decision to demolish more than 4,500 public housing apartments—a move characterized as "the most prominent skirmish in the larger battle over the post-Katrina balance of whites and blacks in New Orleans and how decisions on rebuilding shape the city's demographic future" (Cass and Whoriskey 2006). Noteworthy is that the *New York Times* architecture critic had this to say about New Orleans housing projects, in a plea for restoration: "Built at the height of the New Deal, the city's public housing projects have little in common with the dehumanizing superblocks and grim plazas that have long been an emblem of urban poverty. Modestly scaled, they include some of the best public housing built in the United States. . . . The notion [of dynamiting the projects] is stupefying" (Ouroussoff 2006). And, in a declaration submitted as part of a lawsuit to prevent HUD from going ahead with its plan to demolish these projects, MIT Architecture Professor John Fernandez, following a five-day survey of 140 units in four projects (Lafitte, C. J. Pete, B. W. Cooper, and St. Bernard), asserted: "My inspection and assessment found that no structural or nonstructural damage was found that would reasonably warrant any cost-effective building demolitions. . . . I did not find any conditions in which the . . . residential units themselves could not be brought to safe and livable conditions with relatively minor investment. . . . Replacement of these buildings with contemporary construction would yield buildings of lower quality and shorter lifetime duration, the original construction methods and materials of these projects are far superior in their resistance to hurricane conditions than typical of new construction, and with renovation and regular maintenance, the lifetimes of the buildings in all four projects promise decades of continued service that may be extended indefinitely" (Fernandez 2006).

The centrality of housing to racial issues has been vividly illustrated in many ways following the storms. Racial discrimination has been demonstrated in the following ways:

First, studies by the National Fair Housing Alliance (2006a, 2006b) found that black evacuees were treated less favorably than white evacuees in their attempts to obtain housing. Using standard "paired tester" techniques, the Alliance revealed the litany of standard discriminatory housing market practices in two-thirds of their tests: Some landlords represented to black home seekers that vacant livable units were unavailable or unlivable, while showing several homes to whites; black home seekers were charged more rent and higher deposits than their white counterparts; rental agents failed to return messages to African-American home seekers while returning the calls of their white counterparts; rental agents offered special inducements like lower security deposits to white home seekers, while failing to offer the same to their black counterparts. Parallel racial discrimination in the French Quarter's tourist establishments was revealed in similar testing by the Greater New Orleans Fair Housing Action Center. To wit: African-American customers at Bourbon Street bars and nightclubs receiving less favorable treatment than their Caucasian counterparts and were charged more for drinks; house rules concerning minimum number of drinks and dress codes were more frequently and stringently enforced against black testers than white testers (Korosec 2005; Greater New Orleans Fair Housing Action Center 2006).

The Greater New Orleans Fair Housing Action Center also examined listserv postings for rehousing offers (including one sponsored by FEMA)—most of which reflected admirable charitable instincts, but some of which demonstrated far less admirable, but widely prevalent (and self-deluding), racism in housing patterns (Filosa 2006a). Among the postings:

- "I would love to house a single mom, with one child, but white only."
- "Not to sound racist, but because we want to make things more understandable [sic] for our younger child, we would like to house white children."
- "Provider would provide room and board for $400, prefers 2 white females" (Greater New Orleans Fair Housing Action Center 2006; Korosec 2005).

Second, in September 2006, St. Bernard Parish, right outside New Orleans, passed an ordinance barring single-family homeowners from renting their home to anyone except a blood relative without special permission from the Parish Council. Given St. Bernard's history and reputation as a segregated, predominantly white community, the motives for this extraordinary measure were not hard to decipher. (Nearly 93 percent of the Parish's owner-occupied housing is white-occupied, and potentially thousands of homeowners who left the Parish after Katrina may wish to rent out their otherwise-empty homes.) The Council cited the need to "maintain the integrity and stability of established neighborhoods as centers of family values and activities," and one of the supportive Councilors remarked, "We don't want to change the aesthetics of the neighborhood." The Greater New Orleans Fair Housing Action Center, represented by attorneys from the Lawyers Committee for Civil Rights Under Law and John Relman Associates, immediately filed a motion in Federal District Court for a temporary injunction, claiming a clear violation of the Fair Housing Act, leading the Council to announce it would suspend enforcement of the ordinance (but not repeal it). A second, similarly motivated Council ordinance imposed a year-long moratorium on the redevelopment of multifamily housing, prohibiting renovation without strict screening and pre-approval by the Council itself (Chen 2006; Brazille 2006; National Fair Housing Alliance 2006).

But the overall problem is massive. As Sheila Crowley (2006) writes: "Solving the levee problem may pale in comparison to solving the housing problem. It is impossible to disentangle the housing problems in the Gulf Coast from its other major institutional crises. The challenge for public officials and private enterprise is to restore housing, health care, schools, jobs and commercial establishments in concert with one another. Most people cannot return in the absence of any one of these elements of community life (Rivlin 2006; Sayre 2006). Moreover, rebuilding has stalled because there is not enough housing for the workforce needed for the task" (Martha Carr 2005). And the broader context is that as a nation we do not take housing problems seriously enough. We are light years away from establishing and implementing a right to decent, affordable housing (Hartman 2006). And of course fundamental to the future of housing in the Gulf Coast is the question of who has the right to return. As Sheila Crowley (2006) notes, "While policymakers have been dithering, the modern-day carpetbaggers have moved in. Speculators are buying up property at bargain prices, and multinational corporations are getting richer off of FEMA contracts." Long-time residents sometimes do not have clear title to properties handed down through the generations. Evacuees in far-off places are tempted to take what looks like a windfall of needed immediate cash—usually well below what a knowledgeable on-site seller could command—for their homes.

Education

Almost as important as housing—for families with K-12 children—is schools. Prior to the storm, the system was one of worst in the country, according to Michael Casserly of the Council of the Great City Schools (2006), who observed, "Before Katrina's onslaught, the children of New Orleans were isolated racially, economically, academically and politically in public schools that were financed inadequately, maintained poorly, and governed ineptly." The damage to the educational enterprise on August 29 was enormous, as over two-fifths of the system's schools (disproportionately those in low-income, African-American neighborhoods) sustained severe wind and flooding damage, many beyond repair, and almost as many suffered moderate damage. And so tens of thousands of K-12 students wound up in different school districts and different states, disrupting their curriculum and teacher/student as well as peer relationships. A great many of them missed months of formal education (Dewan 2006c). New Orleans Charter Science and Math High School (2006) produced a collection of personal narratives by the school's students chronicling their evacuations from Katrina. Dewan (2007) describes a moving art therapy program at the largest trailer park for Katrina evacuees, Renaissance [sic] Village, in Baker, Louisiana, which helps children deal with their ongoing posttraumatic stress. Their evocative drawings will be displayed at the New Orleans Museum of Art in an exhibit entitled "Katrina Through the Eyes of Children."

The U.S. Dept. of Education estimated that some 372,000 students—pre-school through college—were displaced from the states hit by the storms. Louisiana alone estimated that some 105,000 of its students were dislocated and not attending their home schools—creating sudden and severe burdens on the receiving school systems, such as overcrowded classrooms. Texas indicated it received some 40,200 out-of-state students as a result of Katrina and Rita; Georgia was accommodating 10,300 students; Florida, 5,600 (Jacobson 2006). These newly arriving students, of course, arrived without academic, discipline, immunization or health records. As of the summer of 2007, just 45 percent of New Orleans's public schools had opened (Brookings Institution 2007). A state school board member is quoted as saying, "The teacher shortage is real. The book shortage is real. We have a labor shortage. There is a shortage of bus drivers. The whole food-service industry is short of workers" (Nossiter 2006b).

A major change in the New Orleans public school system has been state takeover of a large portion of the system and a shift to charter schools, a controversial move and one that has been pushed as a more general goal by market-oriented advocates in the education reform field (Saulny 2006a; Center for Community Change 2006; Adamo 2007). An ancillary result (some claim, a goal) is weakening of the teachers' union; the district's teachers were furloughed in the weeks immediately following Katrina, and their right to return to the system on a seniority basis was replaced by state authority to hire and place teachers in the schools it had seized (Maggi 2005). Teachers in most public charter schools are on year-to-year contracts without collective bargaining leverage. United Teachers of New Orleans has filed suit challenging these arrangements (United Teachers of New Orleands, Louisiana Federation of Teachers, and American Federation of Teachers 2007).

A more recent phenomenon has been a steep rise in violence and misbehavior in the reopened schools, due in large part to the return of teenagers without accompanying parents. Some parents, for a variety of reasons—many job-related—have chosen to remain, at least temporarily, but possibly permanently, in the cities to which they were evacuated, and they gave in to their children's entreaties to return to friends and a familiar environment, making do as best they can with respect to sleeping and eating arrangements. One New Orleans high school, the largest one still functioning, where up to a fifth of the 775 students live without parents, is described as having "at least 25 security guards, at the entrance, up the stairs, and outside classes. The school has a metal detector, four police officers and four police cruisers on the sidewalk." A student observed, "We have a lot of security guards and not enough teachers." Another student added, "It's like you're in jail. You have people watching you all the time" (Nossiter 2006b). One can only imagine the long-range impact of this schooling crisis on the future lives of thousands of angry, lonely, deracinated teens. The new focus on "the school-to-prison pipeline" around the country certainly has taken root here.

The future of the city's school system remains murky, in part because no one can reliably predict how many families will eventually return, who they will be, and to which parts of the city they will return. Experiencing better schooling for their children in another city may be a key decision-making factor for some families. But, as Michael Casserly (2006, 211–12) observes, "One can also see flashing yellow lights on the horizon. The preliminary plans for remaking the city's public schools were designed by people who were substantially different in hue from educational decision-makers before the storm, a touchy issue in these still racially sensitive times. The proposal to replace the currently elected school board with an appointed school board, for instance, is bound to exacerbate concerns among community activists and parents that the schools, along with other city agencies, are being highjacked by alien forces." And Casserly (2006, 213) appropriately extends this warning: "New Orleans is not the only city . . . in which our poorest children are concentrated and isolated in such a way. . . . And it is not the only one that embodies the nation's neglect of its poor. One can see the same pattern in many other cities across the country—if one is only willing to open one's eyes. And, in other cities, we run the same risk . . . whatever the next storm, wherever the next levees."

Health

Another critical service is public health. The storms created their own public health problems—notably, toxics from damage to buildings and vehicles; brackish, sewage-contaminated flood water; decomposing bodies; vermin; and many other sources.

The immediate crisis was described by Dr. Evangline Franklin (2006), Director of Clinical Services and Employee Health for the City of New Orleans:

"Aside from immediate and long-term mold and the lack of water, food, shelter and sanitation facilities, there was concern that the prolonged flooding might lead to an outbreak of health problems in many neighborhoods among the remaining population. In addition to dehydration and food poisoning, there was the potential for communicable disease outbreaks of diarrhea and respiratory illness, all related to the growing contamination of food and drinking water supplies in the area. After dewatering and house-to-house searches for dead bodies and animals, public health concerns centered around acute environmental hazards related to houses standing in water for several weeks (mold, bacteria, concealed rodents, snakes and alligators). This was combined with ruptured sewage lines, refuse, structural instability, debris, the lack of sanitary water (what water they had was usable only for flushing toilets), as well as a lack of gas and electricity. . . . There was concern that the chemical plants and refineries in the area could have released pollutants into the floodwaters. People who suffer from allergies or chronic respiratory disorders, such as asthma, were susceptible to what some health officials have dubbed "Katrina Cough." On September 6, it was reported that *Escherichia coli* (*E. coli*) had been detected at unsafe levels in the water that flooded the city. The CDC [Centers for Disease Control and Prevention] reported on September 7 that five people had died of bacterial infection from drinking water contaminated with *Vibrio vulnificus*, a bacterium from the Gulf of Mexico. (Franklin 2006)

As was the case with the schools, New Orleans was a community at risk well before August 29. An Urban Institute report (Zuckerman and Coughlin 2006) noted that before the storms hit: "According to the United Health Foundation's 2004 State Health Rankings . . . Louisiana ranked lowest overall in the country. It numbered among the five worst states for infant mortality, cancer deaths, prevalence of smoking, and premature deaths...Louisianans also had among the nation's highest rates of cardiovascular deaths, motor vehicle deaths, occupational fatalities, infectious diseases, and violent crime." This majority-black city with extreme levels of poverty produced a de facto caste system of health care, providing unequal, lesser treatment for the poor, the uneducated, the homeless, the immigrant, the uninsured and others who are disenfranchised (Institute of Medicine 2003; Franklin, Hall and Burris 2005). State funding cutbacks beginning in 2004 led to dramatic reductions by more than two-thirds in ambulatory care services for the poorest residents and reduced access to non-emergency care for the uninsured—leading to increasingly congested emergency rooms.

Most of the city's hospitals, located in the center of the city, were damaged or flooded, leading to loss of over half of the state's hospital beds and one of the state's two Level 1 trauma centers (Barringer 2006). As of the summer of 2007, only 13 of New Orleans's 23 pre-Katrina hospitals were open (Eaton 2007b; Brookings Institution 2007). Doctors' offices were rendered unusable, as were pharmacies. As part of general layoffs of City workers, Health Department staff for its clinics went from 250 to 72. Health workers at all levels evacuated, and a great many likely will not return. As of Spring 2006, there were virtually no dentists practicing in the city. Absence of former patient loads of course is a factor influencing health providers' return plans, and physicians need hospitals, support facilities, labs, x-ray units and pharmacies to provide the proper level of health care. One major problem is loss of health records—leading to strong recommendations for development of a system of personal ownership of portable, electronic, transmittable records (Franklin 2006).

Higher rates of illness among evacuees have been reported, especially among children. Mental health problems are rife, with a notable rise in suicides (Turner 2006). The Regional Administrator for Health Unit 2 in Baton Rouge Parish, where some 30,000 persons relocated following the hurricanes, noted that the parish's mental health clinic has seen a 30 percent increase in post-Katrina office visits. "Many experience depression, anxiety, Post-Traumatic Stress Disorder and other mental illness due to hurricane displacement and trauma. . . . Transitional housing areas are reporting problems with child abuse, sexual abuse, domestic violence and substance abuse as people struggle to cope with the loss of their community/support system while living in close proximity to each other in tiny FEMA trailers" (Roques 2007). Decomposed bodies are still being found, adding to the still incomplete toll of storm-related deaths. And toxic waste problems doubtless will persist and show up—Agent Orange-like—in years to come (Dewan 2006a, 2006b; Redlener 2006; Nossiter 2005; Connolly 2005; Cass 2006; Hsu and Eilperin 2006; Barringer 2005; Cole and Woelfle-Erskine 2006; Saulny 2006b; Turner 2006).

A range of political, economic, and social forces have contributed to health care challenges in New Orleans. The city's historic absence of a manufacturing sector prevented the development of a strong labor movement with its demands for health care benefits. Cultural patterns ("*Laissez les bon temps rouler*") and the high-calorie, high-cholesterol local cuisine were contributing factors to the local health picture (Turner 2006b; Franklin 2006).

In sum, the medical problems and unequal access to health care were predictable, just one of the many areas in which poverty and race in our society compound vulnerability (Franklin 2006).

Economic Development

The issue of future (and past) economic development is prominent as well. Pre-Katrina, as Robert K. Whelan (2006) points out, "the local economy was highly polarized, with some professional people doing very well and a much larger number of people employed in low-wage jobs. . . . Traditionally, the New Orleans economy had a tripartite base: the port, oil and related industries, and tourism." Employment growth was stagnant during the 80s and 90s, and the city registered substantial job losses in port-related industries and manufacturing, while gaining jobs in health care, tourism-related industries, legal services, social services, and education (Whelan, Gladstone and Hirth 2002). The metropolitan area lost more than 200,000 jobs in the wake of the storms; in November 2005, the unemployment rate in the New Orleans area was a staggering 17.5 percent.

Rebuilding economically has been hampered by multiple failures on the part of Small Business Administration and FEMA (Nixon 2007), as well the failure of insurance companies to make prompt and full payment, followed by the withdrawal of several key companies from the area with respect to writing new policies. Government clean-up and construction contracts went to firms from Texas and Arkansas, rather than to local firms, which would have had the benefit of shoring up the local economy. Labor contractors and outside firms imported large numbers of immigrant workers, a substantial portion of whose wages did not circulate in the local economy but were remitted to their home countries. And predictably, many were not paid promptly, were paid less than what they were promised, or were not paid at all. MacDonald (2007) offers a case study of Maryland day laborers who traveled to Louisiana and Mississippi, working long hours, for a promised $10/hour, shoveling mud and debris out of the Gulf Coast gambling casinos and other dirty, dangerous jobs—only to have to wait two years to get their paychecks—and then only by virtue of a lawsuit on their behalf brought by a Maryland advocacy organization that assists Latinos (see also Beutler 2007; Browne-Dianis et. Al 2006). For a constructive approach to employment generation and economic development in reconstruction projects—framed around conflicts but applicable as well to other disasters, see Mendelson-Forman and Mashatt 2007. See also Browne-Dianis et al. 2006.

Unequal, racially-related access to credit—residential as well as commercial—has been a serious problem in the past and likely will continue to be. John Taylor and Josh Silver (2006) have documented the extensive redlining that existed pre-Katrina and its relation to unemployment and poverty conditions. In 2004, African Americans received just 15 percent of all market-rate home loans written in the New Orleans metropolitan statistical area, where they comprised 34 percent of the population—leaving them to rely on high-cost, often predatory lending. Had they received market-rate mortgages in proportion to their population, they would have received 4,269 additional loans worth $458 million. In the area of small business lending, during 2004, Community Reinvestment Act-covered lenders made loans to 38 percent of the small businesses in Mississippi's minority neighborhoods, compared to 51 percent of the small businesses in white neighborhoods. Equalizing the 51 percent rate would have increased the number of such loans in Mississippi's minority neighborhoods by 6,588, worth $307 million. While income and creditworthiness obviously play a role, differences in unequal access to credit are rooted in the structural dimensions of race and space, as noted above.

A further important element in the lending picture is the location of bank branches: Such local branches are generally found to boost small business lending, but there are far fewer bank branches in low-income and minority neighborhoods—as an extreme example, the predominantly minority, lower-income Lower 9th Ward and St. Claude neighborhoods of New Orleans have just one branch, while bank branches are clustered around the French Quarter tourist hub and predominantly white neighborhoods across the city. "It is clear," as Taylor and Silver (2006) write, that "the financial sector . . . has yet to address the inequalities between minorities and whites that were magnified by the hurricanes' damage."

WHAT DOES THE FUTURE LOOK LIKE?

What then is the future of New Orleans—and by extension, America's metropolitan areas?

A story in the September 8, 2005, *Wall Street Journal* offers one vision:

> Despite the disaster that has overwhelmed New Orleans, the city's monied, mostly white elite is hanging on and maneuvering to play a role in the recovery when the floodwaters of Katrina are gone. . . . The power elite of New Orleans—whether they are still in the city or have moved temporarily to enclaves such as Destin, Fla., and Vail, Colo.—insist the remade city won't simply restore the old order. . . . The new city must be something very different, Mr. Reiss [chairman of the city's Regional Transit Authority, who helicoptered in an Israeli security company to guard his Audubon Place house and those of his neighbors] says, with better services and fewer poor people . . . , "Those who want to see the city rebuilt want to see it done in a completely different way: demographically, geographically and politically."

This speaks to the replanning process and who is involved in it. Is there to be a true right of return (Wellington 2006)—especially for those who lived in the most rundown and vulnerable parts of the city, such as the infamous Lower 9th Ward? (See ACORN 2007; Nossiter 2007; Solnit 2007.) How can we avoid placing people in danger of future storms and levee failures? Who is responsible for carrying out plans? (An interesting international dimension to these issues occurred in November 2006, when a delegation of Katrina/Rita survivor advocates traveled to Thailand to meet with representatives of those impacted by the 2004 tsunami and the more recent earthquake in Yogyakarta, Indonesia, "to claim their human rights and dignity, while leading the process of rebuilding their communities with full participation and empowerment." Reference was made to government responsibility for such survivors as Internally Displaced Persons, who have special protections under international human rights standards. (See National Economic & Social Rights Initiative 2006.)

Peter Marcuse (2006) asserts that "the principle guiding the planning efforts should not simply be subservience to the desires of the 'monied, mostly white elite,' sweeping the area's past problems under the table and its poorer residents out the door." Rather the process should provide true democratic participation of all those affected by the disaster (involving evacuees who have not returned, as well as those now in New Orleans) and equitable distribution of costs and benefits. That latter goal speaks to economic development for the poor, a true safety net, fair compensation for what has been lost. Beyond New Orleans, "the goals should . . . be . . . moving towards making the cities and region affected a model of what American communities should and could be," and the federal government needs to play the key financing role.(See also Birch and Wachter 2007.)

The most detailed, comprehensive approach—combining democracy and equity, backed by the needed implementation resources—is the Congressional Black Caucus' Hurricane Katrina Recovery, Reclamation, Restoration, Reconstruction and Reunion Act of 2005 (H.R. 4197 of the 109th Congress, with ninety-one cosponsors.) It did not pass, and it was not reintroduced in the 110th Congress, but elements of it—dealing with grants to states to respond to disasters and improvements to the Small Business Administration loan guarantee program—have been introduced as free standing bills.

In December 2006, an elaborate "community engagement" process was held, involving evacuees in New Orleans, Baton Rouge, Atlanta, Houston and Dallas (with satellite gatherings in sixteen other diaspora cities with substantial, but fewer evacuees), produced by America Speaks, designed to produce a comprehensive "bottom-up" rebuilding plan (Warner 2006; UNOP Unified New Orleans Plan 2006). And in the same month, New Orleans Mayor C. Ray Nagin appointed Edward Blakely, a highly regarded urban planner, former Chair of the Univ. of Calif.-Berkeley Urban

Planning Dept., as "executive director for recovery management" for his city (Nossiter 2006c).

John Powell and his colleagues at the Kirwan Institute for the Study of Race and Ethnicity (2006, 60–61) offer the following guidance on what is the most critical issue—the role of race in America:

> Questions about *why* African Americans are more likely than whites to be poor, and why poor African Americans are more likely to live in areas of concentrated poverty, are questions that were neither asked nor answered. . . . There was little critical discussion of how historical patterns of segregation contributed to the racial layout of the city, and how structures worked together to produce racial disparities and economic inequality (Muhammed et al. 2004). . . . Broadening how we think and talk about race is critically important to making sense of today's world. Doing so also raises critical questions about the shrinking middle class, our anemic investment in public space, the meaning of merit in a purported meritocracy, and the promises and failures of the American experiment—all of which concern every American. Once we are able to discuss race and racism in these broad terms, we will be able to construct a response not only to the damage wrought by Katrina, but also to that which occurs across the country every day. . . . [Katrina] created an opportunity for reexamining the connections between race and class, and deciphering precisely how race has been inscribed spatially into our metropolitan areas. In short, it has provided a rare chance to discuss the links between race, equity, justice and democracy.
>
> Race, as a transformative tool, can and should be applied to more than just the rebuilding effort in New Orleans. Racialized poverty, segregation, and the decaying infrastructure of our central cities are common problems plaguing urban areas nationwide. Used properly, race allows us to examine how institutional failings affect everyone, and enables us to re-imagine a society where democracy and democratic ideals are not constricted and undermined by structural arrangements.

We end with this observation by three academics (Frymer et al. 2006):

> The experience of African Americans in New Orleans can serve as the "miner's canary," as Lani Guinier and Gerald Torres argue. Similar to the way in which canaries alerted miners to the specter of poisonous air, the fates that befall people who are disadvantaged by inequalities based on, for example,

race, class, and gender are signifiers of society-wide inequalities. If policy-makers and the public heed the lessons of Katrina and make efforts to address the structural and institutional sources of American inequality, perhaps the brunt of future disasters will not be borne by those who are least able to endure their costs.

Sober words.

References

American Society of Civil Engineers. 2005. *2005 Report Card for America's Infrastructure*. Reston, VA: American Society of Civil Engineers.

Babington, Charles. 2005. "Some GOP Legislators Hit Jarring Note in Addressing Katrina." *Washington Post*. September 10.

Barbour, Gov. Haley. 2006. Testimony before Committee on Appropriations, U.S. Senate. March 6. Retrieved from http://www.appropriations.senate.gov/hearmarkups/gov'stestimony-fullapprops.march06.htm.

Barringer, Felicity. 2005. "Toxic Residue of Hurricane Stirs Debate on Safety." *New York Times*. December 2.

Beck, Chris, and Preston Browning. 2006. "Fables of Deconstruction." Op-ed. *New York Times. November 30.*

———. 2006. "Long After Storm, Shortages Overwhelm N.O.'s Few Hospitals." *New York Times*. January 23.

Blumenthal, Ralph, and Eric Lipton. 2005. "FEMA Broke Its Promise on Housing, Houston Mayor Says." *New York Times*. November 17.

Bonilla-Silva, Eduardo. 2003. *Racism Without Racists: Color-Blind Racism and the Persistence of Racial Inequality in the United States*. New York: Rowman & Littlefield.

Brand, Aaron. 2005. "Rep. Mike Ross Critical of FEMA Mobile Homes Delay." *Texarkana Gazette*. December 15.

Briggs, Xavier de Souza, ed. 2005. *The Geography of Opportunity: Race and Housing Choice in Metropolitan America*. Washington, D.C.: Brookings Institution Press.

Brookings Institution. 2005. *New Orleans After the Storm: Lessons from the Past, a Plan for the Future*. Washington, D.C.

Brooks, David. 2005. "Katrina's Silver Lining." *New York Times*. September 8.

Brown, Michael K., Martin Carnoy, Elliott Currie, Troy Duster, David B. Oppenheimer, Marjorie M. Shultz, and David Wellman. 2003. *White-Washing Race: The Myth of a Color-Blind Society*. Berkeley: University of California Press.

Carr, James H. 2005. Comments at conference on " Predatory Home Lending: Moving Toward Legal and Policy Solutions." John Marshall Law School, Chicago, September 9.

Carr, Martha. 2005. "Housing Shortage Hinders Rebound." *New Orleans Times-Picayune*. October 16.

Cass, Julia. 2006. "For Many of Katrina's Young Victims, The Scars Are More Than Deep." *Washington Post*. June 13.

Cass, Julia, and Peter Whoriskey. 2006. "New Orleans to Raze Public Housing." *Washington Post*. December 8.

Casserly, Michael. 2006. "Double Jeopardy: Public Education in New Orleans Before *and* After the Storm." In *There Is No Such Thing As a Natural Disaster: Race, Class and Hurricane Katrina*, edited by Chester Hartman and Gregory D. Squires. New York: Routledge.

Cohn, Jonathan. 2005. "Trailer Trash: Katrina Victims Need Real Housing." *The New Republic*. September 26.

Cole, Oskar, and Cleo Woelfle-Erskine. 2006. "Rebuilding on Poisoned Ground." *Color Lines*, Spring: 26–28.

Collins, Sen. Susan, and Sen. Joseph Lieberman. 2006. Letter to Secretary of U.S. Department of Homeland Security Michael Chertoff. March 14. Retrieved from http://www.nlihc.org/news/031406collinsletter.pdf.

Connolly, Ceci. 2005. "Katrina's Emotional Damage Lingers." *Washington Post*. December 7.

Crowley, Sheila. 2006. "Where Is Home? Housing for Low-Income People After the 2005 Hurricanes." In *There Is No Such Thing As a Natural Disaster: Race, Class and Hurricane Katrina*, edited by Chester Hartman and Gregory D. Squires. New York: Routledge.

Dewan, Shaila. 2006a. "Storm Evacuees Found to Suffer Health Setbacks." *New York Times*. April 18.

———. 2006b. "In Attics and Rubble: More Bodies and Questions." *New York Times*. April 11.

———. 2006c. "For Many, Education Is Another Storm Victim." *New York Times*. June 1.

———. 2006d. "FEMA Ordered to Restore Evacuees' Housing Aid." *New York Times*. November 30.

———. 2006e. "Storm Evacuees Remain in Grip of Uncertainty." *New York Times*. December 6.

Driver, Anna. 2005. "Some Katrina Victims Face NY Homeless Shelters." *Reuters*. November 18.

Dyson, Michael Eric. 2006. *Come Hell or High Water: Hurricane Katrina and the Color of Disaster*. New York: Perseus Books.

Eaton, Leslie. 2006. "In Louisiana, Graft Inquiries Are Increasing." *New York Times*. March 18.

"FEMA's Latest Fumble." 2005. *Northeast Mississippi Daily Journal*. Editorial. November 18.

Filosa, Gwen. 2006a. Housing Discrimination Hits the Web: Post-Katrina Ads Cited in Federal Complaints. *New Orleans Times-Picayune*. January 3.

———. 2006b. "Displaced Residents Demand Access to Public Housing." *New Orleans Times-Picayune*. June 3.

Fischer, Will, and Barbara Sard. 2006. *Housing Needs of Many Low-Income Hurricane Evacuees Are Not Being Adequately Addressed.* Washington, D.C.: Center on Budget and Policy Priorities. February 27.

Frank, Rep. Barney, and Rep. Maxine Waters. 2005. Reps. Frank and Waters: Where's the Katrina Housing Plan? Press Release. November 8. Retrieved from http://www. house.gov/banking_democrats/pr11082005a.html.

Franklin, Evangeline. 2006. "A New Kind of Medical Disaster in the United States." In *There Is No Such Thing As a Natural Disaster: Race, Class and Hurricane Katrina,* edited by Chester Hartman and Gregory D. Squires. New York: Routledge.

Franklin, Evangeline, Patrick Hall, and Nancy Burris. 2005. *Getting People Healthy in New Orleans,* vols. 1 and 2. New Orleans Health De partment. Unpublished. August.

Frymer, Paul, Dara Z. Strolovitch, and Dorian T. Warren. "Katrina's Political Roots and Divisions: Race, Class, and Federalism in American Politics." *Understanding Katrina: Perspectives from the Social Sciences.* February 1. http://understandingkatrina .ssrc.org/FrymerSrolovitchWarren.

Hamilton, Bruce. 2006. "Bridge Standoff Still Under Scope: Gretna Faces Lawsuit for Stopping Evacuees." *Times-Picayune.* January 4.

Hartman, Chester. 2006. "The Case for a Right to Housing." In Rachel G. Bratt, Michael E. Stone, and Chester Hartman, editors. *A Right to Housing: Foundation for a New Social Agenda.* Philadelphia: Temple University Press.

Hsu, Spencer S. 2006. "2 Million Displaced By Storms." *Washington Post.* January 13.

Hsu, Spencer S., and Ceci Connolly. 2005. "Housing the Displaced Is Rife with Delays." *Washington Post.* September 23.

Hsu, Spencer S., and Juliet Eilperin. 2006. "Safety of Post-Hurricane Sludge Is Disputed." *Washington Post.* February 23.

Hustmyre, Chuck. 2005. "Residents, Evacuees Jam Meeting." *Baton Rouge Advocate.* November 9.

Institute of Medicine. 2003. *Unequal Treatment: Confronting Racial and Ethnic Disparities in Health Care.* Smedley, Brian D., Adrienne Y. Stith and Alan R. Nelson, eds., Washington, D.C.: National Academy Press.

Jackson, Secretary Alphonso. 2006. Testimony before Committee on Banking, Housing, and Urban Affairs, U.S. Senate, answers to follow up questions submitted in writing. Unpublished document. February 15. Retrieved at http://www.nlihc.org/news/042706.pdf.

Jacobson, Linda. 2006. "Hurricane's Aftermath Is Ongoing." *Education Week.* February 1.

Jargowsky, Paul. 2003. *Stunning Progress, Hidden Problems: The Dramatic Decline of Concentrated Poverty in the 1990s.* Washington, D.C.: The Brookings Institution.

———. 1996. *Poverty and Place: Ghettos, Barrios, and the American City.* New York: Russell Sage Foundation.

Jensen, Lynne. 2005. "FEMA Trailer Plans Hit Stoplight in New Orleans." *New Orleans Times-Picayune.* December 1.

"Kafka and Katrina." 2006. Editorial. *New York Times.* December 2.

Katznelson, Ira. 2005. *When Affirmative Action Was White: An Untold History of Racial Inequality in Twentieth-Century America*. New York: W. W. Norton & Company.

Korosec, Thomas. 2005. "Survey Finds Bias in Evacuee Housing: 66% of White Callers Got Better Deals in Houston and 16 Other Cities." *Houston Chronicle*. December 27.

Lipton, Eric. 2006a. "Trailers, Vital After Hurricane, Now Pose Own Risks on Gulf." *New York Times*. March 16.

———. 2006b. "Hurricane Relief From Abroad Was Mishandled." *New York Times*. April 7.

———. 2006c. "FEMA Workers Accused of Bribery." *New York Times*. January 26.

———. 2006d. "FEMA Is Set to Stop Paying Hotel Cost for Storm Victims." *New York Times*. November 16.

Logan, John R. 2006. *The Impact of Katrina: Race and Class in Storm-Damaged Neighborhoods*. Working paper, Brown University, Spatial Structures in the Social Sciences.

Maggi, Laura. 2005. State to Run New Orleans Schools. *New Orleans Times-Picayune*. November 23.

Marcuse, Peter. 2006. "Rebuilding a Tortured Past or Creating a Model Future: The Limits and Potentials of Planning." In *There Is No Such Thing As a Natural Disaster: Race, Class and Hurricane Katrina*, edited by Chester Hartman and Gregory D. Squires. New York: Routledge.

Massey, Douglas S. 2001. "Residential Segregation and Neighborhood Conditions in U.S. Metropolitan Areas." In *America Becoming: Racial Trends and Their Consequences*, edited by Neil J. Smelser, William Julius Wilson and Faith Mitchell. Washington, D.C.: National Academy Press.

Massey, Douglas S., and Nancy Denton. 1993. *American Apartheid: Segregation and the Making of the Underclass*. Cambridge, MA: Harvard University Press.

Mauer, Marc. 2006. *Race to Incarcerate*. New York: The New Press.

McWaters v. FEMA. 2005. Case 2:05-cv-05488-SRD-DEK, Document 38.2005. E.D.La 2005. December 12.

McWhorter, John. 2000. *Losing the Race: Self-Sabotage in Black and White*. New York: The Free Press.

Muhammed, Dedrick, Attieno Davis, Meizhu Lui, and Betsy Leondar-Wright, 2004. "The State of the Dream 2004: Enduring Disparities in Black and White." *United for a Fair Economy*. http://www.faireconomy.org/press/2004/Stateofthe Dream2004.pdf.

National Economic & Social Rights Initiative. 2006. Media Advisory. December 1.

National Fair Housing Alliance. 2006. GNOFHAC and NHFA featured in article about racist post-Katrina policy. E-mail. October 6.

National Low Income Housing Coalition. 2005. "National Housing Advocates Call on Administration and Congress for Action on Housing Hurricane Victims." Press Release. November 30. Retrieved from http://www.nlihc.org/press/113005pr.html.

Nelson, Rob, and James Varney. 2005. "'Not in My Back Yard' Cry Holding Up FEMA Trailers: Emotional Tone of Opposition Hints at Role and Stereotypes of Race, Class." *New Orleans Times-Picayune*. December 26.

Neuman, Johanna. 2006. "The Land of 10,770 Empty FEMA Trailers." *Los Angeles Times.* February 10.

New Orleans Fair Housing Action Center. 2006. Audit of Bourbon Street Discrimination Against African-American Males. Unpublished. November.

"Newsom Slams Bush Decision to Cut Off Housing Vouchers for Katrina Victims at Beginning of Holidays." 2005. *San Francisco Sentinel.* November 17.

Nossiter, Adam. 2005. "Hurricane Takes a Further Toll: Suicides Up in New Orleans." *New York Times.* December 27.

———. 2006a. "F.B.I. to Investigate Red Cross Over Accusations of Wrongdoing." *New York Times.* March 31.

———. 2006b. "Students After the Storm, Left Alone and Angry." *New York Times.* November 1.

———. 2006c. "New Orleans Picks Professor to Lead Efforts on Rebuilding." *New York Times.* December 6.

O'Connor, Alice, Chris Tilly, and Lawrence D. Bobo, eds. 2001. *Urban Inequality: Evidence from Four Cities.* New York: Russell Sage Foundation.

Ouroussoff, Nicolai. 2006. "All Fall Down." *New York Times.* November 19.

Pastor, Manuel, Robert D. Bullard, James K. Boyce, Alice Fothergill, Rachel Morello-Frosch, and Beverly Wright. 2006. "In the Wake of the Storm: Environment, Disaster, and Race After Katrina." New York: Russell Sage Foundation.

Pelletiere. Danilo. 2006. *The Rental Housing Affordability Gap: Comparison of 2001 and 2003 American Housing Surveys.* Washington, DC: National Low Income Housing Coalition.

Perry, James. 2006. Testimony before Subcommittee on Housing and Community Opportunity, U.S. House of Representatives, February 28. Retrieved from http://financialservices.house.gov/media/pdf/022806.pdf.

Powell, John A., Hasan Kwame Jeffries, Daniel W. Newhart, and Eric Stiens. 2006. "Towards a Transformative View of Race: The Crisis and Opportunity of Katrina." In *There Is No Such Thing As a Natural Disaster: Race, Class and Hurricane Katrina*, edited by Chester Hartman and Gregory D. Squires. New York: Routledge.

Powers, Michael P. 2006. "A Matter of Choice: Historical Lessons for Disaster Recovery." In *There Is No Such Thing As a Natural Disaster: Race, Class and Hurricane Katrina*, edited by Chester Hartman and Gregory D. Squires. New York: Routledge.

Redlener, Irwin. 2006. "Orphans of the Storm." *New York Times.* May 9.

Rivlin, Gary. 2006. "Patchy Recovery in New Orleans." *New York Times.* April 5.

Salmon, Jacqueline L. 2006a. "Red Cross, Humane Society Under Investigation." *Washington Post.* March 26.

———. 2006b. "Counterparts Excoriate Red Cross Katrina Effort." *Washington Post.* April 5.

Sarbanes, Sen. Paul. 2005. Letter to Senators Thad Cochran and Robert Byrd. December 8. Retrieved from http://www.nlihc.org/news/120905sarbanes.pdf.

Saulny, Susan. 2006a. "U.S. Gives Charter Schools A Big Push in New Orleans." *New York Times*. June 13.

———. 2006b. "A Legacy of Storm: Depression and Suicide." *New York Times*. June 21.

Sayre, Alan. 2006. "Post-storm New Orleans Economy a Huger Question Mark: Housing Shortages Are on the Minds of Everyone." *Associated Press*. March 28.

Smelser, Neil J., William Julius Wilson, and Faith Mitchell. 2001. *America Becoming: Racial Trends and Their Consequences*. Washington, D.C.: National Academy Press.

Squires, Gregory D., and Charis E. Kubrin. 2006. *Privileged Places: Race, Residence, and the Structure of Opportunity*. Boulder, CO, and London: Lynne Rienner Publishers.

Steinhauer, Jennifer, and Eric Lipton. 2006. "Storm Victims Face Big Delay to Get Trailers." *New York Times*. February 9.

Strom, Stephanie. 2005. "President of Red Cross Resigns; Board Woes, Not Katrina, Cited." *New York Times*. December 14.

———. 2006a. "Red Cross Fires Administrators in New Orleans." *New York Times*. March 25.

———. 2006b. "Bill Would Restructure Red Cross." *New York Times*. December 5.

Taylor, John, and Josh Silver. 2006. "From Poverty to Prosperity: The Critical Role of Financial Institutions." In *There Is No Such Thing As a Natural Disaster: Race, Class and Hurricane Katrina*, edited by Chester Hartman and Gregory D. Squires. New York: Routledge.

Thernstrom, Stephan, and Abigail Thernstrom. 1997. *America in Black and White: One Nation Indivisible*. New York: Simon & Schuster.

Tizon, Tomas Alex. 2005. "La. Trailer Villages Bring Hope, Some Fear." *Los Angeles Times*. December 15.

Torpy, Bill. 2005. "$11 Million Per Night to House Evacuees." *Atlanta Journal-Constitution*. October 15.

"Trailer Trouble Chills New Orleans-FEMA Relations." 2006. *Reuters*. April 3.

Treaster, Joseph B. 2006. "Home Insurers Embrace the Heartland." *New York Times*. May 20.

———. 2006b. "Judge Upholds Policyholders' Katrina Claims." *New York Times*. November 29.

Treaster, Joseph B., and Cornelia Dean. 2006. "Yet Another Victim of Katrina: Federal Flood Insurance Program Is Itself Under Water." *New York Times*. January 6.

Turner, Dorie. 2006. "Mental Health Problems from Katrina Persist." *Washington Post*. November 9.

Turner, Margery Austin, and Shelia R. Zedlewski. 2006. *After Katrina: Rebuilding Opportunity and Equity into New New Orleans*. Washington, D.C.: The Urban Institute.

UNOP (The Unified New Orleans Plan). 2006. Preliminary Report, Community Congress II. December 2.

U.S. Department of Homeland Security. 2006. "FEMA Concludes Short-Term Lodging Program: Longer-Term Housing Efforts Continue." Press Release Number HQ-06-020. February 1. Retrieved from http://www.fema.gov/news/newsrelease. fema?id=23158.

U.S. Department of Housing and Urban Development, Office of Policy Development and Research. 2006. *Current Housing Unit Damage Estimates: Hurricanes Katrina, Rita, and Wilma.* Unpublished document. February 12.

Wagner, Peter, and Susan Edwards. 2006. "New Orleans by the Numbers." *Dollars & Sense* 264 (March/April): 54–55.

Warner, Coleman. "Rebuild Sessions Casting Wide Net." *New Orleans Times-Picayune.* December 1.

Weisman, Jonathan. 2005. "Critics Fear Trailer 'Ghettoes'—Right, Left Target FEMA Initiative." *Washington Post.* September 16.

Wellington, Darryl Lorenzo. 2006. "New Orleans: A Right to Return?" *Dissent,* vol. 3, pp. 23–35.

"'What Next' for Victims of Katrina?" 2005. *Hattiesburg (MS) American.* November 16.

Whelan, Robert K. 2006. "An Old Economy for the 'New' New Orleans? Post-Hurricane Katina Economic Development Efforts." In *There Is No Such Thing As a Natural Disaster: Race, Class and Hurricane Katrina,* edited by Chester Hartman and Gregory D. Squires. New York: Routledge.

Wilgoren, Jodi. 2005. "Vouchers in Their Pockets, Evacuees Find It Hard to Get Keys in Hand." *New York Times.* October 28.

Williams, Linda Faye. 2003. *The Constraint of Race: Legacies of White Skin Privilege in America.* University Park, PA: The Pennsylvania State University Press.

"With Holidays Coming, Evacuees Will Be Sent Packing." 2005. Editorial. *Austin-American Statesman.* November 22.

Zdenek, Robert O., Ralph Scott, Jane Malone, and Brian Gumm. 2006. "Reclaiming New Orleans' Working-Class Communities." In *There Is No Such Thing As a Natural Disaster: Race, Class and Hurricane Katrina,* edited by Chester Hartman and Gregory D. Squires. New York: Routledge.

Zuckerman, Stephen, and Teresa Coughlin. 2006. *After Katrina: Rebuilding Opportunity and Equity Into the* New *New Orleans: Initial Policy Responses to Hurricane Katrina and Possible Next Steps.* Washington, D.C.: The Urban Institute. February.

12

Foreclosing on the Free Market

How to Remedy the Subprime Catastrophe

John Atlas, Peter Dreier, and Gregory D. Squires

It's now official. In January 2008, the American Dialect Society selected "subprime" as 2007's Word of the Year. "Everyone is talking about subprime," said Wayne Glowka, a society spokesman. "It's affecting all kinds of people in all kinds of places."[1]

The word is likely to gain even more currency in the next few years with the accelerating number of foreclosures creating chaos in the housing and stock markets, the banking industry, and the global money markets, triggering skyrocketing consumer debt, tight credit, massive lay-offs, neighborhoods in decline, serious fiscal woes for states and cities, and families and neighborhoods upended by the turmoil.

Business leaders, activist groups, and politicians are calling for our government to do something before the situation worsens. The Bush administration proposed a bail-out for big Wall Street firms, but as of this writing (May 2008) has done little for homeowners except asking banks to voluntarily restructure troubled loans. The subprime crisis has been a hot button issue during the 2008 presidential campaign. The Republican candidates were conspicuously silent, while the Democrats offered reasonable ideas for coping with the symptoms (especially homeowners facing foreclosure), but no major candidate proposed the sweeping reforms needed to address the root causes—four pillars of which are outlined below.

Make no mistake—it *is* a crisis. More than seven million borrowers now hold subprime loans, according to the Center for Responsible Lending (CRL). Most of them involved adjustable-rate mortgages (ARMs) that include an initial low interest rate that quickly "balloons" to a higher rate. The Federal Reserve reported that 2.1 percent of residential mortgage loans held by banks were delinquent at the end of 2006.

In 2007, 405,000 households lost their homes, an increase of 51 percent over 2006. CRL projects that two million families are likely to lose their homes in the next few years. More than 80 mostly subprime mortgage lenders went bankrupt by the end of 2007. Regulators anticipate that between 100 and 200 banks will fail over the next two years.[2]

But it isn't just borrowers and lenders who are losing. Home prices dropped by over 12 percent during a 12 month period beginning February 2007. A Congressional committee projected a loss of $71 billion in housing wealth as a result of the mortgage meltdown. The U.S. Conference of Mayors projected that ten states alone would lose $6.6 billion in local tax revenue.[3]

This mortgage crisis was preventable. Like most economic problems, it was due to corporate greed. Top executives at major banks, mortgage companies, and rating agencies saw an opportunity to increase corporate income and their own compensation by engaging in risky practices. In the short term, their personal compensation was not connected to corporate performance, so they could get away with irresponsible behavior. Eventually, however, these perverse incentives caught up with them. Several CEOs—Countrywide's Angelo Mazilo, Citicorp's Charles Prince, and Merrill Lynch's Stanley O'Neill—were forced out or faced criminal investigations, but not before their firms suffered huge losses. Indeed, they put the entire financial system in jeopardy.[4]

Government is necessary to make business act responsibly. Without it, capitalism becomes anarchy. In the case of the financial industry, government failed to do its job, for two reasons—ideology and influence-peddling. The federal government was dominated by people who didn't believe in regulation of business. Rather, they prefer the burdens of economic change to fall on individuals and families—what Hacker terms "the great risk shift."[5] In addition, the financial services industry—utilizing campaign contributions and lobbyists—wielded influence to weaken regulations and oversight. While federal regulators looked the other way, banks engaged in an orgy of risky loans and speculative investments. Every aspect of the financial industry was so short-sighted and greedy that they didn't see the train wreck coming around the corner.

IT STARTED WITH DEREGULATION

At the heart of the crisis are the conservative free-market ideologists whose views have shaped public policy since the 1980s, and who dominated the Bush administration. To them, government regulation is a misguided interference with the free market. In 2000, Edward Gramlich, a Federal Reserve Board member, urged Federal Reserve Chair Alan Greenspan to crack down on subprime lending by increasing oversight, but his warnings fell on deaf ears.[6]

By the early 1980s, the industry used its political clout to push back against government regulation. In 1980, Congress adopted the Depository Institutions Deregulatory and Monetary Control Act, which eliminated interest-rate caps and made subprime lending more feasible for lenders. The S&Ls balked at constraints on their ability to compete with conventional banks engaged in commercial lending. They got Congress—Democrats and Republicans alike—to change the rules, allowing S&Ls to begin a decade-long orgy of real-estate speculation, mismanagement, and fraud.

The deregulation of banking led to merger mania, with banks and S&Ls gobbling each other up and making loans to finance shopping malls, golf courses, office buildings, and condo projects that had no financial logic other than a quick profit. When the dust settled in the late 1980s, about a thousand S&Ls and banks—including Lincoln Savings—had gone under, billions of dollars of commercial loans were useless, and the federal government was left to bail out depositors whose money the speculators had looted to the tune of about $125 billion. The icing on the cake was the Gramm-Leach-Bliley Act of 1999, which tore down the remaining legal barriers to combining commercial banking, investment banking, and insurance under one corporate roof.

The industry consolidated. Between 1984 and 2004, the number of FDIC-regulated banks declined from 14,392 to 7,511. The proportion of industry assets held by the 10 largest banks increased from 21 percent in 1960 to 60 percent in 2005.[7]

The stable neighborhood S & L became a thing of the past. Banks, insurance companies, credit-card firms, and other money-lenders became part of a giant financial-services industry, while Washington walked away from its responsibility to protect consumers with regulations and enforcement. Into this vacuum stepped banks, mortgage lenders, and scam artists, looking for ways to make big profits from consumers desperate for the American Dream of homeownership. They invented new "loan products" that put borrowers at risk. Thus was born the subprime market.

Wall Street financed many of these mortgages by purchasing loans from originators, packaging them into mortgage-backed securities and selling them to investors who stood to make substantial profits as long as home values kept rising and borrowers paid their mortgages. Because originators sold most of these mortgages, they were less concerned with borrowers' ability to repay than with access to investors to whom they could sell. In effect, the interests of borrowers and lenders were no longer aligned; underwriting standards became much looser (that is loans were made to borrowers who could not afford them). Everyone profited until the housing bubble burst and loans starting "nonperforming."

SURGING INEQUALITY AND PERSISTENT SEGREGATION: INCUBATOR FOR THE MORTGAGE MELTDOWN

The mortgage crisis is best understood in the context of rising inequality and persistent racial and economic segregation. America is experiencing a new Gilded Age—a frenzy of corporate mergers, widening economic disparities, and deteriorating social conditions. It now has the biggest concentration of income and wealth since 1928. Under the Bush administration, the incomes of most Americans fell, but the average income of top wage earners (those above the 95th percentile) increased from $324,427 in 2001 to $385,805 in 2006. Wealth has long been much more unequally distributed than income; that inequality has recently increased.

The American Dream—the ability to buy a home, pay for college tuition and health insurance, take an annual vacation, and save for retirement—has become increasingly elusive. American workers face declining job security. The cost of food, health care, and other necessities is rising faster than incomes. Between 2000 and 2006, for example, the median worker's weekly earnings increased 0.7 percent, while the cost of a typical home grew 80.6 percent.[8] A growing number of families are in debt.[9]

Economic and racial inequality is also reflected by where people live. Between 1970 and 2000 the number of high poverty census tracts (where 40 percent or more residents are poor) grew from 1,177 to 2,510. The number of people in those tracts grew from 4.1 million to 7.9 million.[10] The isolation of rich and poor families is also reflected by the declining number of middle income communities. Between 1970 and 2000 the number of middle income neighborhoods (census tracts where median family income is between 80 percent and 120 percent of that for the metropolitan area) dropped from 58 percent to 41 percent of all neighborhoods. More than half of lower-income families lived in middle income neighborhoods in 1970; only 37 percent of such families did so in 2000. The share of low-income families in low-income areas grew from 36 percent to 48 percent.[11]

Longstanding patterns of racial segregation persist, the result of decades of discrimination by banks, real estate agents, homebuilders, and landlords. Few blacks live in predominantly white neighborhoods. Middle-income blacks are almost as segregated from whites as lower-income blacks. Poor black families are much more likely than poor whites to live in high-poverty neighborhoods. The median census tract income for the typical black household in 1990 was $27,808 compared to $45,486 for whites. A similar pattern exists for Latinos.[12]

UNEVEN DISTRIBUTION OF FINANCIAL SERVICES

These patterns have adverse consequences. Residents of low-income and minority communities live the greatest distance from areas of major job growth. They live in areas with fewer health care services and physicians, lower quality public schools, fewer retail services such as supermarkets and pharmacies, higher prices, and poorer air quality.[13]

Class, race, and geography compound the uneven distribution of financial services and access to credit. Some of these disparities are visible—such as the concentration of such "fringe bankers" as check-cashers, payday lenders, pawnshops, and others located in low-income and predominantly minority urban communities. Some disparities are less obvious—such as the kinds of loans targeted to low-income and minorities residents who live in these neighborhoods.

In fact, a two-tiered system of financial services has emerged, one featuring conventional products distributed by banks and savings institutions primarily for middle- and upper-income, disproportionately white suburban markets and the other featuring high-priced, often predatory products, offered by "fringe" lenders as well as mainstream banks to borrowers in disadvantaged neighborhoods. In addition to what was formerly a conventional fixed-rate 30 year loan, today there are many options including interest only, payment optional, variable rate, and many other types of loans.[14] This two-tiered system is the result, in part, of the failure of government to adequately regulate the evolving financial services industry.[15]

The mortgage meltdown is the result of the dramatic growth in subprime lending and the wave of predatory lending. The media has typically confused these two phenomena.

Responsible subprime lending can help families who would otherwise be considered too risky for a conventional loan to become homeowners. These include middle class families who have accumulated too much debt and low-income working families who want to buy a home in what was an inflated housing market. These loans have higher interest rates and other fees to compensate lenders for the increased risk posed by such borrowers. But the costs are not excessive.

Predatory lending involves an array of abusive practices, targeting those least likely to be able to repay. Predatory loans typically charge excessive fees relative to the risk involved, are aggressively marketed to unsophisticated buyers, and are frequently unaffordable to the borrowers, often resulting in default and foreclosure. Predatory loans have some or all of the following characteristics: Interest rates and fees that far exceed the risk posed by the borrower; loans with low initial "teaser" rates that adjust rapidly upward within two or three years and quickly become unaffordable for borrowers; high pre-payment penalties that make it difficult or impossible for borrowers to refinance when interest rates decline, trapping borrowers in unaffordable loans; loans based on the value of the property with little regard for the borrower's income and, therefore, ability to repay; loan flipping whereby a loan is frequently refinanced, generating fees for the lender but no financial benefit for the borrower; and negative amortization whereby the loan balance increases as borrowers make payments that are sufficient to cover only a portion of the interest but none of the principal that is due.[16] Borrowers face hidden fees masked by confusing terms such as "discount points," erroneously suggesting that the fees will lower the interest rates.

Banks were so eager to profit on these loans that they often failed to require the documentation needed to evaluate the risks, sometimes not even requiring borrowers to report their income or failing to verify it when this information was provided.

Many borrowers who were eligible for conventional fixed-rate loans got snookered into taking subprime loans. Other borrowers were talked into taking loans whose terms they barely understood because the documents were confusing. In many cases, lenders simply lied about the costs of the loans and whether borrowers could really afford them.

Only a decade ago, subprime loans were rare. But, starting in the mid-1990s, led by Household Finance Corporation, subprime lending began surging. Between 1994 and 2005 the annual dollar volume of such loans grew from $35 billion to more than $600 billion. They comprised 8.6 percent of all mortgages in 2001, soaring to 20.1 percent by 2006. Since 2004, more than 90 percent of subprime mortgages came with exploding adjustable rates.[17]

By 2005, the nation's homeownership rate reached a record level of 69.1 percent. But the argument that subprime lending increased homeownership is misleading. Most subprime loans are for *refinancing* rather than purchase, and the number of families losing their homes as a result of default and foreclosure on these loans, which are often predatory, far exceeds the number who became homeowners. The CRL reported that between 1998 and 2006 approximately 1.4 million first-time homebuyers purchased their homes with a subprime loan but projected that 2.2 million borrowers who took out subprime loans have or will lose their homes as a result of foreclosure.[18] By 2006, the homeownership rate was declining as a result of the spiralling wave of foreclosures; the rate had fallen to 67.5 percent by the first quarter of 2008.[19]

Federal Reserve Board researchers found that in 2006, 53.7 percent of blacks, 46.6 percent of Hispanics, and 17.7 percent of whites received high priced loans. In minority areas, 46.6 percent obtained high-priced loans compared to 21.7 percent in white areas.[20] Given current levels of economic and racial segregation, and the prevalence of "fringe" lenders in poor neighborhoods, it isn't surprising that foreclosures have been concentrated in low-income and minority areas, although they have spread to working-class areas and even some affluent areas, such as Greenwich, Connecticut.[21]

The costs are severe. Families can lose their home and their life savings that went into purchasing the home. The costs are not restricted to unfortunate borrowers. However, many spill over into the neighborhood and metropolitan area. Houses become vacant, deteriorate into eyesores, and detract from the feeling of well-being in neighborhoods. Vacant houses attract crime and make it more difficult for neighbors to purchase homeowner insurance. Property values, and thus local property-tax revenues, plummet.[22] A number of cities, including Baltimore and Cleveland, have recently sued lenders, contending that their practices discriminated against black borrowers and led to a wave of foreclosures that has reduced city tax revenues and increased municipal costs.[23]

The consequences are harshest in depressed communities, particularly the Gulf Coast and industrial Midwest. Subprime foreclosure rates in the fourth quarter of 2006 ranged from less than three percent in Washington DC, Maryland, and Virginia, to over 7 percent in Mississippi and over 9 percent in Indiana, Michigan, and Ohio.[24] The weak housing market, lay-offs in the financial industry, and the reluctance of lenders to make loans are careening the nation into a recession.[25]

Not all subprime borrowers are innocent victims. Some were speculators, seeking to profit from the real estate housing bubble with their eyes wide open. They expected to rent their houses or quickly flip them to another buyer in a rising housing market. Others were simply living dangerously above their means, taking on too much debt and occupying houses that, by any reasonable standard, they couldn't really afford. But it would be a mistake to place the primary blame on families who were seeking shelter in what was becoming a financial storm.

WHO IS RESPONSIBLE?

Who is responsible for the mortgage meltdown? In addition to the large-scale economic and social forces—rising inequality, widening economic segregation, persistent racial segregation, stagnant wages and rising home prices—there are also the key players that have played a role in this economic tsunami.

First, and at the bottom rung of the industry ladder, are the private mortgage brokers and bank salespeople who hound vulnerable families for months, soliciting and encouraging them to take out a loan to buy a house or to refinance. There are also independent mortgage brokers who operate in the netherworld of the lending industry, earning fees for bringing borrowers to lenders even if borrowers could not always afford the loans.

These street hustlers earned fees for bringing borrowers to lenders—the larger the mortgage, the larger the fee. They were often in cahoots with real estate appraisers, who inflated the value of homes (on paper) to make the loans look reasonable.

Second, big mortgage finance companies and banks cashed in on subprime loans. In 2006, 10 lenders—HSBC, New Century, Countrywide, CitiMortgage, WMC Mortgage, Fremont Investment and Loan, Ameriquest, Option One, Wells Fargo, and First Franklin—accounted for 60 percent of all subprime loans, originating $362 billion in loans. The top 20 lenders accounted for 90.4 percent of all subprime loans.[26] Executives of some of these companies cashed out before the market crashed, most notably

Angelo Mozilo, Countrywide's CEO, the largest subprime lender. Mozilo made more than $270 million in profits selling stocks and options from 2004 to the beginning of 2007. Between 2004 and 2006, the three founders of New Century Financial, the second-largest subprime lender, together realized $40 million in stock-sale profits.[27]

Third are investors—people and institutions that borrowers never see, but who made the explosion of subprime and predatory lending possible. Subprime lenders collected fees for making the transactions and sold the loans—and the risk—to investment banks and investors who considered these high-interest-rate loans a goldmine. By 2007, the subprime business had become a $1.5 trillion global market for investors seeking high returns. Because lenders didn't have to keep the loans on their books, they didn't worry about the risk of losses.[28]

Wall Street investment firms set up special investment units, bought the subprime mortgages from the lenders, bundled them into "mortgage-backed securities," and for a fat fee sold them to wealthy investors worldwide. (For example, some towns in Australia sued Lehman Brothers for improperly selling them risky mortgage-linked investments).[29]

When the bottom began falling out of the subprime market, many banks and mortgage companies went under, and major Wall Street firms took huge loses. They include Lehman Brothers (which underwrote $51.8 billion in securities backed by subprime loans in 2006 alone), Morgan Stanley, Barclays, Merrill Lynch, Goldman Sachs, Deutsche Bank, Credit Suisse, RBS, Citigroup, JP Morgan and Bear Stearns. These investment banks are now accusing the lenders and mortgage brokers of shoddy business practices, but the Wall Street institutions obviously failed to do their own due diligence about the risky loans they were investing in.[30]

Fourth, the major credit agencies—Moody's and Standard & Poor's—made big profits by giving these mortgage-backed securities triple-A ratings. According to Roger Lowenstein, "By providing the mortgage industry with an entree to Wall Street, the agencies also transformed what had been among the sleepiest corners of finance. No longer did mortgage banks have to wait 10 or 20 or 30 years to get their money back from homeowners. Now they sold their loans into securitized pools and—their capital thus replenished—wrote new loans at a much quicker pace." Almost all of the subprime loans wound up in securitized pools. But the credit agencies had little knowledge of how risky the original mortgages were. Their triple-A ratings were bogus. Moreover, they had a serious conflict of interest, because these ratings agencies get their revenue these Wall Street underwriters.[31]

The entire financial and housing food chain—brokers, appraisers, mortgage companies, bankers, investors, and credit agencies—participated in this greedy shell game. Some of what they did was illegal. But most of it was simply business as usual.

THE JOB FOR THE NEXT CONGRESS

So, what to do now? Washington needs to put a short-term tourniquet on the banking industry to stem the damage, and to get back into the business of protecting consumers, employees, and investors from corporate greed.

First, the federal government should help homeowners who have already lost their homes or are at risk of foreclosure. It should create an agency comparable to the Depression-era Home Owners Loan Corporation, buy the mortgages, and remake the loans at reasonable rates, backed by federal insurance. Created in 1933, HOLC helped distressed families avert foreclosures by replacing mortgages that were in or near default with new ones that homeowners could afford. A modern version of HOLC would focus on owner-occupied homes, not homes purchased by absentee speculators.

Second, Washington should not bail out any investors or banks, including Bear Stearns and its suitor, JP Morgan, that do not agree to these new ground rules. The Fed brokered the deal between Bear Stearns and JP Morgan without any conditions for the consumers who were ripped off. There will be more Bear Stearns-like failures in the foreseeable future—institutions that the Fed considers "too big to fail." But if the federal government is about to provide hundreds of billions from the Federal Reserve, as well as from Fannie Mae, Freddie Mac and the Federal Home Loan Banks, to prop up Wall Street institutions, it should require the industry to be held accountable for its misdeeds. Specifically, such lenders should agree to underwrite all loans for the full terms of the loan, not just for the initial teaser rate (this should apply to originators and purchasers), eliminate all pre-payment penalties, and recommend loan products that are suitable and in the financial interests of borrowers.

Third, Washington should consolidate the crazy-quilt of federal agencies that oversee banks and financial institutions into one agency. Federal oversight has not kept pace with the dramatic transformation of the financial services industry. Four federal agencies—the Federal Reserve, the Office of the Comptroller of the Currency, the Office of Thrift Supervision, and the Federal Deposit Insurance Corporation—have some jurisdiction over mortgage lending. States have jurisdiction over the growing number off nonbank mortgage lenders (which accounted for about 40 percent of new subprime loans) and have no agreed-upon standards for regulating them. States are responsible for regulating the insurance industry (including homeowner insurance), and do so with widely different levels of effectiveness. It is absurd to have so many competing and overlapping agencies involved in regulating these financial services institutions, often at cross purposes.

Fourth, the federal government should be a financial services industry watchdog, not a lapdog. Part of that effort involves supporting (financially and otherwise) initiatives currently being implemented or proposed by several advocacy groups.

The Community Reinvestment Act (CRA), a federal ban on redlining, should be strengthened to sanction institutions that engage in predatory practices and to reward those that engage in responsible lending. The CRA now applies only to federally chartered depositories (e.g. banks and thrifts). This statute should be expanded to cover credit unions, independent mortgage bankers, insurers, and other entities that now account for well over half of all mortgage loans. The Community Reinvestment Modernization Act of 2007, introduced by Eddie Bernice Johnson (D-Texas) and Luis Gutierrez (D-IL) would accomplish this objective. In addition, the Home Mortgage Disclosure Act (HMDA), which facilitates enforcement of CRA, should be expanded to include pricing information on all loans.

A strong national anti-predatory lending law should also be enacted. Currently 36 states and Washington, D.C., along with 17 other local jurisdictions have such laws, leaving most consumers in other states less protected.[32] Again, this statute should apply to those who originate loans and those who purchase loans and mortgage-backed securities for investment purposes.

As of this writing (May 2008), the Fed had issued proposed regulations and Congress has debated several bills to address the immediate foreclosure problems and mitigate their recurrence, but so far no final regulations have been issued and no legislation has been passed.

Congressman Frank and Senator Chris Dodd (chair of the Senate Banking Committee) introduced legislation to address some but not all of these concerns. In May, the House voted 266-154 in favor of Frank's bill. Although the vote went mostly along partisan lines—all 227 Democrats voted "yes" and 154 Republicans voted "no"—39 Republicans bucked pressure from their party leaders and from the White House and voted "yes." (Thirteen members didn't vote.) Most of the Republicans who supported the bill represent districts that have been particularly hard-hit by the mortgage meltdown. The bill would allow homeowners to shift from subprime mortgages they can no longer afford to federally backed mortgages. It would provide $300 billion in federal loan guarantees to lenders who agree to reduce the outstanding principal on loans. In exchange for a new mortgage, backed by the FHA, homeowners must share profits on a subsequent sale of their home with the government. The bill also includes a one-time $7,500 tax credit for new homeowners to be paid back over 15 years, and $15 billion for states and localities to buy and rehabilitate foreclosed properties.

Frustrated with the delayed federal response many states have acted on their own. Nine states have created refinance funds to help borrowers avoid foreclosure. Ten have banned or limited pre-payment penalties. Twenty have created consumer counseling programs. Nine require lenders to represent the interests of borrowers. And 14 states have created foreclosure task forces bringing together lenders, consumers, regulators, and other experts to develop solutions.[33] There is a critical role for state and local governments to play. But an effective, comprehensive solution will require a far more active federal government.

FROM UNEVEN TO EQUITABLE DEVELOPMENT

Getting Congress to adopt regulations to require the financial services and real estate industries to act more responsibly is an important part of the solution. But Congress also needs to address the underlying causes that made so many Americans unable to afford decent affordable housing and vulnerable to the practices of brokers, banks, and others. These include raising the federal minimum wage to the poverty threshold (about $9.50 an hour) and indexing it to inflation; expanding the Earned Income Tax Credit by adding a housing component to the EITC to account for the significant difference in housing costs in different parts of the country; enacting the Employee Free Choice Act, which would strengthen workers' rights to unionize; adopt the Income Equity Act, sponsored by former Minnesota Rep. Martin Sabo, which would deny corporations tax deductions on any executive compensation exceeding 25 times the pay of the firm's lowest paid workers. Congress should also reverse the almost three-decade decline in federal housing assistance to low- and moderate-income families. It could also, by using a variety of carrots and sticks, encourage states and localities to site more mixed-income housing, to increase the supply of rental housing in the suburbs, so that families with rent vouchers could live closer to where jobs are expanding. States and localities could require adoption of inclusionary zoning laws that require developers to set a side a specific share of housing units to meet affordable housing objectives. Such laws have already been implemented in hundreds of localities, particularly in California, but also in Maryland, New Jersey and several other states.

The success of any of these proposals will depend on the capacity of community organizations, labor unions, and consumer groups, to mobilize Americans in the political arena. As Frederick Douglass famously observed, "Power concedes nothing without a demand. It never did, and it never will."

Notes

1. "Linguists Choose 'Subprime' as Word of the Year," *Associated Press*, January 7, 2008.
2. "Subprime Shakeout," *Wall Street Journal Online*, http://online.wsj.com/public/resources/documents/info-subprimeloans0706-sort.html; see also "Take One Credit Crunch. Add Deals, Bills, and Exec Shuffles. Shake Well," *American Banker*, November 30, 2007.
3. James H. Carr, "Responding to the Foreclosure Crisis," *Housing Policy Debate* 18, no. 4 (2007): 837–60; Ellen Schloemer, Li Wei, Keith Ernst, and Kathleen Keest,

Losing Ground: Foreclosures in the Subprime Market and Their Cost to Homeowners (Washington, D.C.: Center for Responsible Lending, 2007).

4. John Cassidy, "Subprime Suspect," *New Yorker*, March 31, 2008; see also "Take One Credit Crunch."

5. Jacob Hacker, *The Great Risk Shift* (New York: Oxford University Press, 2006).

6. Edmund Andrews, "Fed Shrugged as Subprime Crisis Spread," *New York Times*, December 18, 2007; see also Edward M. Gramlich, *Subprime Mortgages* (Washington, D.C.: The Urban Institute Press, 2007).

7. Hubert P. Janicki and Edward Simpson Prescott, "Changes in the Size Distribution of U.S. Banks: 1960–2005," *Economic Quarterly- Federal Reserve Bank of Richmond* (Fall 2006).

8. Data supplied by the Economic Policy Institute, e-mail from Algernon to Gregory D. Squires, May 6, 2008.

9. Hacker, *The Great Risk Shift*; John Leland, "When Health Insurance Is Not a Safeguard," *New York Times*, October 23, 2005; Elizabeth Warren, "Rewriting the Rules: Families, Money, and Risk," Social Science Research Council, Privatization of Risk (June 7, 2006), http://privatizationofrisk.ssrc.org/Warren.

10. Paul Jargowsky, *Stunning Progress, Hidden Problems: The Dramatic Decline of Concentrated Poverty in the 1990s* (Washington, D.C.: The Brookings Institution); Paul Jargowsky, *Poverty and Place: Ghettos, Barrios, and the American City* (New York: Russell Sage Foundation, 2006).

11. Jason C. Booza, Jackie Cutsinger, and George Galster, *Where Did They Go? The Decline of Middle-Income Neighborhoods in Metropolitan America* (Washington, D.C.: The Brookings Institution, Metropolitian Policy Program, 2006).

12. John R. Logan, *Separate and Unequal: The Neighborhood Gap for Blacks and Hispanics in Metropolitan America* (Albany: Lewis Mumford Center, 2002).

13. Peter Dreier, John Mollenkopf, and Todd Swanstrom, *Place Matters: Metropolitics for the Twenty-first Century* (Lawrence: University Press of Kansas, 2004); Chester Hartman and Gregory D. Squires, ed., *There is No Such Thing as a Natural Disaster: Race, Class and Hurricane Katrina* (New York: Routledge, 2006).

14. Allen J. Fishbein, and Patrick Woodall, *Exotic or Toxic? An Examination of the Non-Traditional Mortgage market for Consumers and Lenders* (Washington, D.C.: Consumer Federation of America, 2006).

15. Howard Karger, *Shortchanges: Life and Debt in the Fringe Economy* (San Francisco: Berrett-Koehler Publishers, Inc., 2005).

16. "Market Failures and Predatory Lending," themed issue, *Housing Policy Debate* 15, no. 13 (2004).

17. Robert B. Avery, Kenneth P. Brevoort, and Glenn B. Canner, "Higher-Priced Home Lending and the 2005 HMDA Data," *Federal Reserve Bulletin* 84 (September 2006): 123–166.

18. Michael D. Calhoun, testimony of Michael D. Calhoun before the Financial Services and General Government Subcommittee of the U.S. House Appropriations Com-

mittee, hearing on "Consumer Protection in Financial Services: Subprime Lending" (February 28, 2008).

19. Ellen Schloemer, Li Wei, Keith Ernst, and Kathleen Keest, *Losing Ground: Foreclosures in the Subprime Market and Their Cost to Homeowners*, (Washington, D.C.: Center for Responsible Lending, 2007); Robert J. Shiller, "The Scars of Losing a Home," *New York Times*, May 19, 2008.

20. Robert B. Avery, Kenneth P. Brevoort, and Glenn B. Canner, "The 2006 HMDA Data," *Federal Reserve Bulletin* 93 (December 2007): 73–109.

21. Jennifer Lee, "Subprime Crisis Festers in New York," *New York Times*, February 11, 2008; Christine Haughney, "Pain of Foreclosures Spreads to the Affluent," *New York Times*, April 25, 2008.

22. Dan Immergluck, "From the Subprime to the Exotic: Excessive Mortgage Market Risk and Implications for Metropolitan Communities and Neighborhoods," *Journal of the American Planning Association* 74 (2008): 59–76.

23. Christopher Magg, "Cleveland Sues 21 Lenders Over Subprime Mortgages," *New York Times*, January 12, 2008.

24. David Cho and Nell Henderson, "Where the Wolf Comes Knocking," *Washington Post*, March 15, 2007.

25. *The Mortgage Crisis: Economic and Fiscal Implications for Metro Areas* (Washington, D.C.: U.S. Conference of Mayors, November 2007).

26. EIM Group, "Subprime Mortgages," May 2007, http://www.eimgroup.com/jahia/webdav/site/eim/shared/Sub%20Prime%20Mortgages%20May%202007%20(4).pdf/.

27. Julie Creswell and Vikas Bajaj, "Mortgage Crisis Spirals, and Casualties Mount," *New York Times*, March 5, 2007.

28. Jenny Anderson and Heather Thomas, "Why a U.S. Subprime Mortgage Crisis Is Felt Around the World," *New York Times*, August 31, 2007.

29. Vikis Bajaj, "If Everyones Finger-Pointing, Whos to Blame?" *New York Times*, January 22, 2008.

30. Jenny Anderson and Vikas Bajaj, "Wary of Risk, Bankers Sold Shaky Mortgage Debt," *New York Times*, December 6, 2007.

31. Roger Lowenstein, "Triple-A Failure," *New York Times Magazine*, April 27, 2008.

32. Steven L. Antonakes, "Testimony of Steven L. Antonakes, Massachusetts Commissioner of Banks on Behalf of State Bank Supervisors on Subprime and Predatory Lending; New Regulatory Guidance, Current Market Conditions, and Effects on Regulated Financial Institutions," before the Financial Services Committee Subcommittee on Financial Institutions and Consumer Credit (Washington, D.C.: U.S. House of Representatives, March 27, 2007); Mortgage Bankers Association, "Suitability–Don't Turn Back the Clock on Fair Lending and Homeownership Gains," MBA Policy Paper Series, Policy Paper (Washington, D.C.: Mortgage Bankers Association, 2007).

33. Pew Charitable Trust, *Defaulting on the American Dream: States Respond to America's Foreclosure Crisis* (Washington, D.C.: Pew Charitable Trust, 2008).

Conclusion

War Avoidance and a Peaceful Framework

Marcus G. Raskin

After tens of millions died prematurely in twentieth-century wars; after hundreds of millions were traumatized, maimed, and wounded through war; after the physical despoliation of millions of acres of land; after the physical destruction of the past, and cultures reduced to ashes; and after trillions of dollars lost in war preparation and war, it makes practical sense for third-stage liberals to highlight the tasks and plans leading to the transformation and replacement of the war system. As I have said, this goal is not new, although its character has changed given social awareness, consciousness of the Other, and technology. Ending the war system was a major project of progressives prior to and after the First World War. Before that war it seemed that reason could conquer all things. But World War I taught a different lesson. War, as a system, appeared to be intractable. While radical liberals saw war as a form of slavery, others saw it as either integral to human nature or a necessary instrument to bring about positive social change in terms of human liberation.

For antiwar liberals such as Bertrand Russell and John Dewey it was common sense that to avoid war it was necessary to delegitimate violence, a process that should begin in childhood and would lead to a democratic social character where individual and collective violence would be transformed. Unfortunately, children often live in fear, with parents and educators conflating authority, power, and violence. If there is a strong sense of rebellion on the part of the child, his or her adult life will be taken up with accepting or threatening punishment. Liberals believed that this cycle might be broken through education or through a series of actions that touched the consciousness and empathic sentiment within people. The actions would be linked to one another beyond category and social role. No doubt Christ had this in mind when he protected a prostitute. Christ delegitimated the established social order by embracing the outsider and teaching the importance of social and intellectual boundary crossing. In the American context, this is the tradition that King and the Berrigan brothers, both priests, represented. Contrary to what might be thought, it is very political. Actions such as theirs, which stemmed from bearing witness at personal risk, can lead to delegitimation of the social order. Through their personal risks and actions, people inside of bureaucracies and the citizenry at large can come to believe that the existing social order is out of phase with universal human needs and aspirations. In desperation several career officials in the State Department resigned in protest of the second Bush administration's foreign policies. For the pragmatist, this means finding actions and statements that transcend interest and social role and build on exemplary actions, opening the door to transformation. These actions will be based on prior rhetorical commitments in international law and the entire international legal structure to resolve twentieth-century disputes. In other words, reconstruction is also the means of reinterpreting and applying prior "ought" statements and actions as markers to transform institutional custom and individual consciousness.

For example, as originally contemplated at the end of the Second World War, all use of coercion was to be legitimated internationally prior to the use of force, through the UN, by meeting the test of the "threat to the peace" in Article 2, section 4 of the UN charter. Further, a military staff committee was charged under the Security Council with the responsibility for organizing plans for peace. In the United States at the beginning of the twenty-first century, such ideas sound abstract and unnecessary, for there would appear to be no reason to change the fundamental military and national security stance held by U.S. military supremacy.

In practice, unless propaganda value could be found, the United States has been reluctant to lead on issues of disarmament, a position it committed itself to in seven treaties on arms control.[1] No other major nuclear power presses forward with disarmament proposals, although detailed outlines for them exist and have existed for over a generation.[2] Apparently a disaster must occur to spark the urgency of disarmament even as a public relations flourish. The bombings of New York and Arlington coincided with the second Bush administration's implementation of plans for the appearance of nuclear cutbacks and withdrawal from the anti-ballistic missile (ABM) treaty. The administration set in motion a direction at least as dangerous as the Truman decision to develop the hydrogen bomb by making clear that the United States will fight both preemptive and preventive wars at its convenience. At first glance, the intention of the second Bush administration is as breathtaking as that of other democrats and dictators who have sought to remake the political map of the world. But this is an old reality, as Third World nations know. It had not been codified, however, ever until the current administration. Its interest in demanding that Iraq or other designated rogue or unfriendly states disarm—without touching core of its own arsenal or for that matter even its older weapons—strikes Third World leaders as little more than racism to ensure inequality among nations. The United States continues to place an emphasis on first strike capabilities, with China and Russia remaining in its sights.

Whether the United States can ever give up what it perceives to be its technological advantage is unlikely, especially since there is no agency of sufficient political strength within the United States to make the argument against an augmented national security state, one that does not even have the prudence of careful cold warriors such as George Kennan.

It is said that Americans are the most religious of people and the most advanced technologically. This certainly gives the United States an advantage in ridding the world of Evil. To negotiate with the impure Devil makes one an immoral person or a naïf carrying out a fool's errand. Of course, there are practical, "benign" sides to not negotiating with Evil. The "posture" of the state is that it always needs increased expenditures, especially to withstand Evil. They are usually wasteful expenditures that can count as a "good" in a society given over to wars without end and little if any interest in improving social and economic conditions within the United States and elsewhere. Defense funds operate as a pump-priming instrument for the economy. It would be a mistake with extreme consequences if President Bush's triumphalism were more than rhetoric. His willingness to fight preventive wars is reminiscent of the Axis of the 1930s and 1940s. The United States, restless as it is, finds that its leaders are eager to spread "democracy" to control the unruly and disrespectful in the Third World with few American casualties. That was surely the wish of the Italians in wars against Libya and Ethiopia in the 1930s, when sophisticated methods of terror through air power were perfected.

The heavy reliance Americans place on high-tech weaponry is to further distance the American warrior from the carnage he might otherwise experience or cause in "limited" wars. Thus, it is the hope of American war planners that the American combatant need never wonder about the moral element of any military action, because war is rather like a video game. Nor need he or she contemplate total war and its totalitarian nature, involving whole populations in suffering, at the mercy of their leaders. But the war and strategic planners' hopes are not enough to escape another aspect of the underlying modern condition, namely, the fallibility of military technology; the most modern planes and missiles have a disturbing habit of blowing up and falling apart, just as computers crash. The antiseptic words *surgical strike* and *collateral damage* are hardly enough to save warriors from nightmares and trauma. It is not surprising that some may want to use science and technology to avert as well as fight wars.

Such aspirations take on science fiction attributes. Just as in the twentieth century there were those who insisted that an extra chromosome caused criminal behavior, there will be those computer scientists given over to jamming the signals of other nations, spreading viruses to stop meaningful communication, and hopefully fighting an antiseptic communications war. More pacific-minded bioscientists look for the answer to war in a gene deficiency.

The search for a war criminal gene among leaders is misguided for the same reason the extra chromosome theory is defective. It assumes causal relationships that have nothing to do with the process of nature, outside of what we produce from nature through our social conventions and institutions. In other words, at the level of war making, the institutions and conventions that are produced over time define social character and in turn reinforce the war system. Would American leaders be willing to undergo an examination to ascertain their propensity for war and bellicosity? The probability is that they already do and must exhibit such characteristics. It would be delightful to believe that imaginative thought experiments that generate new ideas and practical scientific activities could be used to wipe away those social habits of the past that embrace the war system. That is not to be.

On the other hand, there are axial attributes of humanity that could be institutionalized throughout the twenty-first century, beginning with the primacy of peaceful resolution of political disputes linked to economic justice and fairness. Can such an idea translate into movements in capitalist nations for Haitian workers who are paid twenty-five cents an hour or millions of other workers who are paid unjust wages and who have been cut off from their own communal roots? The cynical reply is that this amount of money is more than they had before, thereby erasing any responsibility for the past, present, or future, because things are getting "better" for the wretched. How do such ideas resonate in an international currency system in which developing nations have no recourse to stop currency speculation from betting for and against their respective currency, thereby throwing economic plans of nations into turmoil? Or how do the cleptocracies of business and government in Third World nations that been encouraged the United States to have exactly those structures leave the scene without civil wars?

These questions are at the heart of an international market system that has no interest in either human consequences for the many or ends beyond the sale of particular commodities, such as weapons, or profit on betting against or for particular currencies. This is why peaceful settlements must include the means of improving economic conditions through employment, work, and benefits for the poorest in a nation, as well as strict controls over currency speculation. For without considering such questions, conditions of animosity will be created between various economic blocs in the world that will lead to a worldwide Hobbesian nightmare, with Hobbes's solution for the person to surrender total sovereignty to an unaccountable world state. This need not occur, for redistribution mechanisms based on income and need predicated on fairness could become the fundamental global reality. Attempts to this end are not unknown in the United States, as exemplified by liberal attempts at global fairness, such as the positions taken by diverse figures from Walter Reuther, the former president of the United Auto Workers, to Henry Wallace, to the followers of the Swedish Nobelist Gunnar Myrdal. From currency stabilization to the leveling of raw material prices, a guided international market with necessary subsidies could be paid for through a minimal travel surtax.[3] Assessing world economic disparities, world economic growth, and political modes of economic redistribution through the UN or an equivalent is not beyond modern social science, nor is there any reason it should be thought of as beyond nations—especially where there are strong transnational citizen movements showing the intellectual and political way to this end. At the beginning of the twenty-first century there are transnational activists working to organize a worldwide peace and justice movement similar in method to the American civil rights movement and other nonviolent struggles.

Vital to an end to the war system is the recognition that every arrangement made in foreign affairs, to the extent it can be known, and every problem solved peacefully, will be used as the scaffolding for a peaceful international structure. This structure must include attention to economic and social justice as part of any of any settlement conflict. It begins from fairness, as comprehended the international community when it suspends vested interests. In other words, there must be an increasing role for an independent body that speaks for the national "sovereignty." This body would help nations forswear paying protection rackets and buying off the richest and the most powerful elements in any particular struggling nation to ensure peace and development. Its primary monitoring task would be to hold developed nations to policies that neither directly nor indirectly penalize poor and developing nations. To put this another way, it is rich not poor nations, that need monitoring and radical reform of their policies. Attempts were made during the Cold War to achieve some level of economic development. For example, as an answer to socialist claims for world economic development beyond the economic restoration of Western Europe, President Truman proposed a technical assistance program for poor nations that was expanded into an aid program. A decade later, Charles de Gaulle's expanded views of development were based on the idea that a percentage of the West's gross national income would be given over to Third World economic and social development. Other plans called for putting aside savings accumulated through cutbacks in armaments, which would then be funneled to poor nations. In effect, this meant recognition of economic rights for the poor.[4]

Overall, however, managers of rich states wanted to do good and do well at the same time. Their idea was and remains the integration of the poor into world markets. These markets, it was claimed, yielded a better standard of living as judged in terms of more plentiful commodities, especially if the poor nation tied itself to exporting commodities and raw materials. Although this system resulted in greater disparities between citizens, these disparities could be masked by the social system of capitalism itself, which built a middle class through the increase of commodity desire, consumer credit, and then debt. But this method is merely capitalism gluing people to commodities and desires that mask many problems that come with "development," when development is defined as an unfettered market system in which accumulation of private property overwhelms collective need and productive activity.

When "development" becomes more than a phrase in speeches of leaders and diplomats, experience suggests that a planning process will include local community assessments outside of markets to determine what people need for three linked stages of social development, namely, survival, dignity, and decency. Depending on the cultural setting one may be more important than the other. These three stages of development must be constantly reexamined by reconstruction liberals to ensure that they are standing with the bottom 80 percent of the world's population, even though their class position and education are often mediated through elite experiences and elite education.

Liberals are trained in modern forms of knowledge, science, and technology that encourage them to assume, often mistakenly, that their forms and techniques are automatically better than the cumulative knowledges learned over generations in different cultures and settings. Nevertheless, universities and institutes can organize their purpose to formulate and abet nations and communities in their struggles for decency, dignity, and economic and social justice. Such a program of research and action will revivify the university and its social purposes once its members surrender arrogance about other cultures and realize that science and technology may bring disruption but not necessarily efficiency or happiness, just as religious belief may distort reason and political agreement. Like universities, researchers live in a world where current fashions of economic and political thought dominate, often in the face of reality. The result is the peddling of scientific ideas against local cultures where those who have had the ideas are unaware of their own officious certitude, an example being the role of Harvard economists in Eastern Europe after the collapse of the Soviet Union. Indeed, as Janine Weidel points out, the great universities and their economists were not averse to benefiting from the changeover to wolfish capitalism.[5]

TECHNOLOGY AND THE WEAKENING OF NATION-STATE SOVEREIGNTY

What happens where there is no control and accountability over force fields of political energy and legitimate authority and the inquiry process itself are ceded to large aggregates of power, as in the case of international corporations?[6]

The will of governments to regulate international corporations through international mechanisms is virtually nonexistent. There are three reasons for this political force field that seems not to touch the international corporation's legitimacy or, for that matter, illegitimacy. One is the belief that the primary way to achieve international growth and innovation is through international markets that are unencumbered by regulation and publicly debated and formulated definitions of the common good. Second, developing nations in need of capital investment see international corporations as the central element in their own growth. Third, international corporations take advantage of fears that various sectors of the American citizenry have regarding international institutions.

In the United States there is fear, both in the populace at large and among states' rights advocates, that there will be a loss of control to foreign international bureaucratic entities, which could result in a kind of unaccountable international tyranny. These sentiments are shared not only by militia groups within the United States but also by consumer advocates, such as Ralph Nader, who have concluded that hard-won battles in consumer protection will be undercut by international agreements such as the North American Free Trade Agreement (NAFTA) and the World Trade Organization (WTO), which will overrule consumer and worker protections in the name of "free trade." Government officials in the United States fear that they will be bound to international rules that would be internalized in domestic law. Conservative states' rights advocates fear that international standards will result in the application of human rights resolutions and covenants to American law.

On the one hand, in the present atmosphere of attempted American hegemony, without any concert of nations balancing off the reach of American leaders, there is anxiety among rightists about the United Nations as an institution because it could evade the American grasp. This fear occurs even as the United States guides the actions of the UN. In reality, the UN franchises its name to U.S.-dominated activities. On the other hand, where the United States is not interested in having the UN directly involved, it invites the UN "out" of what it considers its sphere, as in U.S.-Latin American relations or the Indochina war.

Nevertheless, the changes in sovereignty that have occurred because of the existence of the UN have emboldened the American Right to press hard to cripple the UN or render it otherwise irrelevant. The Right's concern began almost immediately after the UN's founding, when it became clear that judges in the United States took the far-reaching language of the UN charter as a treaty that, with other UN documents, could affect property and human rights within the United States. These concerns remain more than two generations later and mark an important fault line between conservatives and liberals.

The United Nations as an organization and ideal is both a symbol and a product of cross-cutting forces and ideologies. On the one hand, it is merely the organization of power in service of the most powerful nations. It can even operate as a protector of brutal, corrupt governments that use the international law of sovereignty against the human rights of their own citizenry. On the other hand, it carries an idealistic load, framed in the phrase "We the Peoples," the first three words of the UN charter, which carries the intention and the threat that ultimately it is "we the peoples" who will decide.

The UN's history is a contradiction between both realpolitik and control of the organization by the great powers, especially the United States and the UN's idealistic claim that it serves all of humankind. Dag Hammarskjold, perhaps the most influential UN secretary general, claimed that it was the small nations that needed the protection of the UN, not their powerful counterparts. His argument could have been extended to include the defenseless such as the indigenous peoples of Latin America, Asia, Africa, and the Middle East—the Palestinians—who remain at everyone's mercy, including the nations in which they reside. Ironically, with the events of September 11, 2001, the United States also needs the UN as a defense against its warrior impulses. And if that is the case, then the United States will have to bend its own definition of sovereignty.

It would be mistaken in the extreme if, in the twenty-first century, the crippled United Nations should be understood only as the structural end point of twentieth-century failure. In reality, the UN carries with it the power of a dream of world peace organized through international institutions that cause the individual nations to place more weight on mutual persuasion and dialogue than on the force of arms.

NATIONAL SOVEREIGNTY AND THE PEOPLES

Prior to the twentieth century, attempts at international organization as a means of controlling war failed because proponents did not know how to get beyond the problem of individual state sovereignty. However, embedded in the "We the People" clause of the UN charter is a powerful statement, that in international law and organization, sovereignty is passing from nation-states to peoples. Ultimately, it is they who have the legitimacy. Obviously this change in the narrative of international relations does not mean that the idea of popular sovereignty is accepted in practice. States hold sovereignty for themselves against other states and often their own people. On the other hand, if "we the peoples" become the building blocks of international affairs, it would mean that people, not states, would finally become the subject actors of international law, thereby requiring an entirely different international and transnational legal and economic governance structure.

It should be noted that there are cracks in the meaning of sovereignty, as state leaders and individuals may be brought to the bar of justice in an international tribunal.[7] Official American doubts notwithstanding, one task of the twenty-first century is to expand the jurisdiction of the International Court of Justice, establish regional courts, and hear cases of disfranchised minorities. The depoliticization of disputes and war crimes by turning them into legal cases will have the effect of dampening the flames of passion that define religious struggles, historical injury, perceived slight, and incomplete, useless wars. The paradox of this form of depoliticization is that it can be brought to fruition only by a militant transnational movement that is highly politicized and attuned to the ideals of the UN charter and other such documents.

In the economic sphere the UN has done virtually nothing to regulate international economic corporations. This may be attributed to the American government's intervention on behalf of U.S.-based international corporations that are protected from regulatory interference. This policy complements market economy rhetoric, which has dominated the World Bank and International Monetary Fund (IMF) for over forty years. Neither institution coordinates its activities with the UN or reports to the General Assembly and Security Council. Instead, their responsibility appears to be to the international banking community, which holds tightly to a series of abstract economic dogmas, favoring balanced budgets through cuts in social spending while using the treasuries of nation-states as collateral for loans. These institutions did nothing during the period of the Cold War to dissuade national spending on defense materials or the military of debtor nations. Indeed, World Bank officers were specifically proscribed from touching military budgets of nations because they were invariably used as repressive agents internally and the means for the United States and other European powers to sell their military wares in the Third World, thereby increasing further their debts. The crushing international debt and military budgets have been an important source of economic and social deterioration in the Third World.[8]

A RIGHT TO PEACE

It is incumbent upon the liberalism of reconstruction to present something more than war-free utopias that have no basis in reality, just as it is incumbent on its adherents to do more than accept a frame of reference they know is mistaken in terms of any sensible definition of pragmatism. The corollary is that liberals must surrender the politics of nationalism because it tails off into arrogance, revanchism, and disdain for rules of international behavior and law. Similarly nationalists may describe their policies in idealistic terms, but their practice is war and continuous preparation for it. Peace becomes the hiatus between wars, and military conflicts are to be fought at all times. But to overcome this reality other purposes and objectives, grand in their own right, need champions.

Reconstruction in the international sphere must sustain emphasis on international laws of liberation and social and economic justice in many different venues that directly engage the citizenry. Just as there are domestic laws and assumed rights protecting individuals against murder, similar rights grow out of already existing international law such as the Nuremberg judgments, which held against the crime of aggressive war and crimes against humanity. The crimes of genocide, rape, and pillage are predicates for the conclusion that people have a right of peace. Obviously, with weapons of mass destruction such a right becomes paramount, for innocent civilians are invariably the ones who bear the burden of warfare. Claims of those who fight just wars to obtain a just peace do not absolve the nation that commits war crimes. In this sense the American reluctance to sign onto an international criminal court is related to the notion that it "subjectively" believes that it fights just wars and so cannot be held responsible for murder through bombings or collateral damage. For the United States it is as if a policeman could not be held accountable for killing in the line of duty, which he defines.

The rethinking of organized killing and its purpose is of paramount importance. This is so particularly given the relative weakness of the UN and its inability to end the war system or deal with superpower military and economic threats and dominance, the character of modern weaponry added to old weaponry, and the little change in attitudes on the part of some who assert that war is an ennobling experience. We may be sure that there is a psychological inversion that causes human beings to take their natural fears and translate them into armaments and then find pretexts for doing so, generating threats from others by one's behavior. But there are also material conditions that give added weight to moral reasons against the arms/war syndrome. Although bellicose leaders from past generations have not been terribly concerned with the financial costs of arming and war, this situation is changing, with drops in most defense budgets since 1990, *exclusive of that of the United States.*

Perhaps once democratically chosen leaders comprehend that the reality they shape through their decisions comprises different interactions, opposing histories and perceptions, and a deepened rationality, a system of shared cooperation and moral judgments may emerge through international and transnational relationships that will result in substantially lower defense budgets. But mere cuts in defense budgets where there is a surfeit of existing weapons only begins the solution to the problem of the war system.

For the United States in the twenty-first century, common security and defense are less matters of military defense and more questions of how to make up for the damage done during the Cold War, including the startling problems generated by nuclear waste; how not to prop up outmoded, antidemocratic organizational structures such as the national security state; how to confront, with other nations, problems of ecology and the environment, economic disparity, and control over unaccounted economic power; how to stop manufacturing threats and fantasies as the basis for new weapons systems; and how to compensate broken societies as a result of judgments and actions taken by American leaders during the Cold War in Third World nations.

Concern about such problems as primary issues of the twenty-first century will require a thoroughgoing shift in the style, character, and agenda of foreign policy. Pursuing this course will leave American foreign policy open to the unfulfilled hopes of the twentieth century, namely, that the object of international relations is no longer limited to nation-states but is concerned with women, men, and children who find that they have and want rights to be proclaimed rhetorically and protected in practice. In other words, they seek a double citizenship, one tied to the nation-state; the other being global and attached to all people irrespective of their geographic place, gender, class, or race. There is a serious problem that is not easily confronted or solved. Perhaps more than at any other time in recorded history, states lie. Propaganda will give the unwary the idea that their government is acting according to truthful statements offered to the public and moral axioms. In other words, governments will play on people's decent moral sentiments as if that is what guides what they do. Schools, churches, and unions—the entire civil society (if civil society is more than a scarecrow)—have an obligation to "call things by their right names," which will improve the human condition.

International relations in the twenty-first century can be war, conflict, or cooperation that emphasizes peace. If the century is dominated by conflict, it will be a terrifying time. Even a benign Pax Americana will not be able to contain threats, ethnic and religious wars stemming from hatred, and partition that may result in the subjugation of minorities within a geographic boundary. The likelihood of regional nuclear wars, perhaps accompanied by the use of chemical and biological weapons, will become more than a fantasy. American military planners and warrior-minded presidents will present preemptive military activity as the way to keep "stability" or preempt attacks on the United States. Those who exercise control over the various forms of state violence will be seen as altogether necessary and rational. But what about a citizenry that has other ideas of defense and security? They realize, with the philosopher Alfred North Whitehead, that the "recourse to force, however inevitable, is a disclosure of the failure of civilization, either in the general society, or in a remnant of individuals."[9]

Among international scholars there is support for a right of peace that should be accepted in international and local courts, or the right of exodus, which could be enforced against a warring state by citizens of that state against their respective government or the governments of other states. The right of peace would become part of the ensemble of rights that humanity now expects for itself, through legal, social, and political institutions and ultimately by its own actions. With a right of peace, the burden shifts away from the citizen to blindly follow the call to war, for the nation would be constrained in its activities by those who opt out of the war system. A tragedy of our time is the moral disconnect between the individual's conscience and the activities of government, which are encased in self-serving, moralistic rhetoric and in reality are governed by crude notions of power and domination. Once the right to peace is internationally recognized—with or without American acceptance in the early stages of affirmation by other nations—and such rights are further buttressed by personal accountability for war crimes, which include preparation for war as partially determined by size of defense budgets and the nature of weaponry in an arsenal, there will be far greater weight given by governments to alternatives to the system of war as the fundamental way of protecting interests and settling disputes among nations or within nations. With a right to peace, for example, the taxpayer may assign the portion of his or her tax bill that would typically fund defense to local, state, federal, or international activities that have a peaceful and socially useful purpose.

The right to peace challenges the assumptions of national security and defense policy that have burdened the United States since the Second World War. Personal accountability reins in the idea of impunity of government officials who mask their work behind claims of national sovereignty.

The person's protection from war (arming for it by nation-states) has hardly proved successful in the modern period. War and war preparation by nation-states are thought to be continuous, uninterrupted arming with the most modern weapons, missiles, nuclear weapons, and chemical weapons, as well as more standard weapons of mass destruction. For some the arming and war process is to be legitimated through just rule by the powerful in the executive, such as the National Security Council, who decides when to make war outside of constitutional formalities. For others war is to occur only through the populist process of the majority deciding to go to war, which is accomplished through referendum; the American Constitution calls on Congress to declare war.

Americans have believed that they fight only defensive and just wars.[10] Some argue that wars should be fought only by volunteer soldiers so that the populace at large can opt out of the war. For others, war should come about only through an alliance system that would claim practical paramountcy over the UN even as both the UN and the alliance bend to the will of the United States.[11] Others claim that war is outmoded, and assassination or tyrannicide should be the weapon of choice. For example, note the attempts by the United States to assassinate Mu'ammar Khadafy of Libya or Saddam Hussein of Iraq, or the Israeli use of assassination as a method against Palestinian leaders who sanction suicide missions. And note how in all cases, whether Afghanistan, Vietnam, or Panama, nonmotive language, "collateral damage," is used to describe the killing of civilians. (Otherwise, perhaps, collateral damage would be known as state terrorism because it is aimed at terrorizing innocent civilians.) It is not likely that in common law much of a valid defense can be mounted by a defendant who says that although he meant to kill A he killed B. In war, the modern warrior is equipped to kill A or B, and A and B together.

So it is hardly novel to champion a right of peace. Americans would be in a position to argue in the courts that certain weapons by their nature, or certain actions by the government, violate the individual citizen's right to peace even if he or she is an innocent bystander. The bloody wars since the end of the Cold War may not be able to be stopped by a right of peace. But the existence of such a right delegitimates war and legitimates the individual's rights against the state, which over time may be able to be internalized in all societies. Similarly, class actions could be brought in different venues by nonstate actors who argue that their right to peace and their right of self-defense against war are by the state. In the United States, citizens could require war and law to inhibit a runaway executive. In September 2002, President Bush personalized his difference with Saddam Hussein, claiming that Hussein hated us, by which he meant the Bush family and specifically the first President Bush. It would not appear to be a prudent idea to run a "superpower" on the basis of vengeance and a personal vendetta. There is a Mafia quality to such actions, with the difference being that the Mafia seems to be more concerned with "collateral damage." An executive order has been in place since the Nixon-Carter period that forbids the targeting of heads of state for assassination.

MOVEMENTS FROM THE BOTTOM

In the nineteenth and twentieth centuries, international workers' movements appeared that sought the solidarity of workers, much the way royalty had intermarried across national lines to either expand or stabilize, but at least to sustain, its own power. The aim of transnational movements attached to socialism, populism, and democracy, however, was social and economic justice as well as dignity for all of humankind. Solidarity was no longer to be owned by the few or the royal. There was another difference between royal intermarriage and transnational movements from the Left. Life was to be more than chasing after material goods. There was to be a secular spiritual element, a form of humanism, which is present in the writings of the youthful Marx and followers of his earlier work, such as Erich Fromm.

Until the outbreak of World War I, socialists saw war as integral to the operations of the capitalist system. It was a canon among socialists that participation in war was foolhardy, morally corrupt, and disruptive of any attempts to build an international workers' movement. What conceivable benefit was there, thought Eugene Debs, in workers of one nation fighting the workers of another nation? On the other hand, the French socialists favored patriotic nationalism over class solidarity in the First World War, which effectively ended an international socialist movement. Even as class topped the state with the Bolshevik Revolution, the reality was that the revolution merely made the state stronger, and class in its transnational sense was seen as a fifth column for the Soviet state.

Like so many other beliefs and pronouncements of the time, the First World War destroyed the yearning for class solidarity, as nationalism and xenophobia sabotaged nineteenth-century imperialism. But the world of imperial stability and domination had to collapse once having grafted onto itself the eighteenth-century sentiments of the American and French Revolutions. The zone of difference between stated ideals and lived reality was too great. So long as the pre-World War I imperial framework had no way of including economic and social justice or concern for individual dignity except where it was instrumentally necessary to keep power, imperialists lived their lives trying to subdue others in fear of being overthrown. Peasants vulnerable to bad weather and depressed market conditions augmented the fascist alternative as revolutionary movements demanded a new status for the non-white world, and this status had to transcend being the exploited "burden" of the white world. With the breakup of the world economic and political system during the First World War, and with the melding of war, civil war, and revolution, the tsarist, Turkish, and Austro-Hungarian empires collapsed. The collapse of European empires encouraged the formation of liberation movements in colonized countries. Such movements may be committed to modernizing purposes but with brutal governmental methods, as was the case in Turkey, or may be antimodernist, seeking refuge and legitimation in fundamentalist religions whose most important commandment is hatred of the different, who are thought of as "impure" and "unclean." It is easy to forget that Gandhi had elements of these ideas in his antimodernist, anti-British ideology, as did the Indian leader Chandra Bose.

Before the convulsive changes during and after the First World, the assumption of diplomats and leaders was that relations between states could be frozen in the concrete of alliances and the balance of power. Because of the emergence of Bolshevism, liberation and social movements became more than irritants to status quo nations. For Wilsonians, social movements were to be contained along with Bolshevism in the name of liberal democratic principles. Wilson soon found that concern about the damage inflicted on people through war was secondary to maintaining the status quo. He learned that economic justice and human rights issues were not the concerns of the peacemakers, especially as those terms might apply to the mass of humanity in their day-to-day lives. Because sovereign governments were the only ones who had standing and were "seen" in international law, his hopes for bringing into the field of policy-making the "decent opinion of mankind," to use Jefferson's phrase, had no chance. In any case, his belief in self-determination for new states in practice meant finding and recognizing, for "their" people, the proper course. A single charismatic leader would determine the course of the new nation, with or without the support of public opinion.

The question of public opinion continues to bedevil democracy especially in foreign policy, where those charged with the responsibility of it follow any direction they care to pursue-unless directly inhibited or challenged by authentic mass movements. Transnational movements against the IMF and the World Bank are twenty-first-century attempts to inhibit or stop global capitalism. But they are also movements that are communicating a very powerful message: "We exist and we know as much or more than you do." These movements see globalization as a moving target. That is, they could just as easily confront the nation-state as global corporations. They are also poised to consider social actions around issues of peace. They are a part of a continuous dialogue that will redefine the institutions of the past that have brought humanity to a precarious place. These movements are more sophisticated and likely to be more successful than the socialist movements of the pre-World War I period.

SOCIAL MOVEMENTS AND RESEARCH AGENDAS

During the Cold War it was often stated that the peace movement was bound by its middle class character. This was only partly true, for at various times the labor movement was directly involved in peace activities and in partially funding the peace movement, as in the case of the Brotherhood Workers, the Health Workers, and the United Auto Workers.

Successful social movements have certain characteristics that are not necessarily recognized in their initial stages. They are recognized subjectively and objectively when existential pain is turned into political action by those most in need. In the future, movements in developed nations will cross class, gender, and race lines. Understandably, they will have the difficult task of finding common cause with religious groups and differing religions, outlining a democracy of human rights in economics, and ensuring transparency so that those most responsible in the state and corporate structures of the world can be either called to account for or confronted with their acts, or can be negotiated with. Such movements, even within democratically oriented societies when they seek active engagement from different sectors of society, are not free of physical danger. (Perhaps this is why social movements include young people in activist peace projects, for they require heroism, courage, and boldness against war, features usually assigned to the young.)

Although there are honorable exceptions, at present, governments, peace groups, university faculties, and think tanks are stuck with the assumptions and habits of the Cold War, serving power as it still appears to be. Professors and specialists are not rewarded if they pursue rigorous studies and practical activity to revise the assumptions that have brought humanity to its terrifying situation.[12]

American researchers in the last half of the twentieth century concentrated on war and methods of fighting wars. The presence of nuclear weapons and the attraction of national leaders, bureaucracies, scientists, and the military to nuclear weapons set in motion a world where national leaders and bureaucracies planned the destruction of hundreds of millions of people in a few hours.[13] During most of the Cold War in the United States, university faculties and think tanks took on the responsibility for analyzing and preparing scenarios for war fighting. The social and physical sciences departments of universities spent their intellectual energies on the project of deterrence and war fighting. The type of international law that was not a mere cover story for state violence fell to the margins of legal concern as those peddling the fables about the utility of different forms of warfare and strategic defense moved to the top of influence in Washington. Understandably, this dynamic created an intellectual and moral exhaustion for those who sought to move the discourse away from the war system as a permanent element in the relations of humankind and nations to the war system as a common problem. Social pathologies, if they were presented in terms of defense and security policy, were not only studied but also praised and given impetus to spread.

To their chagrin, reconstruction liberals who did not believe in the Cold War found themselves unable to present nonviolent modes of resolving conflicts without being consigned to the outer reaches of policy discussion or to university fringes and pacifist organizations. Infinitesimal amounts were spent on peace research and scientific inquiries that would have aided in the establishment of a peaceful world system that citizens could have initiated and enforced in their own nations. Instead of this pragmatist mode of rationality, a far different idea of instrumentalism was created, which has had devastating effects lasting longer than our motivations for the original act. Thus, the orgy of building nuclear weapons and strategic "defenses" on the basis of a false premise of political reality will remain with humanity for countless generations in the form of nuclear military waste and nuclear victims, even if there is no future nuclear war, as other nations actively seek nuclear weapons.

The hesitance of national leaders to break with the institutional habits of the past has meant that rational and comprehensive solutions to the war system and armaments acquisition are not on the table of concern, whether in the Kremlin, Quai d'Orsay, Berlin, Tokyo, Beijing, or the White House. Universities and peace groups have abandoned comprehensive solutions, adopting an incrementalist approach that does not touch the war system. To the extent that there are piecemeal solutions, they are highly technocratic and therefore spark no interest except among a very few scientists and military and civilian strategists. This is a surefire way to ensure that no major changes in the assumptions about the war system will occur, since there is no interest in engaging a democratic public with alternative policy frameworks in international affairs. But what about the torchbearers who carry a different seed of development and reconstruction?

In American thought there has been a continuing current for replacing the war system. Mark Twain and William James, Jane Addams, and Emily Balch, appalled and disgusted at American foreign and military policy; Herbert Hoover, in his many addresses to the nation and to other nations; the flawed Woodrow Wilson; Robert La Follette; capitalists who funded Peace ships; John Dewey; and socialists and communists—all sought an end to the war system. Women initiated Mother's Day as a cry against war, the New Left held to principles against war and imperialism. Libertarians such as A.J. Muste, Martin Luther King Jr., Noam Chomsky, and Paul Goodman, whose concerns were hardly different from various thoughtful liberal Democrats in Congress, serve as the "Other" way to organize America's political purpose. We might inquire whether this sentiment carries over into twenty-first-century America. New forces have come into play that suggest the possibility of moving away from the war system. As in the beginning of the twentieth century, women are again playing an increasingly important role in international relations. The role can be a positive one if they are prepared to change the hierarchic structure and consciousness of nations so that the state apparatus with regard to war making will be lessened and transformed. Because war, the state, and sovereignty are so intertwined and both government and people are to take their cues from those who claim the conch of the state such as kings and presidents who usurp constitutional authority, the ambitious will see their power tied to sovereign authority, not to the citizenry. This is a perplexing question.

At one point in the history of the women's movement, it was thought that if more women became active in the public space and in male-established institutions, those institutions, their everyday purpose, and their mission would be altered substantially. For example, women are thought of as more cooperative and less concerned about hierarchies in problem solving and as less violent.[14] However, the interest of the woman pilot Lieutenant Kelly Flinn in flying B52 bombers with nuclear weapons on them, and the willingness of a woman to be secretary of the Air Force, a secretary of state, or national security advisor, suggests that if "new players" are socialized into hierarchic state structures, fulfilling social roles from the past without transforming those social roles or insisting that the structure and purpose of the organization change, democratic inclusivity will have only a modest effect on the day-to-day life of people who must then conform to the social structures.[15] There is nothing to suggest that Madeleine Albright, Benezar Bhutto, or Golda Meir were any less warlike than their male counterparts, so long as the institutional structure stayed the same. On the other hand, women in corporate offices may have a greater tendency to tell the truth when there is clear evidence of fakery than their male counterparts. So it appeared during the corporate scandals that were exposed in 2000 and 2001. It is to be noted that in these cases professionalism demanded truth telling. There are important examples of this truth telling in the work of those scientists who play a crucial role in creating a world consciousness that cannot be easily denied.

The two scientific movements that cannot be easily denied concern health and the environment. It is an important event that health workers organized against nuclear war and for economic justice in the United States. It was a signal event that the World Health Organization brought a case in the International Court of Justice concerning the legality of nuclear weapons and nuclear war. Throughout modern history many health workers have sought a connection between the health of the individual and the health of the nation. The reason seems clear. While modern medicine saw as its task dealing with the health of the particular individual, whether through drugs or other forms of intervention, it is also clear that the health of a nation and of the world, affects the individual, whether it is the starving child in Uganda or those who suffer from the pain of Agent Orange, nuclear poisoning unclean drinking water, or AIDS. As a result, the health professional increasingly has learned that inquiry and its application are social—never outside of the political and values derived from social and community relationships and experiment. The health professionals are those who from standpoint of expertise best know the pathologies that can be laid at war's doorstep.

Similarly, an argument can be made about those in movements connected to preserving the environment. Part of any environment is the protection of the living and of future life. If attention is not paid to war and imperial depredation, foolish modernism of the kind that trapped the Soviet Union into environmental degradation will be missed. The connections inhere in the various parts of the problem. And to the extent that these connections are not made, the chance of anyone feature of the problem being changed and resolved is not very great. We need look no farther than the problem of nuclear waste and its relation to the war system to see the tragic truth of this observation.

AMERICAN SOCIAL GIFTS

The American gift to the world need not be only Big Macs, Coca-Cola, and the socialization of women and non-whites into hierarchic or violent institutions. The gift can be the rethinking of the character of institutions themselves, that is, whether they add to or detract from human well-being and liberation. The United States has a chance like no other nation in modern time to help humanity transcend its past by showing how it will live *within* the framework of international law, disarmament, and economic and social justice. No other nation is in the position of providing others with the knowledge and confidence to do likewise. More than any other, American civilization suggests that humankind wants to and possibly can transcend its own past in favor of good ends. Just as individuals make choices (and close doors to other possibilities), so it is obvious that the institutions of society can foreclose individual choice and social facts (values, in Dewey's terms) of freedom. On the other hand, if the romantics and glorifiers of imperialism are successful in their quest, American society, as I have said, will suffer the fate of empires that did not know their limits or real strengths. The American state in its pursuit of total dominance, world empire "by any means necessary," will lose the chance of being the peace lover and the honest broker that leads by exemplary behavior in international affairs. Just as happened to fifth-century Athens at the end of its golden period, the, United States will lose. In our time American society will not be loved for its freedom and yearning for political equality, economic and social justice, technological innovation, cultural diversity, and caring. It will be known as an arrogant bully, having lost the chance, that is, the choice to open wide the doors of history to decency and dignity. It will have entrapped itself like Icarus, thinking that the mushroom clouds of nuclear weapons are more real than the sun and nature itself and that destroying or threatening to destroy is the same as preservation and reconstruction. Americans will betray the better part of their collective nature if they do not grasp the possibilities that were there for humanity at the end of the Second World War and that have reappeared again in both a tenuous and strengthened form: strengthened in the sense that the orgies of killing and violence have lost their heroic aura; tenuous in that there is a disconnect between this realization and those who believe that the democracy and attendant values are secondary to maintaining the claim, useless and dangerous as it is, of being the "sole superpower."

CONTINUING THE CHALLENGES OF AMERICAN CIVILIZATION

Some who live in a religious tradition speak of the human tragedy from which there is no escape. This tradition recognizes bestiality but does not condone it. Some want to understand tragedy and the fragility of the human condition as a means to excuse particular actions or inaction. But the elements of that tragedy are made unspeakable when we avoid the Other, which is always within ourselves in world politics. We neglect to develop and reinforce institutions that can lift some of the burden of war and economic inequity from humankind. And we reinforce hatred, misunderstanding, and envy felt by the Other. In turn such policies inhibit those elements in all cultures that yearn for liberation and an end to oppression. But who is the "we"? It is that which is most rational and humane in the human species. This is not an easy struggle, within ourselves or our institutions.

Prior to the emergence of modern warfare, thinkers, poets, and dramatists, from Homer to Grotius to Kant to James, sought to demystify war and its results. But this literature, and the work of those most concerned, was unable to overcome the martial values that dominated most cultures. With these values, war became the true test of courage, manhood, bravery, and boldness. Liberals from time to time in the United States have glorified war, as did the reluctant liberal Justice Oliver Wendell Holmes, who praised its purgative powers, its camaraderie, and the belief that the sedentary life is not what challenges men to perform noble acts. After the First World War, however, Holmes's views on war as an uplifting tool changed. Those closest to war, who refused to romanticize it in the twentieth century, knew otherwise.[16]

At the close of the nineteenth century, many ideas on disarmament and international organization were floated that sought stability and security without war for tottering empires. Tsarist Russia promoted international disarmament and an international conference on disarmament in 1899. It was also asserted and "proved" by promoters of the idea of progress at the beginning of the twentieth century that war was a thing the past "civilized nations." Imperial wars by Western nations in non-white territories were excluded from this logic. It was taken for granted by the white imperial nations that they should police non-white controlled lands; the cost was bloodshed among millions of non-whites and sometimes-successful attempts at crushing their psyches.[17] For imperialist nations, putting down revolts was seen as defense of law to protect imperial power and their civilizing mission.

The Left, including liberals, had a more favorable attitude toward revolution than it did toward war. It saw in revolution democratic stirrings and the rejection of economic and social injustice. Often it focused on ends rather than means, believing that if the end were achieved, over time people would forget the suffering that preceded it. But these distinctions become blurred as revolution leads to civil war, which in turn leads to war beyond the borders of the original warring factions, as it did in the French Revolution, the Napoleonic wars, and the world conflagration of the First World War a hundred years later.

Knowing how twentieth-century revolutions and civil wars fold into each other in violent, frightening, and tragic ways makes the fall of Soviet state socialism in a relatively bloodless manner more remarkable. Perhaps autocratic communism didn't die, but it certainly faded away. So now humanity is left with the struggles that have defined American life virtually from its beginning. It is unspeakable that the gains in democracy and equality made for and by people over two hundred years of struggle should be taken away by those eager to recapture the past glories of imperialism, domination, racism, and sexism. It is frightening that those ideas that promised a universalism of dignity and decency, of economic and social justice, might be discarded as if they were the dreams of fools. It is appalling that the second Bush administration should use the language of citizen responsibility and collective self-sacrifice to hide its authoritarian, antidemocratic purposes.

In the case of the United States, the choice is stark and clear. Either American civilization will build out of its exemplars and the great social movements of the nineteenth and twentieth centuries, or American leaders and future generations will confuse force with morality, military technology with good ends, stability with justice, and hubris with knowledge. American civilization will be determined by militarism and global capitalism, and the bell will toll for the better American dream, the one represented by the great abolitionist movements; the art and poetry of Melville, Twain, and Whitman; the courage of those in the labor movement, who reshaped the very meaning of dignity and decency; and the women's movement, whose words and deeds forced male America to surrender some of its power and privilege.

Whether it was Martin Luther King Jr., whose triple purpose was civil rights, antiwar, and economic justice, or Jane Addams, John Dewey, or Eugene Debs, all had a vision of reconstruction that demands to be put into practice in the twenty-first century as the dominant spirit of the age. Given the reality of new problems and unmet needs, their vision will be deepened by other movements of liberation, aided by future problems, programs, and artistic endeavors. Such work could catalyze the beginning of a world civilization that leaves exploitation, war, and economic injustice on the ash heap of history. It is the work and thought of such exemplars that is best able to withstand absolutism, clerical fascism, and criminal irrationality. It will be the machtpoliticans who are political gravediggers.

The twentieth century was a hard teacher. It showed humanity what to reject—if we are prepared to see and listen. It gave us glimpses of the "ought" and told us what "is." Although moving the "is" to the "ought" involves inquiry and the acquisition of socially agreed-upon knowledge, which is judged against a tableau similar to or the same as the UN Declaration of Human Rights and other such foundational documents, its meaning can have optimal value only in concrete situations. For some the "is" and the "ought" can come only from saintly and exemplary action—from those axial people who pay no attention to the conventions of the "is" and who point a different way, as Jesus, Socrates, Muhammad, and Buddha did. That is to say, the unique humane leader or saint sets a course of altruism that others link to, simultaneously introducing new language and a changed vision of what to notice.

But the democracy of the future cannot depend on such individuals alone. Instead, democracy depends on building those sentiments into its institutions and honoring them as they manifest themselves in the everyday life of people. The modern axial position links the well-being of democracy's members to the intelligence and collective judgment of its members.[18]

Democracy is never a completion, but like humanity itself it is always in the process of becoming. If we believe otherwise we will suffer the sin of hubris, as if how we live is the final answer of how to live for all time. In a democracy there must be the continuing recognition of human commonality and revision without surrendering the preconditions of a decent life. Some are conditions and principles that must be intertwined like the linkages in protein strands and genetic clusters of life. They must fall in the category of the necessary and natural, such as air, water, and food. Others are in the secondary category of what is necessary for a decent and dignified life namely education in or out of school; the freedom of wonderment, speech, and association; and that mode of justice that connotes the importance of human dignity in all social actions at all times for all people. What we note is that these are "is" conditions, and when they are denied or unnoticed it is then that they become the "ought" conditions of human struggle.

Let us conclude this section with another look at the question of "is" and "ought." Philosophers have long known that this question is basic to the modern period, to how we see objectivity and evaluation or normative views of ourselves and the world. We are told by Hume and many less luminous figures that we cannot be sure that A causes B in the sciences, except as our senses decide that that is what we perceive to be the case either by intuition, induction, or statistical logic. In everyday life we know that there is a moral sensibility that tells us immediately that to feel otherwise is the result of a deformation as a result of a social role that we feel bound to carry out in such a way as to obliterate the moral sensibility, as, for example, in the case of the custodian of the gas ovens at Dachau. This is a case where social pathology overwhelms the innate capacity for empathy. The question is, in what form of governing is it likely that the moral sense or empathy for the Other can be best exercised, not in the sense of generosity but in the recognition and prosecution of political equality and economic justice that eschews seeing humanity as either prey or predator? It is in democracy critically evaluated that reasoned arguments and passions find the basis for action and behavior. Argument and passion may be frightening to the suffering who have lost hope and accept their colonized status. Similarly, it is frightening to the instigator and those who despise anyone outside of themselves, viewing altruism as either the coin of some primitive society or something that can never exist. But answers can be found and intuitively felt in "political decision time" by yielding to our moral sentiments. These capacities are there within us, and they are our tropes (with shared experience) that cannot easily be denied, whether by the impersonality of technology or social roles that until the twenty-first century, in the way they were constructed and institutionalized, required humanity to be less than what it is and what it could become. It is in the liberalism of reconstruction that some of the answers may be discovered and these capacities may flourish.

Notes

1. For example, the nuclear test ban treaty covering the atmosphere and under water; the Antarctica treaty creating a nuclear-free zone, and the nonproliferation treaty. Note especially Article 6 of the Nonproliferation Treaty ratified by the U.S. Senate in 1970. For a complete listing of relevant disarmament treaties, see Marcus Raskin, *Essays of a Citizen* (Armonk, N.Y.: Sharpe, 1991), Article 9, 235–36.
2. Note the Soviet and American proposals of 1962, the Forsberg proposal, and a comprehensive treaty proposal by this author in *Abolishing the War System* (Amherst, Mass.: Alethia Press, 1992).
3. Note proposals made by the late professor James Tobin in 1978. James Tobin, "A Proposal for International Monetary Reform," *Eastern Economic Journal 4* (1978): 153–59. Former Undersecretary General of the UN, Brian Urquhart, discussion of future responsibilities of the UN, found in *New York Review* 1993, 1994.
4. The 2003 aid and assistance budget given to developing nations by the United States is .07 percent of its annual budget. This is somewhat more than the Clinton administration provided for aid purposes. American aid is conditioned on adopting a "free market" economy. It should be noted that the idea of an international disarmament program that would result in the savings that would find their way into poor nations never got beyond the so-called talking stages. Peace dividends have not fared well internationally or domestically under the power politics paradigm of international affairs.
5. Janine Weidel, *Collision ND Collusion: The Strange Case of East Europe* (New York: Palgrave, 2001).
6. By authority I mean that power legitimately borrowed by government or its agents, who may call in their "political loans" at will, for short periods of time from the sovereign people.
7. However imperfect the mechanism and the ambivalent attitude of the United States in terms of establishing an international criminal court, virtually all nations accept the Nuremberg standards and the UN authorization to bring cases against alleged war criminals. Note the Nuremberg and Asian war crime trials, and recently the UN-authorized trial of Slobodan Milosevich for war crimes.

8. Note the yearly studies of the Swedish International Peace Research Institute during the Cold War, available at www.sipri.se.

9. Alfred North Whitehead, *The Adventure of Ideas* (New York: Macmillan, 1993).

10. The attacks on Pearl Harbor, New York, and the Pentagon add weight to this statement, but when they are fought it should he done with tenacity and the whole hearted support of the citizenry.

11. This method seems inherently unstable, for no nation has been able to govern or guide all others for very long unless it controls the economic and military system of the alliance members.

12. See chapter 3 for comments on the New Left.

13. Hundreds of books and thousands of articles were written during the Cold War on the question of defense and how to fight a nuclear war. Two important books of that period asserted the possibility of fighting a strategic nuclear war: *On Thermonuclear War,* by Herman Kahn (New York: Praeger, 1965), and *Nuclear Weapons and Foreign Policy,* by Henry Kissinger (Garden City, N.Y.: Doubleday Anchor, 1957). With other such books pretending to rationality becomes a demonic activity. For further study on war, see Barbara Ehrenreich, *Blood Rights: Origins and History of the Passions of War* (New York: Henry Holt, 1998).

14. Carol Gilligan, *In a Different Voice* (Cambridge: Harvard University Press, 1982).

15. One brilliant recent exception is Hazel O'Leary, who as the secretary of energy insisted that the Department of Energy make information publicly available about the massive poisoning of American citizens as a result of U.S. nuclear experiments. She was forced to resign.

16. J. Glenn Gray, *The Warriors: Reflections of Men in Battle* (New York: Harper & Row, 1970).

17. Frantz Fanon, *Studies in a Dying Colonialism* (New York: Monthly Review Press, 1962); Kwame Nkrumah, *Neocolonialism* (New York: International Publishers, 1966). An interesting discussion of how anthropologists viewed the Other before the New Left critique can be found in an essay by Kathleen Gough in *The Dissenting Academy*, ed. Theodore Roszak (New York: Pantheon, 1968), 135. But also note the disarray and chaos that have gripped Africa, South Asia, and the Middle East, caught between the free market, starvation, and environmental degradation, where cleptocracy, ethnic rivalry, and absolutism are found in abundance. Robert D. Kaplan, *The Ends of the Earth* (New York: Random House, 1997).

18. Perhaps new political forms beyond democracy will evolve as technology expands and transforms both the public and private spaces of people into face-to-face units, anarcracies, which are self-defining, recognizing new communities beyond the nation-state and global corporation. But even such cases will be only a variant of democracy and democratic spirit.

Index

About the Editors

Marcus G. Raskin is a cofounder and distinguished fellow of the Institute for Policy Studies and a professor of public policy at George Washington University. He served as a member of the Special Staff of the National Security Council during the Kennedy administration, and has since been an avid researcher in the fields of security and nuclear disarmament. Raskin was the chair of the Sane-Freeze Campaign in the 1980s, helped organize the Progressive Alliance, and advises the Congressional Progressive Caucus. Most recently, he helped found Cities for Peace, which has organized local governments and individuals against the Iraq War.

Gregory D. Squires is a professor of sociology, public policy, and public administration at George Washington University. Currently he is a member of the governing board of the Urban Affairs Association, the Washington D.C. advisory committee to the U.S. Commission on Civil Rights, the advisory board of the John Marshall Law School Fair Housing Legal Support Center in Chicago, Illinois, and the social science advisory board of the Poverty & Race Research Action Council in Washington, D.C. He has served as a consultant for civil rights organizations around the country and as a member of the Federal Reserve Board's Consumer Advisory Council.